The First

American Frontier

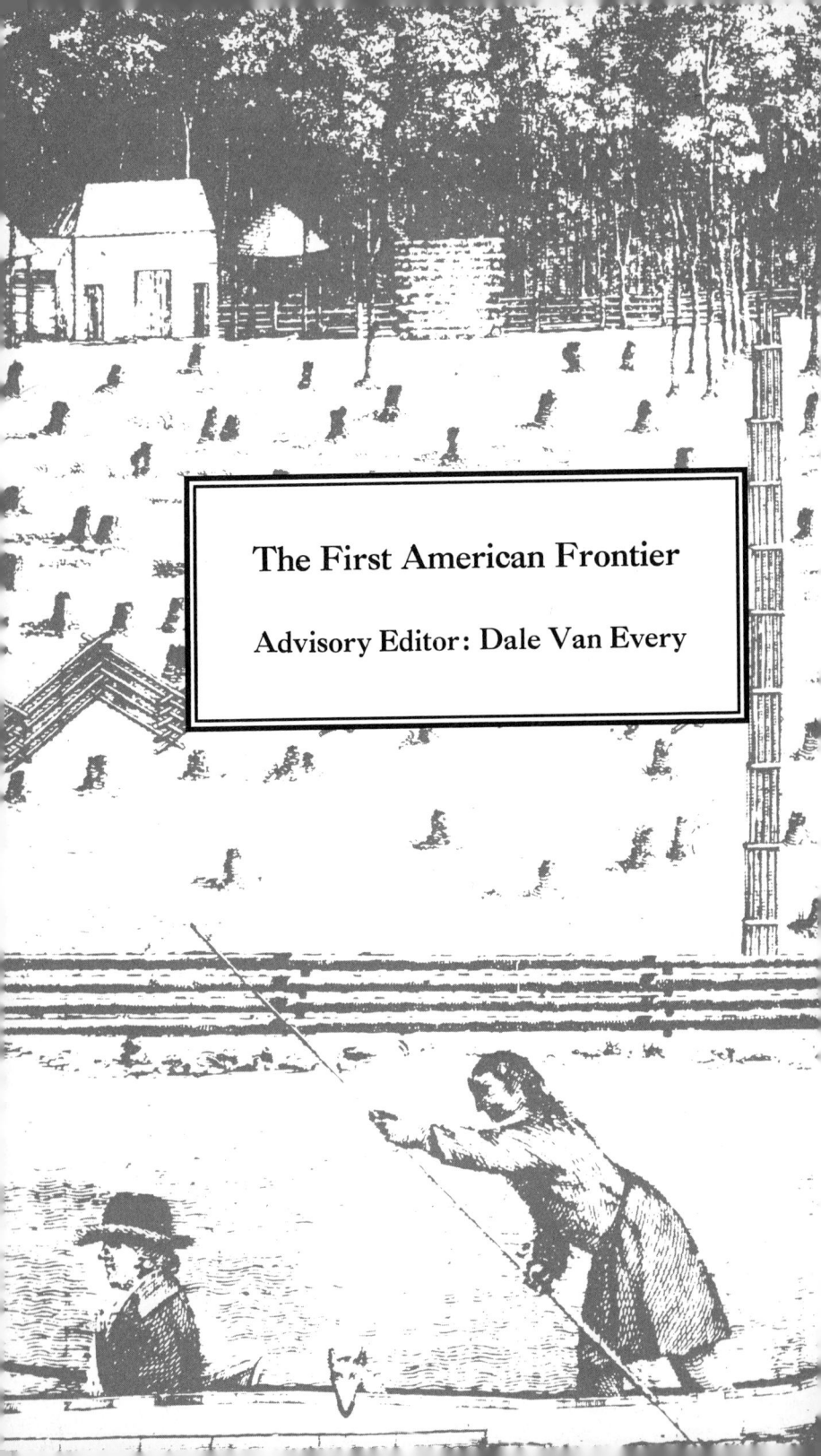

The First American Frontier

Advisory Editor: Dale Van Every

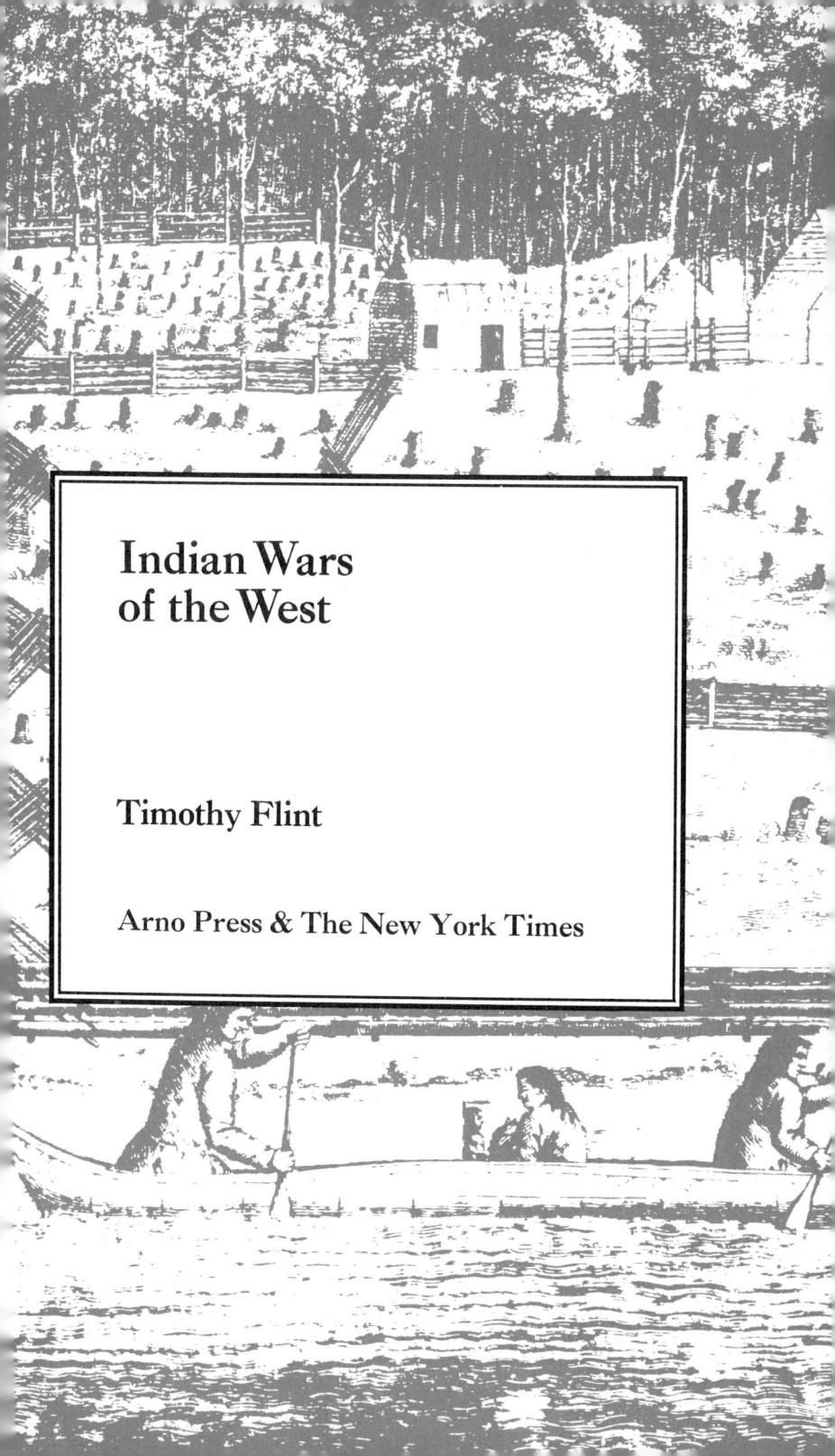

Indian Wars
of the West

Timothy Flint

Arno Press & The New York Times

Reprint Edition 1971 by Arno Press Inc.

Reprinted from a copy in
The State Historical Society of Wisconsin Library

LC #   74-146395
ISBN 0-405-02848-2

The First American Frontier
ISBN for complete set: 0-405-02820-2

See last pages of this volume for titles.

Manufactured in the United States of America

INDIAN WARS

OF THE WEST;

CONTAINING

BIOGRAPHICAL SKETCHES OF THOSE

PIONEERS

WHO HEADED THE WESTERN SETTLERS IN REPELLING THE

ATTACKS OF THE SAVAGES,

TOGETHER WITH A

VIEW OF THE CHARACTER, MANNERS,

MONUMENTS, AND ANTIQUITIES

OF THE

WESTERN INDIANS.

BY TIMOTHY FLINT.

Westward the Star of Empire holds its way.

CINCINNATI:

PUBLISHED BY E. H. FLINT.

1833.

N. & G. GUILFORD & Co., *Printers.*

INDIAN WARS OF THE WEST.

CHAPTER I.

PHYSICAL VIEW OF THE WEST.

THE country, of whose first settlers we propose to give sketches, is now called in common parlance the West, and the Mississippi valley, indicating its position in regard to the elder and more populous country on the shores of the Atlantic. It is the largest, most singular, and most fertile valley on the globe. A profile, or physical section of the vast plain between the Alleghanies and Rocky mountains, places this fact in an impressive point of view.

A line round the edge of the immense basin, commencing at the northern sources of the head waters of the lakes, round the Alleghanies, the gulf of Florida, the mountains that separate the waters of the Rio del Norte from those of the Mississippi, and the central ridges of the Rocky mountains dividing between the waters of the Missouri, the gulf of California, and the Oregon, and thence around the head sources of the Mississippi, to its commencement north of the lakes, would be at least five thousand miles in extent.

This vast surface is watered by the longest rivers on the globe. The Missouri, Mississippi, Arkansas, Red River, Ohio, Tennessee, Wabash, Platte, Kansas, Yellow Stone, Illinois, Osage, and many other of the western rivers, are as different in character from those of the old world, as this valley is more extensive and magnificent than any other. In comparison to their width they have far longer courses, and furnish a navigation less impeded by falls and rapids. These rivers may be considered im--

mense natural canals winding through this vast valley in every direction, at once irrigating, fertilizing, and connecting its remotest points by navigable water communications.   Three of these streams, to wit: the Missouri, the Mississippi, and Arkansas present a continued steam boat navigation of more than two thousand miles in length. Three more, to wit: Red River, the Ohio, and Tennessee have more than a thousand miles.   Of those which are actually ascended by steam boats from three to six hundred miles, the number would be too tedious to enumerate.

Each of these streams is a kind of Nile to the region it irrigates, having a wide alluvial valley along its course, bounded on either shore by bluffs of a peculiar character, generally faced with precipitous limestone walls from two to four hundred feet high.   It is but a few years since steam boats have first begun to be seen mounting with the power of the imprisoned elements between these hoary and ancient parapets of the streams, scaring the water-fowls from their domain, and the wild beasts from their shores.   The discoveries, the peculiar journals and incidents of these long and recent voyages, are too new and voluminous, and we are yet too little acquainted with the new position in which they have placed us, to possess at present all their intrinsic interest.   They will constitute the burden of the history and song of the coming generations.

The peculiar configuration, climate, physical character, fertility, and modes of communication of this wide region, circumstances all having a peculiar bearing upon the character of its inhabitants, have not failed to form a language, and mode of thinking, and manners peculiar to the west, presenting to the eye of a curious observer sufficiently amusing differences between the people of the Atlantic country and the Mississippi valley.   The long jorneys of the inhabitants in steam boats, and by other water conveyances, create the necessity of new phrases, modes of speech, and even habits of thinking and feeling. Among the results may be fairly reckoned greater enterprise, and a readier habit of breaking the ties of home, less pain in doing it, and in general the hardier and more reck-

less habits of soldiers, travellers, and hunters. Time and
circumstances have yet to determine, whether these habits will form, on the whole, a better and more amiable
nationality, than that of the Atlantic people.

They, whose business is on the blue waters of the ocean,
are apt to view the fresh water voyagers of the western
rivers with a sort of contempt. Yet there is no doubt,
that the habitudes of the dwellers on these rivers, accus-
toming them from their earliest years to manage water-
crafts both by the oar and wind, and to consider the waters as furnishing their customary modes of travel and
conveyance, qualify them, when borne down their forests
to the sea, to become sailors at once. Fearlessness, frankness, fluency in conversation, a touch, perhaps, of rough-
ness, smacking of the union of the hunter, soldier, sailor
and merchant, addictedness to cards and profanity form
the prominent traits of the present voyagers on the western
rivers.

The fertility of the greater portion of this valley is as
surprising as its extent. Apparently of more recent formation than the remainder of the continent, it seems less
marked with the curse of sterility. Immense portions are
alluvial. Other portions far from rivers, or the present
courses of waters, show as if they were the deposit of
immense drained lakes, or a vast region of former submersion. Even the pine districts, which are extensive in
the south and southwest of the valley, and towards the
sources of the Mississippi, are not sterile, like the same
tracts in the Atlantic country. They are generally covered in the summer with a luxuriant growth of grass,
herbage and flowers, and bring moderate crops of corn,
wheat, sweet potatoes, and garden vegetables without
manuring. This natural fertility seems to be owing to the
deep loam stratum of the vegetable soil, and its containing uncommon proportions of limestone, triturated, and
perfectly mixed with it. Whatever be the cause, every
traveller has remarked, in proportion as he begins to descend any of the ridges, that form the outline of this valley, that the soil shows a proportionate increase of fertility. It is not pretended, that there are not here, as else-

1 *

where, extensive regions consigned to sterility; but only that the proportion of fertile soil, compared with other countries, is unusually great.

The climate, though every where subject to frequent changes and the extremes of heat and cold, is generally a mild and temperate one, presenting an atmosphere with a fair proportion of cloudless days, and a sky intensely blue and transparent. In winter it no where has the same amount of snow, as in the corresponding Atlantic latitudes. Another feature of diversity from the Atlantic country is seen in the vast western *prairies*. Probably two-thirds of the whole surface of this valley are of this character. The term was furnished by the French, the first settlers of the country, and imports the same as the English word *meadow*. This term to an American ear generally denotes a low and wet grass enclosure. Nothing is farther from the true import of the term prairie, as applied to the grass plains of the west. The savannas of Florida and some of the interior prairies, are wet and marshy; but the infinitely larger proportion is high and dry. Indeed, their destitution of water is in general their greatest inconvenience. They spread extents too uniformly level to admit of springs, and areas too open to evaporation and the direct operation of the sun's rays, to retain moisture. It has been generally asserted, that not far from the shores of the upper Missouri, Kansas, Platte, Yellow Stone, Arkansas, and Red Rivers, the prairies become a sterile and moving sand. More recent discoveries tend to discredit these assertions. The prairies the most remote from rivers are generally found yielding in the season a rank growth of grass, plants, and flowers. When American population shall press upon the means of subsistence, the vast level grass plains with coal beds and salt springs beneath, will be dotted with houses of brick and hedges of thorn, and will be the land of shepherds and cultivators. To encourage this hope, a fact equally new, beautiful, and unquestionable has been settled by experience, that the innocent labors of the cultivator call down the blessing of the sky upon the earth. Between the husbandman, the earth, and the atmosphere there seems a sort of compatibility and contract, that the one shall till, and the others grant moisture and increase. Oppression and disease have no sooner banished man from the plains of Babylon, Persia, and Palestine, than the ground parches, the trees disappear, the beasts, and even the birds depart into exile, and the country, abandoned to sterility, becomes a moving sand. In reverse of this order, when the thousands of square leagues of dry grass plains west of the Mississippi, shall become the resorts of husbandmen, the granges, the hedges, the young orchards, the mulberry groves, forming a new alliance with the sky will generate showers, arrest the clouds, and pour innumerable rivulets over all these green wastes.

In regard to the products of the west, without entering into details foreign to our plan, we remark four distinct species of cultivation, predominating in as many parallel belts, as we descend from the northern extremity of the valley towards the south. The first is a zone with products similar to the northern Atlantic states; and commencing at the sources of the Mississippi, and terminating at Prairie du Chien, it corresponds to the climate between Montreal and Boston. The Indian corn of the northern states, Irish potatoes, rye, wheat, and cultivated grasses are raised in perfection. The winter has an average duration of five months.

The second belt, commencing at Prairie du Chien, and terminating at latitude 36 deg., produces the gourd-seed corn, rye, wheat, apples, pears, peaches, and sweet potatoes. The average winter is four months. The next belt, reaching from 36 to 31 deg., is the region of cotton. From 30 deg. to the gulf of Mexico is the belt of the sugar cane, the orange and fig tree, and the corresponding productions. Sugar and cotton from these districts already constitute a prodigious item in the products of the American soil; and when this valley is peopled and cultivated, as one day it will be, imagination can hardly limit the extent, to which these articles will be produced.

The progress of the population of this country is without any example or parallel in the records of other colonies in ancient or modern times; not excepting even the annals of the advancement of the Atlantic country. We can remember, when all this country, except the ancient French colonies in it, was an unknown and an unpeopled wilderness. The first settlers encountered incredible hardships and dangers. But only open before Americans a fertile soil, and a mild climate, and their native enterprise, fostered by the stimulant effect of freedom and mild laws, will overcome every impediment. Sickness, solitude, mountains, the war-hoop, the merciless tomahawk, wolves, panthers, and bears, dear and distant homes, forsaken forever, will come over their waking thoughts, and revisit their dreams in vain, to prevent the young, florid and unportioned pair from scaling remote mountains, descending long rivers, and finally selecting their spot in the forests, and consecrating their solitary cabin with the dear and sacred name of home.

The following synoptical view will show in a few words, the astonishing advance of this population. In 1790 the population of this valley, exclusive of the country west of the Mississippi and of Florida, which were not then within our territorial limits, was estimated by enumeration, at little more than one hundred thousand. In 1800 it was something short of three hundred and eighty thousand. In 1810 it was short of one million. In 1820, including the population west of the Mississippi, rating the population of Florida at twenty thousand, and that of the parts of Virginia and Pennsylvania included in this valley at three hundred thousand, and it will give the population of 1820 at two millions five hundred thousand. The present population may be rated at four millions. It will be perceived, that this is an increase, in more than a duplicate ratio in ten years.

Some considerable allowance must be made, of course, for the flood of immigration, which can not reasonably be expected to set this way for the future, as strongly as it has for the past. Ohio, with the largest and most dense population of any of the western states, has nearly doubled her number of inhabitants, between the census of 1820 and 1830. During that interval, her gain by immigration has hardly equalled her loss by emigration; and of course, is simply that of natural increase. In the rapidity of this increase, we believe, this state not only exceeds any other in the west, but in the world. It is the good natured jest of all, who travel through the western states, that however productive in other harvests, they are still more so in an unequalled crop of flaxen-headed children, the nobler growth our realms supply!. We have a million more inhabitants than the thirteen good old United States, when, at the commencement of the revolutionary war, they threw down the gauntlet in the face of the parent country, then the most powerful empire on the globe.

Notwithstanding the impression, so generally entertained in the Atlantic country, that this valley is universally unhealthy, and notwithstanding the necessary admission, that fever and ague is prevalent to a great and annoying degree, the stubborn facts above stated, demonstrate, beyond all possibility of denial, that no country is more propitious to increase by natural population. Wherever the means of easy, free, and ample subsistence are provided, it is in the nature and order of human things, that population should increase rapidly. In such a country, though some parts of it should prove sickly, perseverance will ultimately triumph over even this impediment, the most formidable of all. In that fertile region, for its insalubrious districts are almost invariably those of the highest fertility, immigrants will arrive, become sickly and discouraged; and perhaps, return with an evil report of the country. In the productive and sickly sections of the south, allured by its rich products, and its exemption from winter, adventurers will successively arrive, fix themselves, become sickly, and it may be, die. Others, lusting for gain, and with that recklessness to the future, for wise ends awarded us by Providence, and undismayed by the fate of those who have preceded them, will replace them. By culture, draining, the feeding of cattle, and the opening the country to the fever-banishing breeze, the atmosphere is found gradually to meliorate. The inhabitants, taught by experience and suffering, come by degrees to learn the climate, the diseases, and preventives, and a race will finally stand, which will possess the adaptation to the country, which results from acclimation; and even these sections are found in time, to have a degree of natural increase of population with the rest. Such has proved to be the steady advance of things in the sickliest points of the south. The rapidity of our increase in numbers multiplies the difficulties of subsistence and stimulates, and sharpens the swarming faculties and propensities in the parent hive, and will cause, that in due lapse of time and progress of things, every fertile quarter section in this valley will support its family.

Another pleasant circumstance appended to this view is, that almost the entire population of the valley are cultivators of the soil. The inhabitants of crowded towns and villages, the numerous artizans and laborers in manufactories, can neither be, as a mass, so healthy, so virtuous or happy, as free cultivators of the soil. The man whose daily range of prospect is dusty streets, or smoky and dead brick walls, and whose views become limited by habit to the enclosure of these walls; who depends for his subsistence on the daily supplies of the market, and whose motives to action are elicited by constant and hourly struggle and competition with his fellows, will have the advantage in some points over the secluded tenant of a cabin or a farm house. But still, taking every thing into the calculation, we would choose to be the owner of a half section of land, and daily contemplate nature, as we tilled the soil, aided in that primitive and noble occupation by our own vigorous children. The dweller in towns and villages may have more of the air and tone of society, and his daughters may keep nearer to the changes of the fashions. But we have little doubt, that, in striking the balance of enjoyment, the latter will be found to be the happier man, and more likely to have a numerous and healthy family. The people of the west, with very small deductions, are cultivators of the soil. All, that are neither idle, nor unable to labor, have a rural abundance of the articles, which the soil can furnish, far beyond the needs of the country; and it is one of our most prevalent complaints, that this abundance is far beyond the chances of profitable sale.

The extent, to which the commerce of the country has been carried, may be inferred from the fact, that the annual exports from New Orleans average from twelve to fifteen millions of dollars. Among the items in 1831, was one hundred and fifty-seven thousand three hundred and twenty-eight barrels of flour, from fifty to eighty thousand hogsheads of sugar, twelve million pounds of lead, and two million dollars worth of pork, beside the staples of cotton and tobacco. The whole amount of steam boat tonnage exceeds fifty thousand tons. Three hundred and eighty steam boats have been built or run; and more than two hundred are now actually running upon the western rivers.

New Orleans, the chief city of the western country, contains over fifty thousand inhabitants, and more commercial business is transacted in it than in any other of the size in America. Cincinnati, the next largest town, contains over thirty thousand inhabitants; and few towns in the United States surpass it in beauty. Pittsburgh, a town of immense manufacturing business and resources, contains with its suburbs twenty-two thousand four hundred and thirty-three inhabitants. Louisville, a large commercial town of Kentucky, contains upwards of ten thousand inhabitants. St. Louis, Nashville, Lexington, and Zanesville, are large and growing towns; and hundreds of villages are rapidly advancing to the same rank. Towers, churches, manufactories, seminaries, and institutions are springing up on every side.

Before we proceed to present sketches of the adventurous spirits, who preceded in the discovery and settlement of this vast valley, we give in a compressed and tabular view, some of its most interesting physical, moral, and political features.

It contains four-fifths of the area of the United States. The Missouri exceeds three thousand miles in length. The Mississippi has a course of two thousand eight hundred; the Arkansas of two thousand five hundred; Red River of one thousand eight hundred; the Ohio of one thousand five hundred; White River of one thousand two hundred; and Tennessee of the same extent—some of the rivers of the Missouri, as the Platte and Yellow Stone, have courses of equal length.

Proceeding on a less ratio of increase, than that which

has marked the progress of western population from the commencement of its settlement, in the year 1850 this valley will contain ten millions of inhabitants, or more than half the population of the whole United States. Of course, the balance of physical power will be west of the Alleghany mountains. Another interesting circumstance may be mentioned. So far as physical configuration and relative position may be supposed capable of influencing the physical and moral destinies of a country, there is no one of the same extent on the earth, every part of which is so intimately connected with every other part by physical relations and mutual necessities, as the eastern and western, the northern and southern divisions of this great valley. Of course, sectional feeling will be less likely to arise, as a cause of jealousy, severance, and disunion between the several members of the western confederacy. Enlightened nationality is a great political advantage, which this region, in the natural order of things, ought to possess in an uncommon degree. No country has the natural means of such easy and rapid interchange between its remotest extremities, and the inhabitahts have every inducement to become a social people.

There were supposed to be, in 1832 four thousand five hundred churches of the different denominations of Christians, thirty colleges and larger seminaries, with a rapidly increasing number of primary and common schools. The militia in 1832 was about four hundred and thirty thousand.

When we take into view the extent of this valley, the uncounted millions of acres of fertile lands, yet to be redeemed from the wilderness, when we measure the probable increase by the astonishing actual ratio of the past, a measure of increase unparallelled in the annals of colonization, we can not but contemplate this vast, fair, and fertile valley, in the centre of our great continent, with an elevated moral interest. While the broad and calculating reach of anticipation extends to the generations to come, and imagines what will be the influence of this new empire upon the history of the future, we should be lost to ourselves, and the common sentiments of human nature, if we did not turn with a keen and enquiring spirit to ask, who and what were the discoverers and pioneers of this country, who laid the foundations of its present improvements and future prospects?

In the days of ancient fable, discoverers and founders were reputed after their death to be demi-gods. Temples were reared to them; and their achievements were inscribed upon monumental marble and brass. More enlightened, not we would hope at the expense of grateful sensibility, we will place the great names of the founders of our empire before our children. We will cause their eyes to glisten by the recital of their deeds of daring, their spirit of self sacrifice, their heroic conflicts, and their lonely toils. In contemplating the intrepidity, heroism, disinterestedness, and capability of endurance of our forefathers, we present a new and more elevated standard of imitation to their posterity, born in times and under circumstances tending to foster effeminacy and selfishness. It can never be useless to contemplate these images of stern self control, of sublime vigor and perseverance. In seeing what men have been, and may be, we find the best incitements to arrest the downward tendency to indolence, self indulgence, and pusillanimity. We shall attempt, with these intentions, to pass the chief of these mighty and master spirits in review in the following chapters.

CHAPTER II.

DISCOVERY AND CONQUEST OF FLORIDA, AND SETTLEMENT
ON THE MISSISSIPPI.

A sketch of these events, though almost an episode in the annals of western history, from the little influence that Florida has exerted upon the western country, is due to a general and chronological view of the subject. Florida was the first part of this valley known to the inhabitants of Eu-

rope. This country had been discovered and occupied by
the Spaniards nearly forty years, before any definite knowledge of the Mississippi, as the mighty river of the western
interior, had been obtained.

Cuba, as the most fertile and conspicuous of the West
Indies, or Antilles, was among the earliest Spanish settlements. Havana early became the most important city
in this western archipelago, the central point of its communications, the depot of its products, and the arsenal whence
were fitted out its expeditions for discovery and conquest.

So near are the keys of Florida to Havana, that the
naval communications of that great mart could not be kept
up without making the discovery of the Floridas, as an incidental event of course. It is probable, that Sebastian
Cabot, the English navigator, saw the shores of this country, in a few years after the discovery of the continent by
Columbus. But the effective discovery must be conceded
to the Spanish navigator, Juan Ponce de Leon, in 1512;
that is about twenty years after the discovery of America.
The Spanish chronicles relate, that he undertook this voyage in consequence of a popular tradition, which prevailed at Cuba, that somewhere in the interior of Florida, there
was a precious spring fountain, whose waters had the property of imparting rejuvenescence, and afterwards perpet-
uating perennial youth. Having plundered the empire of
Montezuma and the Incas of immense masses of gold, it
would have been an admirable appendage to the acquisition of these greedy adventurers, to have lived in immortal
youth in the possession of their ill gotten gains.

He fitted out a small squadron from Cuba, and steered
across the gulf to the continent, in search of this fountain
of perpetual youth. He discovered land on Easter day,
and gave it the name of Florida, from the Spanish name of
that festival, *pasqua de flores*, the festival of flowers; or,
according to Herera, from the appearance of the country,
which at the time of the discovery, was covered with abundant flowers. If this were the origin of the name Florida,
or the flowering country, the catalpa and magnolia, the wild
pink shrubberies, fringing the shores of the streams, and
the white blossoms of the cornus Florida would indeed give

reason that it should be so called, the aspect of the country in early spring being that of a boundless waste of flowers of the most brilliant colors and fragrant odors.

The adventurer debarked his expedition. He wandered into the interior, and found plenty of fish and game, but no fountain of rejuvenescence. On the contrary, he soon met bands of fierce and determined savages, very different from the docile, timid, and effiminate Indians of Cuba. He was glad to escape these conflicts by a rapid retreat to the shore, whence he debarked for the islands.

Grijalva, Vasques, Garay, Allyon, and Narvaes fitted out successive expeditions for discovery, chiefly in search of mines, between 1518 and 1528. These expeditions present little of interest, except the cupidity and perfidy of the Spanish in their attempt to carry off the natives, as slaves, and the fierce retaliations of the natives. The expeditions all ended in ineffectual explorations, defeats, storms, wrecks, and disappointment.

The attempt of Ferdinand de Soto, governor of Cuba, was a more sustained enterprise, contemplating no less than the conquest and colonization of Florida. He sailed from Havana with a powerful armament of nine ships, manned with a thousand men, and carrying two hundred and fifty horses, and various kinds of live stock, indicating a purpose to establish a colony. This formidable array was headed by a leader, who, unlike most of the Spanish adventurers, sought glory, rather than gold. In a constant succession of skirmishes with the natives, he penetrated the interior, as far as the country of the Chickasaws, returning on his steps from that region to the Mississippi, being probably the first European who ever saw it above the mouth. He crossed it near the point where Red River enters. It is likely, that he had very little idea either of the extent or magnitude of either of those rivers. On the latter he encamped, sickened, and died. He had rendered himself so much an object of hatred and terror to the Indians, that, either to conceal the knowledge of his death, or prevent his body from violation, it was enclosed in a rude coffin, made from the section of a hollow tree, and sunk in the river. His followers, reduced to two hundred

and fifty in number, and brought to the last degree of want
and despair, were glad to fly from these wild and inhospitable forests, and Florida was once more left without an European inhabitant.

The illustrious protestant admiral Coligny, so celebrated in French history, formed the project of establishing
on these remote shores a colony of Hugunots, as the pro-
testants were called in France, in order to furnish them an
asylum from persecution, in the wilderness.   Charles of
France, anxious to get rid of his subjects of this description,
furthered the project.   An expedition to form a settlement
was accordingly fitted out, and the command given to Francois Ribault.   The colonists were landed not far from the
present position of St. Augustine.   On the eastern shore
of the bay of St. Joseph he built a fort, which the French
writers contend, was the first European fortification erected east of the Mississippi river.   In honor of the king of
France, it was called fort Charles, and a number of pro-
testants settled there.

This ill-fated colony suffered disasters from disaffection,
mutiny, and hunger, among themselves, and from intention-
al abandonment by the parent country.   After a considerable interval of time, Ribault arrived with seven ships and
adequate reinforcements from France, but it was only to
draw from the new settlement all the men that could be
spared, for an attack upon the Spanish fleet in those seas.
M. de Laudoniere was left in command; but with a force
unequal to its defence.   In the absence of Ribault, it was
attacked by Don Pedro Menendez, who commanded a Spanish force from the Antilles, charged by the king of Spain
to extirpate the heretics from Florida, and plant orthodox
Spanish catholics, in their place.   He fulfilled his detestable mission to the letter, attacking, and carrying the fort by
storm.   All that escaped the sword, were immediately
hung. with this inscription labelled on their backs: 'not as
heretics, but as enemies of God and the Virgin.'   A respectable protestant gentleman felt his spirit stirred to a-
venge the massacre of his countrymen, and the heirs of his
faith, by his own private resources.   He fitted out a small
armament, sailed to the country, enlisted a number of In-

dians exasperated with the conduct of the Spanish garrison, as allies, attacked the fort, and after a severe resistance carried it. All that survived the assault, were hung on the same trees, from which the miserable French had been suspended, with this retaliating label on their backs: 'not as Spaniards, or soldiers, but as traitors and assassins.' Such are the revolting results of bigotry in all time.

Detailed views of the history of Florida, from their little connexion with the settlement and political fortunes of the west, will not be here introduced. This extensive plain of savannas, lakes, and pine woods soon returned to the possession of the Spaniards, whose possession of Cuba and the Antilles gave them peculiar facilities for retaining it; and it remained in their occupancy nearly half a century. It never reached any considerable extent of population or political importance; and was chiefly valuable to Spain, on account of its cooler and healthier temperature, than Cuba; and its extensive pasturage, furnishing cattle to the garrison and inhabitants of Havana.

The first efficient settlement of the Mississippi valley must be traced to the French, and was a germ of the important colony of Canada. Previously, therefore, to entering on that history, we premise a few brief sketches of the settlement of Canada. The discovery of this country was by Gasper Cortereal, a Portuguese navigator in 1500. He first saw the great river St. Lawrence. He coasted the shores of Newfoundland and Labrador; and while pursuing his explorations in the interior, he and his associates were slain in those inhospitable forests by the natives. The patriarch of the French colonies in North America was James Cartier, an experienced mariner of St. Malo, who sailed April 20, 1534, with two ships and one hundred and twenty-two men for Newfoundland. During this voyage he discovered the bay of Chaleur, and the gulf of St. Lawrence. In 1535 he sailed a second time, under a royal commission, with three ships and a large number of young adventurers, of distinction, elate with the hope of meeting similar golden fortunes with the first Spanish adventurers. On this second voyage he discovered the St. Lawrence, and sailed up that noble stream one hundred

2*

leagues. He made extensive explorations along the shores as far as the Isle of Orleans, ingratiated himself with many of the savage tribes; and by a union of stratagem and force, carried a chief of one of their tribes to France. But being able to raise no expectations of finding gold and silver in abundance, the only inducements in that age, which tempted the cupidity of princes to attempt colonies, the country was abandoned.

Enthusiasm pushed this adventurer to continual efforts to magnify the importance of his discovery, and the utility of colonizing it. In 1540 he persuaded Francois de la Roche, a nobleman of Picardy, to furnish him the means of effecting a settlement in Canada. Cartier was appointed to the command of five ships, and countenanced by a royal commission. Ou the 23d of August, 1540, this expedition arrived at St. Croix, and sailed up the St. Lawrence four leagues above that point, where he built on a high cliff the first fortification, called Charlesbourg, at no great distance from the present position of Quebec, where he passed the winter. The journal of the first winter spent there speaks of ice two fathoms thick, and snow more than four feet deep; and of that bitter and unrelenting severity of a Canadian winter, too well confirmed by subsequent acquaintance with the climate. This extreme severity, pressing upon unacclimated adventurers, poorly supplied with comfortable shelter and comforts, produced the natural results of wasting and mortal sickness. Yet the banks of the magnificent St. Lawrence furnished a rich soil, and delightful habitations, during the brief warm summer of the climate. The connexion of this mighty river with the vast northern lakes, and the valley of the Mississippi, the immense mart thence opened for trading with the natives, and the consequent resources of the fur trade, together with the peculiar aptitude of the French for that trade, and for conciliating the savages, soon gave solidity and importance to the settlements in this inclement region. These advantages enabled the colony to surmount the severity of the climate, occasional wars with the Indians, and even the conquest of the English, to whom the colony surrendered in 1628, one hundred and thirty years before its final conquest by Wolfe. It was shortly after restored to France; and continued to advance in population, wealth, and importance. Lying in the rear of New England and New York, and encircling the northern frontier of those provinces, it continued for the space of a century to menace the conquest of those colonies, and to send forth expeditions of French and Indians, to plunder and harass those incipient settlements; and to fill their early annals with chronicles of the border wars with the Canadians. From the earliest periods of the foundation of Quebec and Montreal, the French aptitude to ingratiate themselves with the Indians had been conspicuous. The colonists began early to cohabit with the Indian women, and to display that inclination for hunting, and trapping, and becoming, in their phrase, expert *coureurs du bois*, or woodmen, which has marked their character from that time to this. They were not slow in discovering the astonishing and instinctive shrewdness of the Indians, in pursuing their long excursions through forests, and along rivers and lakes, in pursuit of furs and game. Associating and identifying themselves with them, the French soon became more expert hunters and trappers than the natives themselves. Adopting their manners and tastes at first from policy, they soon imbibed them by inclination and temperament, becoming a great community of woodmen. In their hunting and trapping expeditions along the vast shores, and numberless waters, and unexplored forests, and deserts of the northern lakes, they were not long in obtaining some indefinite conceptions from the Indians of a river of vast length and magnitude, which pursued a course directly opposite that of the St. Lawrence, and which rolled through almost interminable forests into an unknown sea.

We have seen, that the English had seen the mouth of the Mississippi, soon after the first discovery of America. But it was only to discover an apparent arm of the sea, winding through the vast marshes of the Balize. The Spanish colonists of Florida must have often seen the Mississippi. But they had never surveyed it much above the mouth of Red River, that is to say, only a short section of its lower course, through its deep swamps and forests. The ex-

tent of the vast stream, the almost numberless rivers that
enter it, the great and fertile valley watered by it had not
even entered their conceptions.

The honor of the efficient discovery of the Mississippi,
probably belongs to the fathers Marquette and Joliette,
two French missionaries from Canada, who were detailed
for that object by M. de Talon. They started on their
journey of discovery from Quebec with three associates.
They traversed the immense lakes in a birch bark periogue,
ascended lake Michigan to the bay of St. Joseph; and
thence, it is supposed, over the present accustomed portage
from that bay to the Ouisconsin, and down that river to the
Mississippi, and thence down that stream, through its forests, and passing the mouths of its tributaries, to the Arkansas. Those early French discoverers seem all to have been
distinguished by a full measure of the vivacity of their national enthusiasm. That imagination must be cold, that
does not kindle in view of the grandeur of the forests, tributaries, precipices, prairies, animals, and birds discovered
in a summer descent of that river, even at the present time,
when the visions of fancy all have yielded to the often repeated surveys of experience. We need not admire, that
those explorers saw in the numberless swans and water-
fowls on the undisturbed bosom of the stream, in the fishes
beneath its pellucid wave, in the tangle of grape vines
on its shores, in the buffaloes and other wild animals of its
forests and prairies, in the numerous tribes of red men a-
long its shores, in its majestic sweep down its dark woods,
in the grand bluffs, the influx of the mighty and turbid Missouri, the grand-tower, and other precipices not far above
the mouth of the Ohio, the entrance of that majestic and
placid stream, in short, of forest, prairie, bird, beast, and
production along such a prodigious length of unexplored
empire of the fancy, ample materials for all the exaggerations, which we find recorded in the journal of their
voyage.

It could not be expected, that these fathers on their return, would undervalue the merit of their discovery, or un-
derrate the beauty and advantages of the river and country,
they had explored. M. de la Salle, commandant of fort

Frontiniac on lake Ontario, a needy adventurer, possessed of rank, courage, and talents, yielded his imagination to the contemplation of this discovery. To explore the Mississippi, which had as yet only been discovered, promised fame, wealth, success. The exhausted condition of his finances offered sufficiently formidable obstacles to an enterprise, which could not be prosecuted without money. At the close of the summer of 1669, by the greatest exertions, he had built, and equipped a small vessel, called the *Griffin*, at the lower extremity of lake Erie, near the present position of Buffalo. It was the first structure of the kind, that had ever been seen on these unexplored inland seas. The company consisted of thirty-four men, among whom was father Lewis Hennepin, a Franciscan friar, and the interesting chronicler of this voyage. In their progress along the lake coast, they were joined by many other woodmen, eager to explore the country west of the lakes. By the time their vessel had reached the bay of St. Joseph, it was already full-freighted with a valuable cargo of furs and peltries; and debarking the adventurers on the western shore of the lake, the vessel was despatched back with her cargo. But as she stopped on her return, she was arrested, and burned by the savages, and all her crew massacred. By this disaster the number of the adventurers was reduced to thirty-four, and their communication with Canada in a measure cut off. From lake Michigan they ascended the Chicago; and, passing through the table lake at its source, they descended the des Plaines and the Illinois to Peoria lake, where they built a fort, and passed the winter. They called the fort *Creve cœur*, or broken heart, either, as some say, from their own want and sufferings, during the winter, or, as others affirm, from its being the position of a bloody battle between the Iroquois and Illinois Indians, in which the latter were defeated, and, beside the slain, suffered a loss of eight hundred prisoners, carried by their enemy into captivity. In the spring de La Salle returned with those men to Canada, to procure supplies and reinforcements.

In the absence of the commandant, the father Hennepin was instructed to ascend the Mississippi to its sources;

while La Salle on his return proposed to descend the river to its mouth; so that between them, the exploration of the river might be complete.

The father left the fort in the spring with two associates, to accomplish his part of the plan. He reached the Mississippi, March 8th, 1680. Having arrived there, whether he found it easier to descend, than ascend the current, or whether he deemed that more fame would result from the downward, than the upward exploration, does not appear. But he descended the Mississippi from the mouth of the Illinois to the Balize in sixteen days. The discrepancies and exaggerations in his journal, and the very short period occupied in the descent, have induced some historians to view his whole narrative with doubt. But a periogue with a moderate use of oars, during the spring floods, and floating night and day, would easily descend the river from that point to the Balize in sixteen days. His journal records a fact of more difficult credibility, than the rapidity of his descent, to wit, that on his return he ascended the river from the mouth of the Illinois to the falls of St. Anthony. Thence he returned to Canada, and embarked immediately for France. He there published his travels in the most splendid style, and dedicating his book to the great minister Colbert. The country received the name of Louisiana, in honor of Louis XIV, then on the throne of France.

La Salle, in the mean time, delighted with the country of the Illinois, put in requisition every resource, which his exhausted means would allow, to furnish another expedition to that region. A crowd of adventurers joined him to push their fortunes in these unexplored countries. They reached the Mississippi in 1683. With these associates he founded the villages of Kaskaskia and Cahokia, in the fertile alluvion near the Mississippi, since called the American bottom; and these are the oldest settlements in what may be properly called the Mississippi valley. Having given his friend M. de Tonti the command of this little colony, he hastened back to Canada, and thence to France, in order to enlist the French ministry in co-operation with his views.

One of his first objects was to convince the ministry of the existence of that astonishing inland water communication, which nature has furnished between the gulf of St. Lawrence and of Mexico, which unites these distant points by an almost unbroken chain of nearly four thousand miles in length. He first comprehended, and suggested that plan, upon which the French government afterwards so steadily acted, of extending a chain of communications from one point to the other, thus drawing a hostile arch, like a bow, round every point of the English colonies, save that which was shielded by the ocean: and thus insulating these settlements within this impassable barrier. Communications being thus formed between Canada, the lakes, and the upper Mississippi, it was necessary to the completion of this plan to commence an establishment at the mouth of the river.

La Salle obtained from the king the command of a squadron to explore the mouth of the Mississippi by the Mexican gulf. The expedition sailed, August, 1684; but steering too far to the westward, instead of reaching the mouth of the Mississippi, they made land more than one hundred leagues west of the Balize, in the bay of St. Bernard, in the present country of Texas. One of his vessels was stranded on the bar at the entrance of the bay. He finally succeeded in landing his followers on the banks of the Gaudaloupe. They soon raised a fortification, which protected them from the continual assaults of the savages. But they were visited with disease; and in want, and in utter ignorance of their position on these desolate prairies, they found their condition inexpressibly lonely and hopeless.

The unquenchable spirit of this brave man impelled him to incredible efforts to rescue the band of associates, thus attached to his fortunes, from impending destruction. His first effort was with twenty followers to reach the Mississippi, and ascend it to the colony of his friend M. de Tonti. The nearest point of the Mississippi on the line of his march was not less than five hundred miles. His route was through a country wholly unknown, and peopled with various tribes of Indians; and presented an endless succession of swamps, forests, prairies, and rivers. In advancing into these unknown solitudes, the Indians received them with the utmost kindness; domesticating the wanderers, and offering them their wives, their game, and the shelter of their cabins, with a boundless hospitality. Four of his licentious followers left him to domesticate themselves with the savages. Sickness, desertion, and weariness compelled him in weakness and discouragement to retrace his way to the fort of St. Bernard.

In a few days they resumed courage to renew their attempt to journey over land to the Illinois. Two long months they wandered in a north-west direction through the unknown forests and prairies. At length they encamped in a beautiful plain, where game abounded, and where they were welcomed by a tribe of Indians. De La Salle here halted, to allow his exhausted companions relaxation and repose. The Indians made them free of their cabins, as on their former journey. Delighted with this unbridled license, wearied with toil, and excited by the example of the deserters on the former trip, these unprincipled recruits from the populace of a French city, abandoned their commander and joined the Indians. Upbraided by their commander, to treachery they added murder. They first assassinated a party which La Salle had sent out to hunt, among which was his nephew. La Salle, aware of this mutinous spirit, and uneasy about the fate of the hunting party, set out in search of them. His gloomy presentiments were soon realized. Scarcely had he discovered their dead bodies before he fell himself under the fire of the mutineers. Thus died this distinguished adventurer, identified with the earliest periods of European acquaintance with the Mississippi valley, alike illustrious by his merits, his courage, and his misfortunes. History has not clearly settled at what point of his route he fell. Some of the ill-fated colony, which he left at St. Bernard, were murdered by the savages, and the remainder were carried captive into the interior of Mexico, by a Spanish detachment from New Leon.

The mutineers soon quarrelled among themselves. In the quarrel the two persons that fired upon La Salle, in the re-action of justice, inflicted death upon each other. Two priests of the party became penitent for having winked at the assassination, and furnished these incidents. Seven of the company only remained, who, guided by these priests, and conducted by the Indian tribes on their way, finally reached the Arkansas, where they found a French colony from Canada, that had just formed a settlement there.

Charlevoix throws a melancholy interest over the fate of the other great discoverer of Louisiana, father Marquette. Previous to his discovery of the Mississippi, he had been a laborious and devoted missionary among the Canadian tribes of Indians. He was still prosecuting his travels with great ardor. On his return from Chicago to Michilimacinac, he entered a river of lake Michigan, which bore his name. He requested his followers to land, intimating a presentiment that he should end his days on that lonely shore. They landed, and at his request raised a rude altar, at which he celebrated mass, afterwards requesting, that he might be left to offer thanks to God alone for half an hour. When they returned, the apostle of the wilderness had expired.

Both La Salle and Marquette furnish affecting examples of the evanescence of human records. The place where they were buried, is unknown.

The Spaniards and the French seem to have been alike aware, that these beginnings would be the germ of a great empire. The whole policy of each nation sufficiently intimates, with how much jealousy the one nation watched the colonial movements of the other. The Spaniards of Florida had founded Pensacola in west Florida, obviously as a military post, to watch and overawe the French colonial attempts in these regions. Ibberville, by order of the king of France, sailed for Louisiana, accompanied by three considerable ships of war. In March, 1699, after exploring much of the Florida shore, they entered the Mississippi. On that river they became acquainted with many of the native tribes, and entered into amicable negotiations with them. The expedition terminated by establishing a colony at Biloxi, in Biloxi bay, a position equally remarka-

3

ble for its health and sterility. It was fortified, garrisoned by a few soldiers, buccaneers, and Canadians, and left in the command of M. de Bienville.

In May following, the governor of Biloxi set out on an exploring expedition on the Mississippi. In that river he discovered at eighteen leagues from the sea, an English vessel named the *Ban,* which had left a consort at the mouth of the river. The English captain assured him, that he wished to plant a colony there under the protection of the French, if he could obtain for it liberty of conscience, in which case four hundred families would emigrate to it from Carolina. He was assured, that the king of France had not expelled heretics from his kingdom at home, to establish them in a republic in the new world. The Englishman was in doubt, whether he was in the Mississippi or not; and Bienville, glad to avail himself of his ignorance, assured him, that this was not the Mississippi, which was much farther to the west, but a river of Canada under the jurisdiction of his master. Deceived in this way, the English captain was induced to put his ship about, and to leave the river. This point has hence borne the name of the *English turn.*

In December, 1699, Ibberville arrived with two large ships of war from France. With him came thirty miners, and sixty Canadians accompanied by M. de Seuer, who had been an extensive traveller in Canada; and they were enjoined to ascend the Mississippi, and form an establishment near its sources, and particularly to explore a mine of *terre verte,* which had been discovered in that region by M. de Thuillier. With this force M. de Seuer ascended the Mississippi, and established a fort on an island in the Mississippi, reputed to be two hundred leagues above the mouth of the Illinois. It was, probably, that which is now called Rock island, at the mouth of Rock river. It was intended to overawe the Indians at the sources of the river, and along the shores of lake Superior. He returned thence to Montreal, taking with him chiefs of the Sauteurs and Sioux, being the first of those tribes, that had ever been seen in Canada. They were won by the gifts and kindness of the governor of that city, to whom they presented as many arrows, as they numbered warriors in their tribe. These were the secrets by which the French gained such an unbounded influence over the Indians of the Mississippi valley.

Ibberville, informed of the attempt of the English to establish themselves on the lower Mississippi, determined to anticipate them. He embarked on that river with four small vessels, loaded with provisions, and manned with fifty men, in January, 1700. In a position eighteen leagues above the Balize, he built a fort on the bank of the river, near the present position of Placquemine.

Accompanied by M. de Bienville he set out from this fort to visit the famous tribe of Natchez, and another Indian tribe inhabiting a lake south-west of the Mississippi, believed to be that at present denominated Sicily ilsand. On the third day of their ascent, they reached the chief town of the Natchez, situated near the present town of that name. They found a missionary from Canada already among them. The great *sun chief* of the Natchez visited them in state, borne on a litter, and accompanied by six hundred men. They noted in the manners of this chief more dignity and native politeness, than they had yet seen in any of these petty sovereigns. His authority was despotic. On the decease of a chief of hi srank, it was the custom for his domestics and wives to devote themselves to death, to be ready to serve him in the *land of souls,* as on earth. Their traditions affirmed, that their former population had exceeded two hundred thousand; and that they had then possessed nineteen hundred sun chiefs; though at this time the number was reduced to seventeen. They had a temple of the sun, in which they preserved a perpetual fire, and on the altar of which they offered the first fruits of their harvest, and of the proceeds of their game. It was an article of their faith, that brave warriors, who had killed many men and buffaloes, would dwell in the world to come, in a charming country, abounding in abundance of fish, game, and fruits, and enjoying perennial sun shine; while the spirits of the imbecile and peaceable would be exiled to a land of lakes and marshes, where all their subsistence would be fish and alligators. We may remark, in passing, that at this time the Mississippi forests abounded with buffaloes and other game, rendering the subsistence of these first French expeditions on the river, affairs of comparative ease. During this visit of the French, the temple of the sun was struck by lightning and burnt. To appease the Great Spirit, supposed to be angry, the Natchez sacrificed four children in the flames, and would have offered more, but for the determined opposition of the French.

About this time Bienville conducted an exploring expedition far to the west. He ascended the Washita to the point of the Warm Springs and crossed thence to Red River, passing through a pleasant country, and becoming acquainted with many Indian tribes before unknown, particularly the Natchitoches. Biloxi was visited by a Spanish expedition, attempting in vain to expel the French from that post. It was soon after voluntarily abandoned by the French, and a fort established at Mobile in its place.

The Canadian wanderers of the woods and waters, in exploring the St. Peters of the upper Mississippi, had failed to find ores of copper in the *terre verte.* But they had become well acquainted with the Sacs, Sioux, and the various dwellers with barbarous names in those far wildernesses. They had been most egregiously deceived by the confident tales of an impostor, who pretended to have discovered mines of unexampled richness on the Missouri. Search for these mines brought them acquainted with the extensive lead mines, which, however, yielded gains too slow and moderate to satisfy their greedy and inflamed imaginations.

In 1702 news arrived in these forests, that France and Spain had declared war with England. In 1703 the English made an unavailing effort, with a fleet of seventeen vessels, aided by two thousand savages, to take St. Augustine in East Florida. At an early period in the annals of these settlements, it became a part of the French policy to gather from the streets and magdalens of the French towns poor girls, and to send them to this remote colony, where they were generally married to the colonists on the night of their arrival. The history of one of the girls, thus sent out, presents a series of incidents surpassing in interest and pathos the fictions of romance. About this time the annals of Louisiana begin to give details of the wars between the Choctaws, in alliance with the French, and the Chickasaws, who were friends of the English. An incident, which occurred near Mobile in 1705, affords striking views of savage character.

The Chickasaws had sold a number of families of the Choctaws, who had visited them in time of peace, as slaves to the English. This exasperated the latter to revenge. It happened, that seventy Chickasaws of both sexes were on a visit to the French fort at Mobile. In returning home, they were obliged to pass through the country of the Choctaws, now at war with them. In their embarrassment, they besought M. de Bienville to grant them an escort of French soldiers, to protect them on their return. He consented, and a captain and twenty-five soldiers were detailed for this service. They arrived near the chief Choctaw town. The Choctaw chiefs invited the Chickasaws to a talk, assuring them, that they did not mean to hinder their return, but only to reproach them for their perfidy in the hearing of the French. The Chickasaws had it not in their power to refuse, and gathered to hear the talk.. The Choctaw chief placed himself in a large open space, surrounded by an immense circle of three thousand of his warriors. He then began his harangue, reproaching them in the most cutting terms with the falsehood and cruelty of their late attempt upon his people. When he had exhausted his stores of invective, he lowered his calumet, as the signal for their death. Instantly thousands of arrows were despatched at them, and they fell. In circumscribing the circle, and in the fury of their revenge, many Choctaws were killed by the arrows of their own people. Among others, Bienville was slightly wounded. He was escorted back to Mobile by three hundred Choctaw warriors.

Ibberville, the great patron of this first French colony, died in 1707, and La Salle, one of the patriarchs of Louisiana, in 1710. In this year an English buccaneer with his crew, made a descent upon Isle au Dauphine, plundering it of fifty thousand dollars. About the same time the French and Spanish settlers began to be embarrassed by the interference of the English of Carolina with the Indians in their vicinity, contracting alliances with them, and presenting a menacing aspect upon their eastern borders. In 1716 Bienville had orders to establish settlements at Natchez, and even as high as the Wabash. In a quarrel with the Natchez, five French were slain by them and six made prisoners. Arriving there, Bienville summoned the chiefs to a conference, in which they readily consented to give up their prisoners, but made more difficulty about surrendering the authors of the murders. Upon this, the murderers were immediately imprisoned by the French. He then obtained the promise, that White-head, the chief of the murderers, should be put to death. Another chief of inferior rank immediately offered himself to die in his stead. Bienville finally proposed peace to them, on condition, that they should send him the head of Big-beard, one of the murderers, and build a fort for the French, with which they complied, and thus became accessories to their own subjugation.

In October of 1716, M. de St. Denis, after having travelled to Mexico, arranged a plan in concert with the Viceroy of that country, to establish missions among the tribes of natives at Nacogdoches, Adayes, and Ayache; and M. de La Motte was sent to commence an establishment at Natchitoches on Red River. At this time, the colony of Mobile numbered seven hundred souls, and possessed four hundred horned cattle. Hitherto agriculture, the most essential interest of a colony, had been almost entirely neglected. The government at length became enlightened to see the advantages of establishing a colony on the Mississippi, that should devote itself to raising provisions. The growing of silk, indigo, rice, and tobacco were the first articles proposed. It was judged also, that Florida could furnish the parent country with pitch, tar, and other naval supplies. New Orleans was selected as the spot on which to commence the new agricultural colony. The settlement was commenced in 1717. The forest trees were cut down, and about one hundred and fifty persons were established in cabins among the dead trees, where that great commercial city now stands.

CHAPTER III.

ANGLO-AMERICAN SETTLEMENTS.

THE first efforts towards the settlement of the Mississippi valley were made by the French, at its three remotest and opposite points, on the Illinois, and at Kaskaskia, whence their settlements extended across the Mississippi to St. Genevieve and St. Louis; on the Mexican gulf at Biloxi and Mobile, and on the lower Mississippi at New Orleans.

In pursuance of their great plan of occupying this whole valley, and connecting their settlements from Canada to the Mexican gulf, by a line of posts with water communications, like the chord of an immense semicircle, stretching along the whole rear of the English settlements, they gradually extended their fortifications to the south side of lake Erie, erecting one at Presq'sle, on the present site of Erie, and another on Boeuf, on French creek, between that point and the Ohio; and a third at the delta of the junction of the Alleghany and Monongahela. The advantages of that admirable position did not escape the eyes of a people remarkably acute to discern the advantages of posts. By it they proposed to command the trade, and awe the obedience of the Indians of the Ohio and the lakes, and connect the southern Canadian posts by the long and unrivalled communication of the Ohio with the settlements of the Wabash, Illinois, and lower Mississippi.

Indeed, they had a double motive to the occupancy of this fine position. The Ohio Company, formed in England, had for its express object the occupancy and settlement of the country on the Ohio. At the recommendation of General Washington, they sent out a party to erect a stockade fort on this very delta, where the Ohio commences. This party, accompanied by a detachment of militia from Virginia, arrived at this point in 1753. They were driven off by the French, who immediately proceeded to anticipate them by erecting a fort on the present position of Pittsburgh, named Du Quesne, after the governor of Canada. So important was the occupancy of this point deemed in England, that the ministry ordered the assemblage of a powerful regular force, under the command of General Braddock, to take it; who, aided by a large body of the provincial militia, set off through the dark forests, and over the pathless mountains for the west. From the time this army had crossed the Alleghanies, its movements were continually watched by spies from fort Du Quesne, whose garrison was thus daily and almost hourly acquainted with its route and progress. General Braddock, stubbornly devoted to the precision of European tactics, moved down from the mountains through the forests in close order, as though marching on the hostile plains of Europe. His army had just crossed the Monongahela, and were defiling from its alluvion through a ravine. On its upland summit lay the French and Indians, concealed among the high grass and timber. The Indians exulted, and assured their French allies that they would shoot them down like pigeons. Washington, thus early provident in council, foresaw the issue, and by his persuasion attempted in vain to avert it. The brave but obstinate English general rushed on to his fate. The Indian yell was raised, and an invisible and invulnerable enemy poured a fire upon them, which literally mowed down their ranks. Washington was spared, apparently as by a miracle. The forest resounded with the groans of the dying. The commander soon received a mortal wound, and a complete rout ensued. The provincials commanded by Washington were the last to retire, covering the retreat of the regulars, and saving all that escaped that ill-fated day. The loss of the English amounted to sixty-four officers out of eighty-five, and about seven hundred privates. The result of this battle gave the French and Indians a complete ascendency on the Ohio. The incursions of the savages extended along the whole western frontier of Virginia, and even excited the apprehensions of the settlements east of the Blue ridge. But in 1758 the tide of war again began to turn against the French. Fort Frontiniac, an important

French post on lake Ontario, was taken by a British detachment under Colonel Bradstreet. This facilitated the reduction of fort Du Quesne on the Ohio. General Forbes was ordered for that service, assisted by a body of provincials and Virginia regulars under Washington, then a colonel.

Before the main army moved from Raystown, in Pennsylvania, Major Grant was detached with eight hundred men, partly regulars and partly provincials, to precede the main army, and reconnoitre the country and the fort. This force, like Braddock's, imprudently advanced into an ambuscade of the' French garrison of fort Du Quesne, was surrounded by the enemy, and after a brave but unavailing struggle, lost three hundred men killed and wounded, and Major Grant and nineteen officers taken prisoners.

General Forbes, with the main army, amounting to eight thousand men, at length advanced from Raystown, slowly marching towards the Ohio, which they did not reach until November. The French, incapable of resisting a force so formidable, abandoned the fort the evening preceding the arrival of the army, and escaped in their boats down the Ohio, to join the colony on the Illinois. The English immediately took possession of this important post, which, in compliment to the popular and successful British minister, they named fort Pitt, and afterwards Pittsburgh. This was the first English establishment on the Ohio. From that period we date the commencement of Anglo-American settlements in this valley.

But even previous to this, an attempt had been made by two men of the name of Tygart and Files to establish their families on an upper water of the Monongahela. The valley in which they selected their abode, still bears the name of Tygart's valley, and his name has been given to the east fork of the Monongahela. The family of Files soon fell victims to the Indians, and that of Tygart, warned by their fate, abandoned the country in 1754.

Not long after, Thomas Eckerly and two brothers, of the sect denominated Dunkards, emigrating from Pennsylvania to the west, and encamped at the mouth of a creek emptying into the Monongahela, ten miles below what is now Morgantown, from that circumstance called Dunkard's creek. These harmless religionists here passed years in sylvan abundance and solitude, unmolested by the Indians, who were carrying desolation among the white settlements in every direction. Their being thus remarkably spared, subjected them to the suspicion of being in confederacy with them, and acting as their spies. The sect was odious, and the elder Eckerly, on his return from a visit to the old settlements, was imprisoned. It was with difficulty that he at length prevailed on the officer of the nearest frontier post, with a guard, to accompany him to his establishment. On approaching the solitary abodes of these inoffensive people, their cabins were found in ashes, the mutilated bodies of the inhabitants strewed the yard, and the ruthless vengeance of savage desolation had swept over their pleasant little fields. It was an affecting testimony to their innocence of the charge of confederacy with the Indians. Mr. Eckerly abandoned the country.

In 1758, a party conducted by Thomas Decker, commenced a settlement on the Monongahela, at the mouth of what is thence called Decker's creek. But in the ensuing spring, the Delawares and Mingoes assaulted it, murdered most of its inmates, and completely broke up the establishment. Soon after the capture of fort Du Quesne, a small fortification had been established at the present position of Brownsville, on the Monongahela, then known by the name of Redstone fort. It was commanded by Captain Paul. One of the survivors of Decker's company reached there, with the intelligence of the destruction of that settlement. The garrison was too weak to send a detachment in pursuit of the murderers. But Captain Paul despatched a runner with the intelligence to fort Pitt. Captain Gibson of that fort, started with thirty men in pursuit of the Indians. Although the perpetrators had retreated beyond his reach, he overtook a small party of Mingoes near the present site of Steubenville. The Little Eagle, a Mingo chief, headed this party. Captain Gibson came upon them at day-break. As soon as the American leader was discovered by the Indian chief, the latter raised the war-hoop and fired upon him. The ball passed through Captain Gibson's hunting shirt, and wounded a soldier behind him. The chief, in return for his fire, received from Gibson a sword cut of such prodigious force as completely to sever his head from his body. Two other Indians were killed, and the remainder escaped.

There were a number of captive Americans at the Mingo towns, when Little Eagle's discomfitted party returned. Several of them were sacrificed to appease his shade. The remainder were restored at the peace of 1765. They stated, that the survivors of Little Eagle's party affirmed that Captain Gibson had cut off that chief's head by a single stroke of his long knife. A war dance ensued, interspersed with cries for revenge on the *long knife* warrior. The name thus elicited went into a general appellation, and the Virginia warriors, and the Anglo-American militia in general, were thenceforward designated by the western Indians as the *long knives*.

In presenting an outline of the annals of the first settlement of west Pennsylvania and west Virginia, we must not forget, that Pittsburgh, Redstone, and the first Virginia settlements west of the Alleghanies, were the germs of the Anglo-American settlements in the great Ohio valley. Thence proceeded the pioneers, who settled Ohio and Kentucky. Thither they returned, in the hour of defeat and dismay, to recruit their numbers, and to resume courage for a return to their abandoned cabins, in the far and fertile wilderness. The names of fort Pitt, Redstone, Point Pleasant, and Powell's valley, recur at every period of the Kentucky and Ohio annals, as the homes of security and supply, to which the settlers fled from Indian plunder and massacre, and whence expeditions returned to resume their forsaken enterprises.

But to enter with any particularity into the relation of individual efforts and sufferings, and less important triumphs and defeats, would only render our chronicles a confused mass of rencontres of the rifle and tomahawk, of burnings, murder, captivities, and reprisals, which confound by their number, and weary by their monotony and resemblance. A few more prominent events only can be selected, as samples of the rest. A few names only, from the long catalogue of pioneers, can be transferred to this summary. The memory of the hundreds, necessarily omitted, lives, where they would have wished it to live, in the winter's evening cabin recital, in the rustic mountain ballad, in the rude but interesting chronicles of border warfare.

A dreary uniformity of incident marks all the story of the commencing settlements in every part of our country, from Plymouth to Jamestown, and from the lakes to the Balize. There are examples, indeed, which present the French forming colonies among the Indians, and remaining in profound peace. But it was by amalgamating with them, losing their own identity, and becoming savages. The case of the colony of William Penn, presents only a seeming exception. It grew out of circumstances, that never occurred before or since; and, when analyzed, will be found to be no anomaly from the general aspect.

In the whole history of the incipient settlement of our country, not one solitary instance of an attempt to settle an unoccupied tract, claimed by the natives, is to be found, which was not succeeded by all the revolting details of Indian warfare. It is of little importance to enquire, which party was the aggressor. The natives were not sufficient civilians to distinguish between the right of empire and the right of soil. Beside a repulsion of nature, an incompatibility of character and pursuit, they constantly saw in every settler a new element to effect their expulsion from their native soil. Our industry, fixed residences, modes, laws, institutions, schools, religion, rendered an union with them as incompatible as with animals of another nature. The crime of aggression, force, and final extinction, charged upon the whites, in relation to the natives, and discussed on the narrow principles of crimination and recrimination, has only been discussed hitherto in a manner worthy of congress wranglers, and in a style of narrow puerility. In the unchangeable order of things, two such races can not exist together, each preserving its co-ordinate identity. Either this great continent, in the order of Providence, should have remained in the occupancy of half a million of savages, engaged in everlasting conflicts of their peculiar warfare with each other, or it must have become, as it has, the domain of civilized millions. It is in vain to charge upon the latter race results, which grew out of the laws of nature, and the universal march of human events. Let the same occupancy of the American wilderness by the municipal European race be repeated, if it could be, under the control of the most philanthropic eulogists of the savages, and every reasoning mind will discover, that in the gradual ascendency of the one race, the decline of the other must have been a consequence, and that substantially the same annals would be repeated, as the dark and revolting incidents which we have to record. We do not say, that the aggression has not been in innumerable instances on the part of the whites. We do not deny, that the white borderers have too often been more savage, than the Indians themselves. We abhor injustice as much when practiced towards the whites as the Indians; and we affirm an undoubting belief, from no unfrequent nor inconsiderable means of observation, that aggression has commenced in the account current of mutual crime, as a hundred to one on the part of the Indians. It has been the intercourse of a race more calculating, more wise, with ampler means, it is admitted, but without the instinct of gratuitous cruelty, or a natural propensity to war as a pursuit, with another race organized to the love of the horrible excitement of war and murder for their own sake. Circumstances, fear, impotence may restrain them. But still in the Indian animal and moral structure, their ancient propensities would be found, we doubt not, as vigorous as ever among those remnants the most subdued and modified by our institutions. Give them scope, development, and an object, place them in view of an equal or inferior enemy, and their instinctive nature would again raise the war-hoop, and wield the scalping knife, and renew the Indian warfare of the by-gone days.

The chronicles of the commencing settlements of West Pennsylvania and Virginia redeem from oblivion many traits, hitherto almost unrecorded by history, of the activity, vigilance, and efficiency of General Washington, in advancing these settlements, and repelling or punishing

border aggressions. All the great enterprises for this purpose seem to have been suggested, and many of them carried into effect by him.

Among the actual warrior pioneers, we find the conspicuous names of Col. Lewis, Capts. Hogg, Paul, and M'-
Nutt. They furnish striking examples of that hardy race,
who were the advance guard of the subduers of the wilderness, whom no certainty of labor, solitude, or suffering
could deter, and no form of danger or death daunt, so as to
induce them to abandon their purpose to fix their families
in the remote wilderness.

The first expedition from Virginia, to avenge the destruction of the Roanoke settlement by a party of Shawnese in 1757, was headed by these intrepid borderers. Beside the chastisement of the Indians, it had for its object
the establishment of a post at the mouth of the Big Sandy
of the Ohio; and to check the Indian communications between the upper French forts and Galliopolis, a French
settlement on the Ohio. The expedition, after encounter-
ing every form of suffering from famine and fatigue, wholly failed, many of the party perishing miserably from hunger. The destruction of Sivert's fort on the upper tract
of a water of the Potomac, and the treacherous massacre
of its inmates. after they had surrendered on the promise
of being spared, and the massacre of 1671, on the settlements of James river are passed over, as these events did
not happen in the valley of the Ohio.

The escape of Mrs. Denis, who had been taken captive
in the James river settlement, in 1761, presents a parallel
to similar narratives of female captives in the early history
of the settlement of New England. Her husband having
been slain, after being taken captive, they conducted her
over the mountains and through the forests to the Chili-
cothe towns north of the Ohio. There she seemed to con-
form to their ways, painted and dressed herself, and lived
as a squaw. Added to this, she gained fame by attending
to the sick, both as a nurse and a physician; and became
so celebrated for her cures, as to obtain from that very superstitious people the reputation of being a necromancer,
and the honor paid to a person supposed to have power with
the Great Spirit.

In 1763 she left them, under the pretext of obtaining medicinal herbs, as she had often done before. Not returning at night, her object was suspected, and she was pursued. To avoid leaving traces of her path, she crossed the Scioto three times, and was making her fourth crossing forty miles below the towns, when she was discovered, and fired upon without effect. But in the speed of her flight, she wounded her foot with a sharp stone, so as to be unable to proceed. The Indians had crossed the river, and were just behind her. She eluded their pursuit by hiding in a hollow sycamore log. They frequently stepped on the log that concealed her, and encamped near it for the night. Next morning they proceeded in their pursuit of her; and she started in another direction as fast as her lameness would permit, but was obliged to remain near that place three days. She then set off for the Ohio, over which she rafted herself at the mouth of the Great Kenhawa, on a drift log; travelling only by night through fear of discovery, and subsisting only on roots, wild fruits, and the river shell fish. She reached the Green Briar, having passed forests, rivers, and mountains more than three hundred miles. Here she laid down exhausted, and resigned herself to die, when providentially she was discovered by some of the people of that settlement, and hospitably treated at one of their habitations.

The settlement paid a dreadful penalty for this hospitable act. Sixty warriors came to it, pretending the most perfect friendship, for it was a time of peace. While the inhabitants were feasting these seeming friendly Indians, they rose and killed nearly every man in the settlement, carrying the women and children into captivity.

An affecting incident occurred from an assault of fifty Delaware and Mingo warriors upon the settlement of Big Sandy in 1761. Having committed a number of massacres, they were pursued by a party under Capt. Paul. He overtook an encampment of a division of this party, who were guarding some prisoners. It was night. Unconscious that there were prisoners among them, Paul fired upon them, killing three warriors, and wounding more. The remainder fled. Capt. Paul rushed on the camp, to secure the wounded and arrest the fugitives.• One of the party, seeing what appeared a squaw, sitting in a sort of composure of defiance, was about to dispatch her with his tomahawk. Capt. Paul threw himself between the assailant and the victim, and received the blow intended for her on his arm, remarking, that it was a shame to kill a woman, though she were a squaw. It was Mrs. Gunn, an English lady, who had been an inmate in the family of his father in law; and who had been made a captive a few days before, when her husband and her two children were slain. When asked why she had not made herself known, she replied, 'my parents are dead, my husband and children are slain; I have none for whom I wish to live, no wishes, no hopes, no fears. I would as soon die as not.

CHAPTER IV.

ANNALS OF WEST PENNSYLVANIA AND VIRGINIA.

SOME circumstances of horror occurred at this time in these annals, of a new complexion even in the history of Indian warfare. A scalping party of fifty savages in 1754, returning from their customary murders and burnings with twenty scalps and some prisoners, on the Susquehannah they murdered the whole family of Jacob Miller; proceeding thence to the house of George Folk, killing him, his wife and nine children, and deliberately cutting their bodies into small fragments, and throwing them, piece by piece, to the swine. Two of their prisoners were tied to trees, around which fires were kindled, and the victims were gradually scorched to death. A third was placed, with his arms closely pinioned, in a hole in the earth, the soil of which was closely rammed round his body, so that his head only was above the ground. He was then scalped; and after a long interval, a fire was kindled near his head. The victim declared that his brain boiled in his head, and implored instant death in vain. His agony continued, until the pupils of his eyes burst from their sockets.

These sickening horrors sometimes drew down retaliation upon the innocent, as well as the guilty. An association, denominated the 'Paxton Boys,' broke into a settlement of Conestoga Indians, noted for their harmlessness. The whole, to the number of forty, were massacred. The christian Indians of Naquetank and Nain were preserved from a similar fate only by the interposition of the government, and their removal to safe keeping in Philadelphia.

The peace of 1765 did not put an end to the Indian war. The hostile savages continued in force east of fort Pitt. It became necessary to furnish that place a supply of provisions. A quantity was forwarded under a strong guard, commanded by Col. Boquet of the regulars. The Indians assailed the guard at Turtle creek in a narrow defile, and a most obstinate conflict ensued for many hours. The fierceness of the assault may be calculated from the fact, that the British loss in killed and wounded exceeded one hundred; and that of the savages was reputed at nearly the same number, among whom were many of their most noted chiefs and warriors.

This repulse saved fort Pitt, humbled the savages, and disposed them to a peace, by which three hundred prisoners were immediately redeemed, and the redemption of many others in dispersed positions stipulated.

An amusing incident occurred at this time, calculated to divert attention from these revolting details. By a royal proclamation, every person was forbidden to trade with the Indians, to prevent their obtaining guns and ammunition. In despite of this, a cavalcade of many wagons, laden with ammunition, was despatched from Philadelphia for fort Pitt. Capt. Smith, a distinguished backwoodsman, who had been in a long captivity among the Indians, and conspicuous in the border wars, collected a number of his friends, called 'black boys,' from being painted as Indians. These men he distributed behind the trees, and as the cavalcade began to approach Sideling hill, they were ordered to fire upon the horses. The conductors finding the horses falling under them, came to a halt, and capitulated with Capt. Smith. They were allowed to take their private property; but all the rest, consisting of powder, lead, warlike stores, and various articles for traffic with the Indians, was burned or destroyed. The discomfitted traders obtained from a neighboring post a party of highland soldiers, who arrested and imprisoned some of these 'black boys,' as robbers. Capt. Smith was not a person to leave his enterprise in an unfinished state. He collected three hundred riflemen, marched to fort Loudon, where his companions were imprisoned; sat down against it, commenced retaliation, and under a flag of truce, soon obtained the release of the prisoners, who returned in joy and triumph to their homes. On the occasion, verses not unlike Yankee doodle, were composed, and sung in commemoration of the 'black boys' triumph, to the tune of *'Black joke!'*

From the peace of 1765, the country about fort Pitt and Red Stone on the Monongahela, began to settle rapidly. We can merely indicate the names of some of the more conspicuous pioneers. Tegard, Province, Crawford, and Hardin settled at Red Stone in 1767; the Pringles, Cartwrights, Hacker and Rule, on the upper waters of the Monongahela in 1769. Van Metre, Swan, Hughes, and others, settled about the same time near the mouth of Muddy creek of the Monongahela; and the Zanes, distinguished in the settlement of West Virginia, commenced establishments at Wheeling. With them were associated in this settlement Seffer, Doddridge, Biggs, Greathouse, Baker, and Swearingen. In 1772 the beautiful country, called Tygart's valley, on the east fork of the Monongahela, was settled, and the names of settlers in West Pennsylvania become too numerous to particularize. From these points the emigration began to overflow into Kentucky.

From the peace of 1765 to 1774 was a period of comparative peace and repose to the frontier settlements. The Indians then renewed hostilities, stimulated by repeated outrages and murders practiced upon them by the whites, during this interval. The murders at Captina, those inflicted by the notorious Ryan, the unprovoked killing of the *Bald Eagle*, and various other murders were of the number. It was about this time, that Logan made his famous speech, to which the pen of Mr. Jefferson has given so much celebrity. Logan was distinguished for his elo-quence, and was the son of Skillemus, a distinguished Cay-uga chief, who set his son an example of devoted attach-ment to the English. After the close of Dunmore's war, in which Logan lost all his relatives, he became melan-choly and addicted to drunkenness and mental derangement. It was in such a, frame of mind that he affirmed, that he would not turn on his heel to save his life. On his route from Detroit to Miami, he was murdered in a way that is not related.

The necessary brevity of these sketches induces us to pass over most of the memorable incidents of Indian war-fare in these regions, allowing us only space for a short narrative of the celebrated action at Point Pleasant, at the mouth of the Big Kenhawa, in September, 1744.

A campaign had been in preparation, to chastise the savages for their numerous and remorseless border assaults in time of peace. The army destined for this expedition, was composed chiefly of volunteer militia, collected west of the Blue ridge. One division was commanded by Lord Dunmore, and the other by General Andrew Lewis. The forces started from camp Union, now Lewisburg, nine miles west of the White Sulphur Springs.

They were nineteen days in marching through the rug-ged and mountainous forest to the Ohio; and not without heart-burnings and separations and divisions from the dif-ficulty of settling the point of priority of command. One division only, that commanded by General Lewis, reached Point Pleasant. The forces under Lord Dunmore pro-ceeded in another direction, intending to cross the Ohio, and march against the towns of the Shawnese.

General Lewis was ordered to join forces, and proceed with him to that point. Accordingly he made prepara-tions for crossing his troops to the north bank of the Ohio, when news were brought him, that a body of the enemy had been found drawn up in close order, and covering four acres of ground. Cols. Lewis and Fleming were imme-diately ordered out to meet them. They formed their troops into two lines, and had scarcely advanced a few hundred yards, before the action commenced. At the onset both the colonels fell wounded, and the advance fled. They were rallied by a reinforcement under Col. Field. Never was savage obstinacy displayed more unyieldingly. Forming a line across the delta between the rivers, and sheltered by logs in front, they maintained the contest from sunrise till evening, repelling frequent and the most impetuous charges. A fortunate movement on the part of the Virginia troops decided the day. Three companies, under the command of Capts. Isaac Shelby, afterwards governor of Kentucky, George Matthews, and John Stewart, were detached by General Lewis to ascend Crooked creek, a water there entering into the Kenhawa, and under the covert of its banks and high weeds, move down upon the rear of the Indians, and attack them in that direction. Finding themselves between two fires, and supposing that the attack upon their rear was by the expected force of Colonel Christian, which had not yet arrived, they commenced a precipitate retreat, having fought from morning until sunset.

Scarcely had the action ended, when Col. Christian arrived with his expected reinforcements. Bodies of the enemy had, also, been seen on the opposite shores of the Ohio and Kenhawa. But this seasonable arrival of Colonel Christian, and the bloody repulse they had met, not only hindered them from resuming the action, but, in its decisive results, disposed them to peace. It was a dearly purchased victory, seventy-five of the Virginia troops being killed, and one hundred and forty wounded. The loss of the Indians was, probably, as great, consisting of the prime warriors of the Shawnese, Mingoes, Wyandotts, and Cayugas, led on by Cornstalk, the head chief of the confederacy, and a warrior of great fame. Among the distinguished officers in the battle of Point Pleasant, were Generals Isaac Shelby, and Campbell, and Col. Campbell, heroes of Kings Mountain, Generals Evan Shelby, Moore, Tate, Wells, and Matthews, and Colonels Herring, Stuart, McKee, Steele, and Cameron, all of them afterwards distinguished as warriors, or statesmen.

It was about this time, that the seeds of the revolution began to germinate, and that the colonists, who had hitherto had the strong arm and the ancient glory of Great Britain to protect them, found in this power, hitherto regarded as a parent, an enemy, and a new element of apprehension united in innumerable ways with the savages against us. It is at this period, that we begin to hear of the infamous Simon Girty, and the equally detestable Colony united with Lord Dunmore and his savage allies. If it is cause of admiration, that the feeble commencements of white men in the wilderness were not extirpated, root and branch, how much more is it matter of astonishment, that the inhabitants of the frontiers, and of the western woods were not entirely cut off, when Great Britain united her terrible power with the savages against them. We find Lord Dunmore strongly impressed with the difficulties of the new position, in which the first harbingers of the revolution placed him. He was in the Indian country with a large hostile force, and exceedingly anxious to make a peace with the Indians, that he might return home, and prepare for new emergencies. White-eyes and Cornstalk, but chiefly the latter, were deputed on the part of the savages to treat of peace. Cornstalk had manifested the bravery of a hero at Point Pleasant. At Lord Dunmore's tent he displayed the powers of a consummate orator, and an adroit statesman. While he met Lord Dunmore's criminations with recriminations but too well founded, while he sketched the wrongs and the declining star of the red people, in contrast with the cunning and oppression of the whites, a competent judge, who was present, affirmed, that Patrick Henry, or Richard Henry Lee had never produced finer bursts of oratory. This son of the forest was decidedly one of those favorites of nature, to whom she has been pleased, under her own sign manual, to grant a patent of nobility. In this speech he protested against the allowance of sending the 'fire water' of the whites among them. In his own camp, to induce his own people to accede to the terms of the whites, he adverted to the constant advance of the one, and the decline of the other. 'What shall we do?' asked he. 'Are we ready to kill all our women and children, and then go out, and fight them, till not a warrior remains?' The question was met with sullen silence. 'Then,' he continued, striking his tomahawk against the post, 'I will go in, and make peace.' The peace of 1774 was accordingly concluded.

The enlightened and generous chieftain soon after fell a victim to the misplaced vengeance of the whites. He was on a visit of business at the garrison at Point Pleasant. He had been engaged in delineating, on the floor of the garrison, a map of the country between the Missouri and the Mississippi, and the various streams of those mighty rivers, with which he seemed perfectly acquainted. A voice was heard from the other side of the river, which he recognized to be that of his son, Ellinipsico, and who, uneasy about his long stay at the garrison, had come to enquire about him. Never was meeting more affectionately filial and parental. Just at this moment news arrived, that one of the hunters of the fort had been slain by Indians lurking behind the bank. His bloody body was soon brought to the garrison, with the charge, that Indians had accompanied Ellinipsico, who had committed the murder. It was in vain the affectionate son averred that he came alone; in vain that many of the garrison wished to save the magnanimous chief. The fury of revenge in the garrison was equally blind and unrelenting. The son was agitated. His father evinced the utmost composure. 'My son,' said he, 'the Great Spirit has sent you here, that we should die together. Let us submit to his will;' and turning to meet the exasperated multitude at the door, he received seven bullets in his body, and fell without a groan. Ellinipsico met his fate with the same dignity and composure. But the Red Hawk, a young chief, who was present, concealed himself in the chimney of the cabin. He was dragged down, and cut in pieces. Thus fell the noble Cornstalk, chief of the Shawnese, the victim of a revenge as unjust and as savage, as that of the red men. He seemed to have a presentiment of his death; for on the day previous, he observed in council, 'when I was young, and went to war, my thoughts often told me at each adventure, that it might be my last. I still lived on. Now I am in the midst of you. Kill me, if you choose. I can die but once; it is alike now, or hereafter.'

All the cruelties of Indian warfare were immediately renewed; and after numerous detached massacres and burnings, the concentrated fury of the savages fell upon Wheeling. Round the fort at this place had grown up a flourishing settlement with surprising rapidity. There were already thirty houses in the village, round which were smiling pastures and fields, and abundant flocks and herds. Capts. Ogal and Mason, with a small party, had been reconnoitering the approaches to the settlement. Captain Ogal returned to the fort, affirming that there was no enemy at hand. But in the course of the night, the Indians, to the number of nearly four hundred, arrived. Seeing many lights, and apprehensive that the garrison were prepared for them, they ambuscaded the road of approach to the fort, by two concealed parallel lines of their number. In the centre they placed six savages, to decoy the garrison to come against them, by the smallness of their numbers.

Early in the morning, two men from the fort came near these Indians, unconscious that greater numbers of them were at hand. One of them was shot dead, and the other purposely allowed to escape, that he might return to the fort, and decoy others into the ambuscade. Capt. Mason, understanding that this assault had been made by only six Indians, marched out with fourteen men to attack them. Passing into the ambuscade, most of his men were mowed down. Capt. Mason, severely wounded, concealed himself behind a tree. After a severe personal conflict with an Indian, whom he killed, Capt. Ogal, with twelve men, rushed out to their relief; but met the same fate with the preceding party. Of twenty-six only three escaped death, and two of these were severely wounded.

The garrison were thus forewarned of the assault preparing for them. Scarcely had they been made aware how many of their number had been slain, before the enemy appeared before their walls, and they were summoned to surrender by the renegado Girty. He vaunted the number of his forces, called on them to renounce the colonial cause, and submit to Great Britain, denouncing the utmost fury of savage vengeance, if they resisted, or fired a gun. He then read them governor Hamilton's proclamation, and allowed them fifteen minutes to deliberate on his promised terms, if they would surrender. Col. Zane assured him, that they were all resolved to perish, rather than to surrender to any force, with him at their head. Girty resumed his boasts of the magnitude of his force, and the impossibility of restraining the savage fury of the assault. A shot discharged at the orator caused him promptly to withdraw.

The fort contained thirty-three men, and the assailants numbered three hundred and eighty. The women stationed themselves beside the men, moulded bullets, loaded, and handed the guns. The less firm or robust performed the cooking, and brought provisions and drink. The assailants, finding that they could make no impression upon the fort, and finding that a sufficient force would soon collect from the country against them, killed every thing, that had life, upon which they could lay their hands, amounting to more than three hundred cattle, swine, and horses, burned all the dwellings and buildings outside the fort, and decamped on the morning of the next day. The forces, that soon collected for the relief of the place, found twenty-three unburied dead about the fort, and witnessed a most affecting sight of desolation.

Bodies of Indians still lurked about the fort. One of these enticed a party of patroles into an ambuscade, by scattering some Indian trinkets in sight, so as to seduce them from their path. The company stopping to look at the ornaments, the Indians in ambush opened their fire upon them, by which in a few moments twenty-one were killed, among whom were Capt. Foreman and his two sons, and a number more were wounded. The whole would have been cut off, had not Capt. Lynn appeared suddenly with a small party on an adjoining eminence. Discharging their guns with loud shouts, they induced the Indians to believe that a large reinforcement was at hand; and they produced a precipitate retreat of the assailants.

About this time a conspiracy of the tories in the vicinity of Wheeling and fort Pitt was discovered. The rumor was, that these tories, aided by Girty and the Indians, were to murder the whigs in the settlements, and march in triumph to Detroit. The exasperated whigs were not slow in action. The usual remedies of corporeal punishment, imprisonment, and confiscation were promptly applied.

CHAPTER V.

FIRST SETTLEMENT OF KENTUCKY.

TENNESSEE asserts her claim to priority of settlement. But it is immaterial to these annals, whether we commence with those of the one state or the other. It is convenient to the only order of which this narrative seems susceptible, to begin with those of Kentucky. The people of this state have impressed their name, character, and spirit in a great degree upon the whole west; and our attention is naturally turned to the commencement of this settlement, as the third era in the order of time, but the first in importance, in the history of the population of the Mississippi valley.

It takes its name from the Indian appellation of one of the chief rivers Kan-tuck-kee, importing the *dark and bloody ground.* It was first visited in 1763, by Finley, of North Carolina. In this adventurous and remote journey into an unknown wilderness, beyond a vast barrier of mountains, by a few congenial spirits, strongly endowed with the wandering propensity, and the same fondness for the wild existence of a hunter in unpeopled and remote forests, it is uncertain, whether they were led by any vague expectations, so common in the minds of adventurers at that time, of finding Peruvian mines. They found treasures equally refreshing to the spirits of hunters, rich cane breaks, wild clover fields, beautiful lawns, and a charming open landscape; a flowering forest alive with buffaloes, elk, bears, deer, panthers, wolves, wild cats, foxes, turkeys, and

5

unhappily, with red men among the rest. They made their way to Big bone lick, the huge organic remains of which excited their utmost astonishment. After an extensive exploration of this fine country, seen in all its native attractions, they returned to North Carolina, to tell the traveller's tale, describing the country, as a terrestrial paradise, full of game, the soil of which was covered with cane and clover, and its forests with blossoms.

These descriptions of the newly discovered region excited, as may be supposed, abundant conversation in Virginia and North Carolina, the inhabitants of which naturally wished to secure the possession of a domain so extensive and fertile.

After the lapse of two years, Daniel Boone, the celebrated western pioneer, accompanied Finley in another visit to the country. After their return, it is matter of regret, that we henceforward hear little of the first discoverer of Kentucky. As the name of the latter will be forever identified with the annals of the state, and as it occupies the most conspicuous place among the records of the primitive western backwoodsmen, we shall take leave to introduce in this place a sketch of his character. He stands at the head of a remarkable class of people, almost new in the history of the species, trained by circumstances to a singular and unique character, and in many respects dissimilar to that of the first settlers of the shores of the Atlantic. The thoughts of these backwoodsmen expatiated with delight, only when they were in a boundless forest, filled with game, with a pack of dogs behind them, and a rifle on their shoulders. Yet much as their characters seemed dashed with wild recklessness, they were generally as remarkable for high notions of honor and generosity, as for hardihood, endurance, and bravery.

Daniel Boone is reputed to have been born in Maryland, about the year 1756. His first dawning indications of character intimated the preponderance of that ruling passion for hunting and the woods, which followed him through life. But as he advanced to manhood, the partially settled frontier forests of Maryland became too beaten and sterile of game, to afford range to his spirit. His parents removed by his persuasion, to the deeper forests of Virginia, and subsequently to the still wilder regions of North Carolina. But all the eastern declivities of the Alleghanies presented the ascending smokes of incipient cultivation. In following Finley over those mountains into the untouched and fertile wilderness of Kentucky, he found in the clover and cane brake lawns, enlivened with bears, buffaloes, and turkeys, the cherished home of his imagination. In 1769, we find him seeking to select the spot on which to build his family cabin, for he was now married. Though uneducated, in the sense in which that phrase is now understood, he possessed a quickness of apprehension, a stern firmness of decision, a strength of character, a self possession, which stamped him with pre-eminence in his peculiar walk, and eminently fitted him at once for command and self dependence. The great hunter of Kentucky was equally remarkable for an unwavering and an unconquerable fortitude, which bade defiance to pain and death, and for gentleness of manners, and humanity of disposition. All his peculiar traits of character were fortified by his long cherished habits of wandering for days together with no other companionship than his rifle and his own thoughts.

His first exploration with Finley, without accident, was one of unmixed pleasure. But in his second journey there, his sufferings commenced. As he and a single associate named Stewart, had started for a morning hunt, they were taken prisoners by the Indians, who first plundered them of every thing, and then led them into captivity, by long and severe marches through the wilderness. They were generally watched with unsleeping vigilance. But their captors, relaxing it for a moment on the morning of their eighth day's march, they escaped, and returned to their plundered camp; where, having neither guns, ammunition, nor food, they would have perished with hunger, had it not been that at the exact period of their return to their camp, they were visited by a brother of Boone, who furnished them a timely supply. Soon after, they were fired upon by a considerable body of savages, and Stewart was killed. The brothers escaped; and with their tomahawks built themselves a cabin of poles and bark, in which they spent the winter. In the spring of 1770, Boone's brother returned to North Carolina, and left him alone in the woods, the only white man in Kentucky. He had neither bread, nor salt, nor even a dog for a companion. During this absence of his brother, he made an exploring trip to the Ohio, returned on his steps, and in July met his brother coming from North Carolina, according to his agreement, when they parted. They then explored the country together, as far as the river Cumberland, and in 1771 returned to their families, with the intention of removing them to Kentucky.

In the autumn of 1773, Daniel Boone returned with his family, joined by five other persons. In Powell's valley the party received an accession of forty other persons, all confiding in the guidance and management of Daniel Boone. The party thence advanced into the wilderness in high spirits, until the 10th of October, when the Indians fired upon their rear, and killed six men. Among the slain was the eldest son of Daniel Boone. They faced upon the foe, and drove them off, but not until their cattle were dispersed. The immigrants themselves were so much afflicted and disheartened, that it was deemed expedient to retire to the settlements on Clinch river. Here Daniel Boone continued to hunt, until June, 1774.

At this time he was requested by the governor of Virginia, to whom fame had made him known, to repair to the Falls of Ohio, to conduct thence a party of surveyors, whose stay there was deemed unsafe, on account of the recent hostility of the northern savages. With a man of the name of Stoner for his companion, he made his way through the woods in safety to the Falls, and piloted the surveyors away, according to request. He was absent from home two months. This year the Shawnese and other northern Indians commenced open hostilities upon the frontier settlements. Daniel Boone was ordered, with the rank of captain, to take command of three contiguous forts, where he discharged his assigned duty, until peace was declared with the Indians. Being released from this duty, he was solicited by Henderson and company of North Carolina, as their agent, to attend a meeting of the southern Indians.

which they had convoked, with a view to purchase of them lands south of Kentucky river. In 1775 he met the Indians, pursuant to his appointment, and made the purchases. He was then requested to head a party, sent to take possession of the lands. He opened a road from Holston to the Kentucky, with their assistance; but was attacked by the Indians, and four of the party were killed, and five wounded. It was in the early part of the summer, that the survivors reached Kentucky river. A fort was commenced at the lick, where Boonesborough now stands; but the party, enfeebled and discouraged by their loss, were sometime engaged in its erection.

Leaving some men to guard the fort, Boone took the remainder to Clinch settlement, to escort his family to the country; and his wife and daughter were the first white women who arrived in Kentucky. Here he remained a number of years, aiding and encouraging those who were bold enough to follow his example, and to choose his mode of life. The Indians were continually harassing and murdering the new settlers; and he was always ready to head the parties of woodsmen, who sought revenge, to put them on the trail of their foe, and give them a chance to retaliate. The future historical incidents of his career are naturally interwoven with the events in the progress of the settlements in the west. With the following brief sketch of his character, we shall return to the order of those events.

The very name of Daniel Boone is a romance in itself. A Nimrod by instinct and physical character, his home was in the range of woods, his beau ideal the chase, and forests full of buffaloes, bears, and deer. More expert at their own arts, than the Indians themselves, to fight them, and foil them, gave scope to the exulting consciousness of the exercise of his own appropriate and peculiar powers. He fights them in numerous woods and ambushes. His companions fall about him. He is one of those peculiar persons, whom destiny seems to have charmed against balls. When, by daring or stratagem, he comes off safe from a desperate conflict, it affords him a delightful theme to recount to his listning companions around the cabin fire, or as feasting on the smoking buffaloe hump, on a winter evening, his strange

5 *

adventures and his hair-breadth escapes. At length he is taken. But the savages have too much reverence for such a grand 'medicine' of a man as Boone, to kill him. He assumes such an entire satisfaction along with them, and they are so naturally delighted with such a mighty hunter, and such a free and fortunate spirit, that they are charmed, and deceived into a confidence that he is really at home with them, and would not escape if he could. It is probable, too, that his seeming satisfaction is not altogether affected. The Indian way of life is the way of his heart. It is almost one thing to him, so that he wanders in the woods with expert hunters, whether he takes his diversion with the whites, or the Indians. They are lulled into such confidence, as to allow him almost his own range. He seizes his opportunity, and in escaping, undergoes such incredible hardships, privations, and dangers, as nothing would render credible, but the most indubitable evidence, that they had been actually so endured.

Boone thought little of titles and courts of record. Fences, butts, and bounds, and partition lines, and all the barbarous terms invented by the spirit of *Meum* and *Tuum;* and the paltry lets and hindrances of civilization were terms of unhappy omen in his ear. He finds himself circumvented by those who had thought with more respect of these things; and in his age, he fled from landholders and lawsuits in Kentucky, to the banks of the Missouri. Here, on a river, with a course of something more than a thousand leagues, all through wilderness, an ample and a pleasant range was opened to his imagination. We saw him on those banks. With thin, grey hair, a high forehead, a keen eye, a cheerful expression, a singularly bold conformation of countenance and breast, and a sharp and commanding voice, and a creed for the future, embracing not many articles beyond his red rival hunters, he appeared to us the same Daniel Boone, if we may use the expression, 'jerked' and dried to high preservation, that we had figured, as the wanderer in woods, and the slayer of bears and Indians. He could no longer well descry the wild turkey on the trees; but his eye still kindled at the hunter's tale; and he remarked, that the population on that part of the Missouri was becoming too dense, and the farms too near each other, for comfortable range; and that he never wished to reside in a place, where he could not fall trees enough into his yard to keep up his winter fire. Dim as was his eye with age, it would not have been difficult, we apprehend, to have obtained him as a volunteer, on a hunting expedition over the Rocky mountains. No man ever exemplified more strongly the ruling passion strong in death.

In 1770, a party of nine persons, headed by Colonel James Knox, reached Kentucky with a view to hunt, and explore. It is not known that Knox and Boone ever met, or had any knowledge that the other was in the country. This may be accounted for by the circumstance, that their different attempts were made in different parts of the country. Boone saw the country only with the eye of a hunter, with very little forecast of its future value and destiny. Knox and his party viewed this fair region with different eyes, and saw it in the aspect of its value under the hands of cultivation and habitancy. While they, however, were meditating, whether it were better to induce a great body of their countrymen to immigrate with them, or to enter on their enterprise alone, the whole country, which had hitherto been claimed by France, passed by ceded transfer to the possession of England. The Virginia troops, who had served in the Canadian war, received bounties in these western lands; and were anxious to survey them, and ascertain their value. The claimants, with their surveyors, arrived in the country, in 1773, to view and select their lands. They descended the Ohio from fort Pitt to the Falls, and explored the country on the Kentucky side of the river. They examined some of the salines, or licks, and among others 'Big bone lick;' and contemplated, with astonishment, those enormous organic remains found there. They returned delighted with the appearance of the country. About the same time, General Thompson, of Pennsylvania, commenced an extensive course of surveys of the rich lands on the north fork of Licking. In 1774, other surveyors followed the same route. After reaching the Falls of Ohio, they travelled up both sides of Kentucky river, as far as Elkhorn, on the north, and Dick's river on the south.

This year, the first cabin for family habitancy was built on the present site of Harrodsburg, by James Harrod. This habitation answered the double purpose of a house and a fort. The occupants were emigrants from Monongahela. All the Indians north-west of the Ohio were now at open war with the Virginians. A severe battle, which we have already noticed, was fought between the parties at the mouth of the Great Kenhawa. It terminated in favor of the Virginians. The battle field was called Point Pleasant. Many of the soldiers returned to the south-western parts of Virginia through Kentucky. Governor Dunmore, who then commanded the main army of militia, who had not been in the action of Point Pleasant, marched into the Indian country. Peace was soon after made between him and the Indians. The surveyors were again able to execute their commissions. While the government of Virginia made use of these means to render the country safely habitable, individuals in several places built cabins, inhabited them one season, and then returned to their homes; in this way giving themselves a future claim to the land, upon which they had built. Harrodsburg, Boonesborough, and Logan's camp, near the present site of Stamford, were the first permanent settlements. The two latter settlements were made under the auspices of Virginia. Henderson and company had been induced, by exaggerated accounts of the fertility of the soil, to wish for some claim, to enable them to monopolize the profits which would accrue from the occupancy and sale of the new country. They accordingly made that purchase of lands from the Indians, to which we have referred, and in which Boone was their agent. Boone was now upon the ground. A fort was built, and a land office opened by Henderson and company, for the sale of their lands. The purchasers were to receive titles in virtue of that which Henderson and company had received from the Indians. This would have been a golden speculation indeed, could this company have realized their expectations. Virginia had as yet attached little value to her western possessions. The great conflict between the colonies and the mother country had occupied all her chief thoughts and energies. Things so remained, until in common with the other states, she proclaimed herself free and independent, and alone possessing the right of extinguishing the Indian claims within her territory, and making sales of her lands.

The legislature of that state declared Henderson's purchase null, as far as concerned the validity of the claim; but effectual so far as related to extinguishing the claims of the Indians within her territories. To indemnify Henderson for his loss, they made him a compensation of two hundred thousand acres of land, lying at the mouth of Green river. The association was satisfied with this grant; and the settlers under titles received from them in other parts of the country, looked to Virginia for protection in their rights. The legislature at the same time confirmed a purchase, made by Colonel Donaldson from the six nations, of the country north of Kentucky river. The Indian claim to the whole of Kentucky, north of the Tennessee, was now extinguished by purchase. James Harrod and his men joined the Virginians at the battle of Point Pleasant. After peace with the Indians, he returned to Harrodsburg, and gathered around him a sufficient number of woodsmen to render Harrodsburg a safe retreat of refuge for travellers and immigrants. A road, sufficiently wide for a single file of pack horses, had been opened by Daniel Boone from the settlement on Holston to Kentucky river. He removed with his family and followers to Boonesborough. Several families moved to Harrodsburg in the month of September, 1775. Three women with their husbands and children, came this year to encounter all the dangers of the savage wilderness, the privations and hardships of a backwood's life, and the severe confinement of being shut up in the limits of a fort. These permanent settlements were viewed by the Indians with extreme jealousy. They seem to have been perfectly aware, to what results these things must lead. They commenced a systematic course of murdering all whom they could find unprotected, and beyond the limits of the forts.

James Harrod, the founder of this settlement, was another character like Boone, exactly fitted for the duties and calls of the relation, which he sustained to the colony. It was not ambition that placed him at the head of a party, and his little colony; but the call of the people, and an intimate and deep feeling, that he was more qualified for those duties, than any one around him.   He was a brave and expert huntsman, and a man of generous, frank, and independent character.   He possessed, in an eminent degree, that instinctive keenness of tact, to seize the clue and circumstances, that guide the hunter in a straight and safe direction through the pathless woods.   He united the instincts of an Indian to the calculations and reasoning powers of civilized man.   Any one, at all conversant with the scenes of a first settler in the wilderness, and the requisite traits for counsel and guidance in the leader of such an establishment, can see at once what an invaluable acquisition such a man would be to such a settlement.   When the Indians had committed thefts or murders, he was always at hand to head an expedition of retaliation, or recovery. When a family made known, that their stock of provisions was running low, he was ready to shoulder his rifle, and to scour the woods to hunt for a supply.   The hunting of lost cattle and horses in the woods is a profession in which the genius and skill of a backwoodsman has a peculiar field of development.   Those who live in the old settlements can never imagine the skill, which men in situations like his, acquire in that way.   The finding of cattle, lost in the woods, is a thing of vital importance to the first settlers in such a country.   They who had lost them, repaired to Mr. Harrod.   He sallied forth, availing himself of his peculiar resources in this sort of experience, and their cattle were found.

So dear did this way of life become to him, that after this primitive state of things had all passed away, after he had obtained the commission of colonel, had a family, friends, and comforts of all kinds multiplied around him, he used to leave his house, and repair to those parts of Kentucky, that were still wide and waste wilderness abounding in game.   He would there remain, in the depth of woods, two or three weeks, secluded from the sight of every human being.   In one of these expeditions he lost his life; but how, or where, is not exactly known.   He left a daughter, and an ample estate in lands. The early stages of the settlement of this state were fruitful in producing characters of this kind. Their names, exploits, and hair breadth escapes will remain themes of interest in the narratives of their descendants around the evening fire.

The third station, as we have mentioned, was at Logan's camp. Benjamin Logan was by birth a Virginian. By the death of his father, when he was only fourteen, he was left with the care of a large family. He provided for the support of his mother; saw his family settled, left Virginia, and repaired west of the mountains, to these new regions, to provide for himself. He purchased lands, married, and commenced improvements on the Holston. He was with Lord Dunmore, when he made peace with the Indians, in 1774. The next year he visited Kentucky, selected the spot where he afterwards built his fort, and in 1776, removed his family to the country. These three settlements of Boone, Harrod, and Logan were the grand rallying points for the solitary settlers dispersed over all the country. The Indians were considered as enemies, for there was no security by day or night, but in these stations.

The 14th of July, 1776, a daughter of Daniel Boone, and two daughters of Colonel Calloway, were encountered by the Indians, beyond the precincts of the fort, and were carried away prisoners. Daniel Boone collected a party of eight men, and immediately followed them. On the 16th of the month, they were retaken uninjured, and two of the Indians were killed. It would be useless to attempt to describe the joy of the parents and their lost daughters at this meeting. It is a scene which no words can paint. The narrative of their recapture, had we space to give it, would be one of extreme interest.

Soon afterwards, the settlers ascertained that the Indians had brought a considerable force into the country, and had divided it into small bodies, with which it was intended to attack and destroy the settlements in detail. They had no knowledge of the modes of bringing and sustaining a considerable force in the field. They can not make great efforts in a pitched battle, or in besieging a fort. But they are cunning, persevering, and terrible beyond conception, in carrying into effect the injuries and murders, which they meditate in this way. It is inconceivable, with what dexterity they provide for their own safety, while they plan the murder of their enemy. They conceal themselves in a thicket, among the weeds, behind a fence, or any covert. Here they lie through the whole day or night, to way-lay the path, where they suppose the object of their revenge will pass. When they imagine their aim is sure, they fire, and if circumstances warrant, dart on their victim and take his scalp. If they dare not do this, they slide back to their ambush, retreat, and are gone, carrying with them the pleasant thought, that they have destroyed one or more of their enemies. They cut off the supplies of a garrison, by killing or driving off their cattle. They secrete themselves in ambush near the springs and watering places, that they may kill or capture those who repair there, unconscious of their danger. In the night, they place themselves near the gate of the fort, and watch patiently, until the morning, that they may kill the first person that comes forth. They are remarkably adroit in stratagems, to decoy the garrison out on one side, while they enter on the other, and kill the women and children. When they have exhausted their stock of provisions, they supply themselves anew from the chase, and return to the siege, in the hope of getting another scalp. Their object is in this way, to kill the garrison, or destroy the settlement in detail.

When at this distance of time we contemplate the horror of women and children, in conceiving such an enemy always about them in the pathless wilderness, it astonishes us, that settlers could ever have been found, who would put their lives in their hand, and march so far away from their native country and home, to encounter these dangers. We are surprised that they could cheerfully meet the labors of cultivation and the field, constantly surrounded by these dangers; and still more that they would expose themselves to the greater dangers of hunting, under such circumstances. But notwithstanding all these difficulties and dangers, in number and magnitude not to be described, the population of Kentucky was constantly increasing. The country was so extensive, that the numbers of the Indians were not sufficient, to allow them to spread over the whole of it. Consequently, the solitary family that plunged deep into the wilderness, although far from the protection of the forts, might escape, through the ignorance of the Indians of their situation. It appears from the records of pre-emption rights, that more improvements were made in 1776, than any preceding year. Many of those, who afterwards filled the most conspicuous places in the country, were immigrants of this year. Among these we may name George Rogers Clark. Leestown, situated a mile below where Frankfort now stands, and so named from Willis Lee, who had been killed by the Indians, was established this year, as a rendezvous for the hunters and improvers on the north side of the river. It was at first nothing more than a cluster of cabins. Some of the other establishments that have since become considerable towns were inferior even to this. These isolated settlements could not withstand the fury of the Indian attacks, and were all deserted during the first year of them. Virginia was now so much interested in these remote settlements, and the country which she claimed here, that during the session of her legislature, in 1776, a law was passed, constituting that part of the country which had hitherto been a part of the county of Fincastle, in Virginia, a separate county by the name of Kentucky. The boundaries of the new county were defined, and constituted much the same country which now composes this state. The act gave the inhabitants of the new county a right to a county court, with the customary jurisdiction, and all the usual civil and military officers.

The county was duly organized. A court of justice was established, to hold quarterly sessions at Harrodsburg, which was composed of six or eight men, respectable for talent and information. They were, *ex officio*, justices of peace. They could, besides, hold monthly sessions for the despatch of ordinary business. Benjamin Logan was of their number. They were duly attended by their sheriff. The officers for a regiment of militia were commissioned. They immediately classed the citizens, whether resident or not, in companies or battalions. The military operations were under the control of a county lieutenant, with the title of colonel.

During the winter the Indians were forced into a kind of truce by the severity of the season. The return of spring brought with it the renewal of Indian hostilities. Benjamin Logan removed to his own camp, which he fortified for defence. Although the Indians were in the country, this camp escaped attack until May. Harrodsburg was attacked in March. From the beginning this had been the strongest post in the country. Unfortunately, at the time of the assault, some of the men that belonged to it were absent. The 6th of March, a large party of Indians, marching privately through the woods, surprised three persons who were making an improvement. One was taken prisoner. One was killed and one escaped, and gave information to the garrison of Harrodsburg, of the appearance of the Indians. He was a mere youth, by name, James Ray, the same who was afterwards General Ray. The Indians, aware that the place was forewarned, and prepared for them, deferred the attack until the next day, when Harrodsburg was infested, after the Indian method of warfare. The notice, short as it was, had enabled the people to put the place in the best order for defence. The fire commenced, and some were wounded on both sides. The assailants soon became satisfied with their reception, and withdrew, leaving one of their number slain behind. This fact always indicates great discomfiture on the part of the Indians, or greater rashness on the part of the slain. For it is well known to be their most sacred and invariable custom, to remove their dead and wounded. This custom, probably, has its origin in a purpose to prevent the enemy from ascertaining their loss.

After their repulse, the Indians encamped in a body near the fort. They were in too great numbers to be pursued. On the 15th of April, Boonesborough in turn was attacked by one hundred savages. They were received there with such a determined spirit, that they retired after having killed one person, and wounded four. Their own killed and wounded were withdrawn, so that their loss could not be ascertained. Nearly the same number, and proba-

bly the same force that had besieged Boonesborough, soon
afterwards attacked Logan's fort. It contained fifteen persons, of whom two were killed, and a third wounded. The
enemy's loss, as before, was not ascertained. The forts
of Boone and Harrod were about equi-distant from Logan's; and they were the only places, whence help could
be expected. These places, besides, were kept in such
continual alarm, that it was useless to look for help from
them. The little garrison suffered greatly. They were
sustained by the dauntless example of Logan, and a consciousness of the result of capture. The savages hung
pertinaciously round the fort, as though determined to reap
the full measure of vengeance, of which they had been disappointed at the two other forts.

At the moment of attack, the women were without the
fort, milking the cows. The men were guarding them.
The Indians approached them under covert of a thick cane
brake, which had not been cleared away around the cabins. Thence they fired upon the people, and killed two,
as we have mentioned. A third person was wounded.
The remainder with the women reached the fort unhurt.
As soon as they reached the fort, the Indians, unwilling
to lose their powder and lead, relaxed their fire. An affecting incident occurred, which, as strongly illustrative of
Indian manners, and the circumstances of these kinds of
warfare, we will relate.

The besieged, looking from the fort, perceived that one
of those whom they had supposed killed by the Indian fire,
was still alive, and struggling to crawl towards the fort.
He evidently dreaded being mangled and scalped by the
Indians; and yet seemed to feel that if he made exertions
to drag himself to the fort, they might be sufficient to at-
tract the attention of the Indians, and yet not sufficient to
enable him to accomplish his purpose. The unhappy man,
meanwhile, knew that he had a family in the fort, and
that deliverance was within a few rods of him. The generous feelings of the intrepid Logan would not allow him
to see him making these ineffectual struggles, without an
effort to aid him. He tried to raise volunteers from the
garrison, to go out with him, and make an exertion to bring

the wounded man in. But such was the probability that death would be the forfeit of the exposure, that none could be found, but a certain man, named Martin, who had prided himself on the reputation of a soldier, to offer his services. The man raised himself upon his knees, and seemed to be struggling forward. The two intended deliverers proceeded together to the gate. At that point Martin recoiled and turned back; Logan was left alone. He saw the poor man, after crawling a few steps, sink to the earth. His compassion could not sustain the sight. Collecting his powers, and putting his life in his hand, he rushed forth, took up the half dead victim in his arms, and bore him amidst a shower of balls into the fort. Some of the balls were buried in the pallisades close by his head.

But along with this happy omen, another of a different aspect was seen. On the return of the wounded man, the garrison discovered that they had but a few more shots of ammunition left; and there was no chance of replenishing their stock, nearer than the other two forts. They were aware at the same time, that these garrisons would need all they had for themselves. To detach any of their number to go to the settlement on Holston, would be so to weaken their number as to leave them almost a certain prey to the invader. To sustain the siege without ammunition, was impossible. To go to Holston was the elected alternative. As the life of every member of the garrison depended upon the success of the expedition, it was necessary to select on the party, men who could judge with promptness and decision, what was best to be done in cases of emergency; and who were expert woodsmen, and capable of sustaining every kind of fatigue and suffering.

Logan, indispensible as his presence was in the garrison, was unanimously elected to head the party, to be despatched on this still more important expedition. It would be difficult for imagination to group a more affecting picture, than the parting of this small forlorn hope from their families, left in the desolate forests thus reduced in numbers, and without ammunition, and surrounded by a savage foe. We can see them looking back upon the pale faces of their families, and contemplating from the thick

cane brake, the pathless wilderness, which their imaginations would naturally represent filled with their ruthless
enemies. But these men of iron sinew, although they had
generous and tender hearts, had sound judgments and
strong minds. They felt that the step was necessary.
They might be allowed to drop 'natural tears,' and to cast
fond looks behind, as they went forth with stealthy pace
from their weeping friends, to thread their way through
the woods without being seen by the besieging savages.
They took for this purpose, an entirely untrodden track
through the forests; and crossed the Cumberland mountain by a route, which had, probably, never been trodden
before. We presume it never has been since.

They reached Holston in safety; and obtained the requisite supplies. Logan entrusted them to the remainder
of his small party, with directions how to proceed; and
started on his way home alone, preceding the slower advance of this party, to carry in ammunition. Within ten
days from the time of his departure from the fort, he performed this long, hazardous, lonely journey, and reached
the fort again. It was still invested by the savages, and
almost in despair. His return seemed an interposition
of Providence, and naturally tended to invigorate and encourage the besieged. The return of the party soon after,
with ammunition, yielded them the physical means of annoying the enemy, and sustaining the siege..

A new difficulty arose. The garrison was approaching
a state of starvation, and must hunt to relieve their necessities. This new difficulty once more spread the gloom of
despair over their prospects. But as they were resign-
ing their hopes of escaping the savages, Colonel Bowman
arrived at the fort with an hundred men, and dispersed
them. The Canadians left a proclamation which had been
prepared by the governor of Canada. It seemed to be intended for circulation among the people. It offered protection to those of the people who would abjure their allegiance to the revolted colonies, and threatened those who
would not. The paper was carried to Logan, who concealed it carefully through fear of the effect it might work
upon the minds of the people.

6 *

The arrival of the force under Colonel Bowman, and the consequent dispersion of the Indians, was calculated to raise the spirits of the garrison. But in the midst of their exultation and joy, they learned that his men were enlisted but for a short time, great part of which had been consumed on their march to their relief. They foresaw that the departure of this force would be the sure renewal of the horrors of the Indian invasion. They were again in want of ammunition; and Logan again undertook the long and lonely expedition to Holston; and once more returned with a supply. Nothing inspires animation and intrepidity in men, like seeing by experiment what may be done by patience and courage, in sustaining or vanquishing difficulties, and being found equal to all emergencies. About this time, too, they were animated by being joined by Mr. Montgomery with a party of soldiers.

On the 4th of July, the Indians, untiring and determined in their hostilities, again attacked Boonesborough. To prevent this fort from receiving assistance from the two others, they had recourse to their customary plan of annoyance; and sent detachments from their main body, to intimidate each of the forts, so as to prevent its aiding the other. In this siege the Indians killed one man, and wounded two others. It was ascertained that they lost some of their own number, although the killed were removed, according to custom. They kept up the siege with great vigor two days and nights; but finding all their efforts to take the place ineffectual, they suddenly disappeared.

On the 25th of this month, a party consisting of forty-five men, joined Boone from North Carolina. In the intervals of these sieges, the inhabitants of the forts cleared and cultivated their fields. A part kept guard, while the other part labored. This state of continued hostility naturally inspired a spirit of adventurous revenge; and gave to these contests all the interest, which the strongest feelings of the human heart can impart. The continued recurrence of danger, created a natural callousness and indifference to it; and it became a point of keen and intense study, which party should see each other first, and get the first shot. In this species of dexterity the woodsmen were quite as close and sure marksmen as the savages. The latter began to acquire a respectful caution, in reference to meeting the former, and were very shy in approaching the garrisons. The Indians had already denominated the Virginians, as has been seen, 'Long Knife.' They could now add that they were close shooters. Winter returned, and the Indians as usual left them. The term of service, also, of the militia men of whom we have spoken, expired this autumn, and they returned to their homes. There remained at Boonesborough twenty-two, and at Harrodsburg sixty-five, and at Logan's fort fifteen men.

The 1st of January, 1776, Boone with thirty men, went to the lower 'Blue licks' to make salt for the different settlements. The 7th of the next month, while he was in the woods, on a hunt to supply the salt makers with food, he came upon a party of one hundred and two Indians, marching to the assault of Boonesborough, the third attempt upon this ill-fated place. It was clearly of all the settlements, the object of their most settled dislike and revenge. Boone fled, but the savages pursued and took him prisoner. They then advanced upon the licks and made twenty-seven of the salt makers prisoners by capitulation. The Indians, delighted with this signal success, marched their prisoners in triumph through the forests, and across the Ohio to Chillicothe. On this march the weather was exceedingly inclement, and suffering from its severity in common with their prisoners, induced the savages to show lenity to them. If, instead of marching home with their spoils, the savages had bent all their efforts against Boonesborough, weakened as it was by the loss of so many of its men, it is probable that they would this time have succeeded in capturing the place. Flushed by this success, they would have vanquished the other two forts, and, no doubt, would have murdered the inhabitants, as they threatened, and would thus have broken up the settlements for this time. But though the savages generally manifest sufficient cunning, they appear to want combined thought; and seldom make use of one advantage, as a mean of obtaining another; and notwithstanding their own exultation, and the depression of the settlers, in consequence of this great success, they left the forts unmolested for a considerable time afterwards. Could the savages have realized all the misery which the inhabitants suffered, in consequence of the carrying off so many of their numbers into such a dreadful captivity, even their vindictive spirit would have been satisfied with the extent of the suffering inflicted.

In the month of March, eleven of the prisoners, among whom was Boone, were led away from Chillicothe to Detroit, and presented to the British commandant, Hamilton. The governor offered them an hundred pounds, as a ransom for Boone, intending, as he said, to set him at liberty on a parole; for the reader will not need to be informed that this was at the commencement of the revolutionary war. They refused it. A situation more vexatious to a spirit like his, than that in which he was thus placed, can not easily be imagined. The least attempted movement towards escape would alarm the vigilant savages, and on the other hand he refused the offer of supplies of indispensable necessaries by the British, as enemies of his country, and as never expecting to be able to repay them. The companions of his captivity were left to the British at Detroit, and he was compelled to return with his savage masters to Chillicothe. Soon after his return to that place, he was adopted into the family of one of the principal men of the tribe, and wisely appeared to be reconciled to his new way of life, and to accommodate himself to it with cheerfulness. Such deportment by such a mighty hunter and untamed spirit, could not but win the confidence and affection of his masters. When challenged to a trial of his skill with the rifle, he found it much less difficult to surpass them in the closeness of his shooting, than to vanquish the envy and ill will created by this visible superiority in a point of so much importance in the eyes of that race. He proved himself a most successful hunter. He found it easy to ingratiate himself with the king chief of the Shawnese, by showing great apparent deference to him, and by always granting him a share of the proceeds of his hunt. Thus leading a life in accordance with his instinctive propensities, and acquired habits, and in great honor among that primitive race; it is probable, that his seeming acquiescence to his lot would have become real, had it not been for the remembrance of his wife and children at Boonesborough. But these cherished recollections haunted him, and continually prompted the desire and the purpose to escape. In June following his captivity, he was taken to the Scioto salt works, and there employed so diligently in making salt that he found no means of escape.

On his return with his masters to Chillicothe, he found four hundred and fifty warriors, in all their horrible painting and war garnish, prepared for an expedition against Boonesborough. With all the love of country and family, natural to such a man, he now for the first time rejoiced in his captivity, as it enabled him to obtain such information respecting the objects of this expedition, as, could he transmit it to the fort, might save it from destruction. He determined to put in execution his long meditated purpose of escape. He arose early in the morning, and was allowed to go forth as usual to hunt. He contrived to secrete a little food, enough to answer for one meal, and with this slender provision made his escape. In less than five days he traversed a distance of one hundred and sixty miles, in which distance, besides other rivers, he crossed the Ohio. He made but one meal on the journey. The fort was found in no state of preparation for the formidable attack that was preparing for it. But this forewarning, a distinct perception of the danger, and the energy and industry of Boone soon put it in as high a state of defence as their means and the shortness of the time of preparation would allow.

Having made their preparations, the garrison were now anxiously awaiting the appearance of their enemy. The escape of one of Boone's companions from captivity brought news of the expedition to the fort, and informed that in consequence of his escape, the expedition had been deferred three weeks. Fortunately, the garrison had received accessions of considerable numbers, since the captivity of Boone. Meanwhile, Boone determined to anticipate their movements. With nineteen select associates, he set out from the fort, on an expedition to surprise 'Paint creek town,' an Indian village on the Scioto. Having arrived within four miles of that place, they were met by thirty Indians, who were marching to join the main army, now on its way to Boonesborough. A battle was immediately commenced, which terminated in the flight of the savages. Not a man of Boone's party fell. Boone immediately marched back towards Boonesborough, with all possible despatch. On the sixth day of his march, he passed the main Indian army unperceived, and on the seventh arrived at the fort.

The day after his arrival, the Indian force appeared, commanded by Captain Duquesne, eleven other Canadian Frenchmen, and a number of savage chiefs. The British flag was displayed in their centre. They immediately invested the fort and sent a regular summons, requiring Boone to surrender. This was by far the most imposing force that had ever been seen in the country; and it was natural that the first view of it should produce consternation. Boone requested two days, in which to consider the propriety of a surrender; and the savages weakly granted the request. The garrison consisted of fifty men, and the odds in numbers was fearful. Boone assembled them; harangued them and placed before them the chances of their alternatives ; on the one hand victory or defeat, in case of resistance; and on the other hand the entire plunder, and the hopeless condition of captivity, in consequence of surrender. The consultation was short, and the answer unanimous, that as long as one man lived, the fort should be defended. It may be supposed that the garrison diligently employed these two days of truce, in completing their defences. They had collected their cattle and horses, and driven them into the fort. At the expiration of the time, Boone, from one of the bastions, thanked the commander of the Indians, for the time allowed him for preparation, and proclaimed the result of the determinations of the garrison. Duquesne, disappointed in the expectation of surrender, endeavored to carry his point by duplicity. He declared that he was charged by governor Hamilton, to take the garrison prisoners; but not to treat them harshly, and that if nine of the principal men would come out, and enter into parley with him, he would withdraw, upon condition that the garrison would swear allegiance

to his master.   To treat upon such terms would at least
gain time, and Boone consented.   The conference was
opened within fifty yards of the fort gate.   The articles
were few, explicit, and soon settled.   But it was remarked
that many of the Indians, who had nothing to do in the treaty, stalked about the contracting parties, under suspicious
circumstances.   The articles were signed.   Boone was
informed that it was customary in such cases, that two
principal Indians should shake hands with one of each of
the whites.   This, too, was granted; and two approaching
each of the nine, endeavored to drag them off as prisoners.
Boone instantly perceived their purpose.   He and his men,
by a violent struggle, disengaged themselves from the grasp
of the Indians, and made for the fort.   A volley of balls
was fired upon them, and one man was wounded.   The
enemy immediately resumed an unremitting attack.   The
besiegers soon attempted to undermine the fort.   This attempt was probably dictated to them by their French commander; for they knew little of war, except the use of gunpowder and brute force.   The garrison discovered that
their enemy was attempting to undermine the fort, on the
side of the river, by remarking that the river, which was
clear above, was turbid below, with the earth and clay
thrown out by the excavation.   To counteract the effect of
this mine, the garrison dug a trench within; and by throwing the earth of the trench over the wall, manifested to
their foe that they penetrated their purpose.   Perceiving
that they were not like to carry their purpose, either by
fraud or force, the enemy decamped on the 20th of August.
Two men were killed, and four wounded in the fort.   The
savages had thirty-seven killed.   The number of their
wounded could not be ascertained from the circumstance
that they were immediately carried off.   This was the
last combined and powerful effort against Boonesborough.
The assailants were to the besieged, as six to one.   They
had skilful leaders, and were not deficient in ferocious
courage.   The walls of the fortification were combustible,
and but twelve feet high; and the garrison no better armed or supplied than their foe.   It was a striking example
of the difficulty of conquering a small force of intrepid
men, who have determined never to surrender.

In the succeeding autumn, Boone made a journey to
North Carolina to bring back his wife, who, during his
captivity among the Indians, had returned to her father's
house, despairing of his return. The Indians had made
no open attack upon Logan's fort, during this period. He
had, however, casual skirmishes with them, as his men
met them at different points in the woods. In one of these
rencontres he was severely wounded. That these infant
settlements survived these sustained hostilities of the savages, and continued to increase in the woods, so far away
from the protection of the parent state, evidences the intrepidity and spirit of these primitive nurslings of storms
and dangers. All this while, the parent state was engaged
in a struggle for existence with the gigantic force of Great
Britain; and could do little more, than look occasionally
from her own suspended conflicts, with admiration upon
the bravery of her children in the new country, contend-
ing with hosts of savages, headed, urged on, and supplied
by the British of Canada, with the means of annoyance.
But in 1778, having a moment of breathing time, Virginia
felt that sound policy, as well as maternal and good feeling, called upon her for some efficient measures, to render
a residence in the woods of Kentucky more safe and desirable. It was within the scope of her policy, to reduce
the British posts on the frontiers of the Ohio country, and
of the Wabash, whence the savages were supplied with
arms, munitions, and incitement to sally forth, and make
incursions upon the new settlements. For this purpose
she raised a regiment of troops, and gave the command to
George Rogers Clark. The force consisted of between
two and three hundred men. Colonel Clark was intimately acquainted with the topography of the western country,
and, as after events abundantly showed, admirably qualified for a command of this kind. His main force descended by water from the Monongahela to the Falls of Ohio,
where he was joined by some troops from Kentucky. Thirteen families accompanied him on this expedition, who fixed themselves on an island near the Falls, called since,
'Corn island.' This was the germ whence sprang the
flourishing town of Louisville.

CHAPTER VI.

FIRST SETTLEMENT OF KENTUCKY CONTINUED.

THE settlement which Colonel Clark left at 'Corn island' had a deep interest in his success. They were sixty or seventy miles distant from any aid in Kentucky. They were equally exposed to the attacks of the British and Indians; and dared not remove from the shelter of the island, until after the capture of Vincennes, by Colonel Clark. They then removed to Louisville, fixing themselves just below the mouth of Beargrass. Being the head quarters of Colonel Clark, and otherwise a naturally eligible situation, it soon received such accessions of strength and numbers, as to become an important settlement, and the nucleus of various others.

We may, perhaps, in this place most properly introduce another of the famous partizans in savage warfare, Simon Kenton, *alias* Butler, who from humble beginnings, made himself conspicuous by distinguished services and achievements, in the first settlement of this country, and ought to be recorded as one of the patriarchs of Kentucky. He was born in Virginia, in 1753. He grew to maturity without being able to read or write; but from his early exploits, he seems to have been endowed with feelings, which the educated, and those born in the upper walks of life appear to suppose a monopoly reserved for themselves. It is recorded of him, that at the age of nineteen he had a violent contest with another competitor for the favor of the lady of his love. She refused to make an election between them; and the subject of this notice indignantly exiled himself from his native place. After various peregrinations on the long rivers of the west, he fixed himself in Kentucky; and soon became a distinguished partizan against the savages. In 1774, he joined himself to Lord Dunmore, and was appointed one of his spies. He made various excursions, and performed important services in this employ.

7

He finally selected a place for improvement on the site where Washington now is. Returning one day from hunting, he found one of his companions slain by the Indians, and his body thrown into the fire. He left Washington in consequence, and joined himself to Colonel Clark in his fortunate and gallant expedition against Vincennes and Kaskaskia. He was sent by that commander with despatches for Kentucky. He passed through the streets of Vincennes, then in possession of the British and Indians, without discovery. Arriving at White river, he and his party made a raft, on which to cross with their guns and baggage, driving their horses into the river, and compelling them to swim it. A party of Indians was concealed on the opposite bank, who took possession of the horses as they mounted the bank, after crossing the river. Butler and his company seeing this, continued to float down the river on their raft, without coming to land. They concealed themselves in the bushes until night, when they crossed the river, pursued their journey, and delivered their despatches.

After this, Butler made a journey of discovery to the northern regions of the Ohio country, and was made prisoner by the Indians. They painted him black, as is their custom, when a victim is devoted to torture; and informed him that he was destined to be burned at Chillicothe. Meanwhile, for their own amusement, and as a prelude to his torture, they manacled him hand and foot, placed him on an unbridled and unbroken horse, and turned the animal loose, driving it off at its utmost speed, with shouts, delighted with witnessing its mode of managing under its living burden. The horse, unable to shake off this new and strange incumbrance, made for the thickest covert of woods and brambles, with the speed of the winds. It is easy to conjecture the position and sufferings of the victim. The terrified animal exhausted itself in fruitless efforts to shake off its load, and worn down and subdued, brought Butler back to the camp amidst the exulting yells of the savages.

Having arrived within a mile of Chillicothe, they halted, took Butler from his horse, and tied him to a stake, where he remained twenty-four hours in one position. He was taken from the stake to 'run the gauntlet.' The Indian mode of managing this kind of torture was as follows: The inhabitants of the tribe, old and young, were placed in parallel lines, armed with clubs and switches. The victim was to make his way to the council house, through these files, every member of which struggled to beat him, as he passed, as severely as possible. If he reached the council house alive, he was to be spared. In the lines were nearly six hundred Indians, and Butler had to make his way almost a mile in the endurance of this infernal sport. He was started by a blow; but soon broke through the files, and had almost reached the council house, when a stout warrior knocked him down with a club. He was severely beaten in this position, and taken back again into custody.

It seems incredible, that they sometimes rescued their prisoners from these tortures, adopted them, and treated them with the utmost lenity and even kindness. At other times, ingenuity was exhausted to invent tortures, and every renewed endurance of the victim seemed to stimulate their vengeance to new discoveries of cruelty. Butler was one of these ill-fated subjects. No way satisfied with what they had done, they marched him from village to village, to give all a spectacle of his sufferings. He ran the gauntlet thirteen times. He made various attempts to escape; and in one instance would have effected it, had he not been arrested by some savages who were accidently returning to the village from which he was escaping. It was finally determined to burn him at the lower Sandusky, but an apparent accident changed his destiny.

In passing to the stake, the procession went by the cabin of Simon Girty, who had just returned from an unsuccessful expedition to the frontiers of Pennsylvania. The wretch burned with disappointment and revenge; and hearing that there was a white man going to the torture, determined to wreak his vengeance on him. He found the unfortunate Butler, threw him to the ground, and began to beat him. Butler, who instantly recognized in Girty a former companion of his youth, made himself known to him. His savage heart relented. He raised him up, and promised to use his influence to save him. Girty had a council called, and he moved the savages to give Butler up to him. He took the unfortunate man home, fed, and clothed him, and Butler began to recruit from his wounds and torture. But the relenting of the savages in his favor was only momentary. After five days, they repented of their relaxation in his favor, reclaimed him, and marched him to Lower Sandusky to be burned, according to their original purpose. By a surprising coincidence, he there met the Indian agent from Detroit, who from motives of humanity, exerted his influence with the savages for his release, and took him with him to Detroit. Here he was paroled by the governor. He escaped, and by a march of thirty days through the wilderness, reached Kentucky.

In 1779, while the states generally were struggling with the taxes and burdens of the revolutionary war, without means or resources, Virginia discovered that she possessed an unwrought mine in her rich western lands. In this year she opened a land office for the sale of these lands, prescribing the terms of conveyance; and found that after all legal claims and grants were filled, an immense extent of country still remained at her disposal. The successes of Colonel Clark, and the clearness and security of the offered titles, induced many immigrants to repair to the country. Some settled near the old stations; and some scattered themselves in new positions in the woods, as their fancy led them to select; and the general and promiscuous settlement of the country may be said now to have fairly commenced.

In April, 1779, a block house was built on the present site of Lexington. Several stations were selected in this vicinity, and in that of the present position of Danville. Settlements were also made this year on the waters of Beargrass, Green, and Licking rivers. A station was a collected parallelogram of cabins, united by palisades, so as to present a continued wall on the outer side; and the cabin doors opened into a common square on the inner side Of course, these stations were the strong holds of the settlers. They united the strength, furnished the society, and cemented the friendships of the inhabitants; and were often the germs of populous and busy villages. Adventurers crowded upon the country, some selecting lands for imme-diate and permanent settlement; and others choosing spots on which they purposed hereafter to build, returned to their native place.

The Indians, though they must now have perceived the impossibility of arresting this advance of population, and the permanent occupancy of these hunting grounds, con-tinued their pertinacious purpose of revenge, by their cus-tomary modes of detached aggression, and the murder of individuals and families. It is astonishing, how little the frequent recurrence of these terrible catastrophes seems to have retarded the settlement of the country, and the stea-dy advance of the settlers in building and improvement. The people began to be conscious of their strength, and of the necessity of an efficient union, to put an end to the aggressions of the savages. An assemblage of the settlers was called at Harrodsburg, to devise the means of carry-ing their purposes into effect. The result of the common council was to carry the war into the enemy's country; and, as the Shawnese had been most conspicuous in their hostilities, it was determined to fit out an expedition against old Chillicothe, which was their chief town. The volun-teers were to unite at Harrodsburg, and the command was assigned to Colonel Bowman. Logan, Holder, Harrod, and Bulger commanded under him. Some of the most re-spectable citizens of the country served as privates. The united force amounted to two hundred.

They reached Chillicothe undiscovered in July, towards sunset. After deliberation, it was determined to defer the attack, until the dawn of the succeeding morning. The force was divided into two detachments, one commanded by Colonel Bowman, and the other by Captain Logan. The one party was ordered to march to the right, and the other to the left; and upon a given signal, to surround the town, and attack it in concert. The party commanded by Logan repaired to the assigned point, and waited in vain for the signal. The attention of the Indians was drawn to this point by the barking of a dog. At this mo-

ment one of the other party discharged a gun.   The whole
village of course was alarmed in a moment.   The women
and children were hurried into the woods, through a path
not yet occupied by the assailants; and the warriors collected in a strong cabin.   All this passed under the eyes
of Logan's party, who immediately took possession of some
of the deserted cabins.   It was now day light, and frequent shots were exchanged between the parties.   The
expedient of Logan, to march safely to the assault of the
cabin was an ingenious one; and as far as our reading extends, original.   He proposed to his party, to tear off the
Indian cabin doors, and each to carry one before him as a
breast work, in advancing upon the Indian cabin, where
the warriors were assembled.   As they were marching
upon the foe behind their moveable wall, Colonel Bowman
perceiving that their plan of surprising the Indians was
disconcerted, sent them an order to retreat.   Captain Logan's party were astonished at this order, and reluctant to
obey it.   The retreat must take place over an open prairie, exposed to the covert fire of the Indians.   Instead of
a concerted retreat in good order, every one endeavored
to make the best of his way from the danger, in the mode
dictated by his own judgment.   Each one started away
from behind his concealment; and made for the wood at
his utmost speed.   Some of their number fell by the bullets, which the savages showered upon them as they fled
over the prairie.   The stragglers assembled in the woods,
and resumed something like order.   The Indians sallied
out upon the invaders, commanded by their chief, Black
Fish.   They were much inferior in numbers, not exceeding thirty; yet Colonel Bowman's force, once intimidated,
continued to fly before them under the impulse of terror,
and were severely pressed.   His force was brought to a
halt, in a low and sheltered ground.   His fire upon the
surrounding enemy, who were protected behind bushes,
produced little effect.   Captains Logan and Harrod, and
others mounted some pack horses, and made a charge upon the Indians.   This assault somewhat staggered them.
Black Fish was killed, and the Indians in their turn took
to flight.   The men pursued an unmolested march home-

wards. In this ill managed expedition nine men were killed and one wounded. The Indian loss was comparatively small. Only two or three were known to be killed.

The winter of 1779 and '80, was remarkable for its length and severity, and the accumulation of ice and snow. Many families immigrating to the country, in their transit over the mountains, were arrested by the snows, and suffered exceedingly from cold and hunger. Their cattle perished; and in some cases the owners were compelled, by starvation, to feed upon their bodies. When they arrived in Kentucky, they found, indeed, plenty of animal food; but the grain of the country had been all consumed. They were introduced to the new modes of a backwoods life, by being obliged to subsist upon milk and meat. The arrival of so many new settlers in the spring, rendered all the stations so crowded, that it was found necessary to establish many new settlements in the forests. The old stations, in the central parts of the state, were, of course, the safest from Indian attack; and the country had now an interior and a frontier; a safe and an exposed region. Many of the settlers at the close of this year, had a rustic abundance of all that the country could supply. Some of the immigrants of this year were men distinguished for talents and standing in the regions from which they came. Among them we may name Colonel Thomas Marshall, who had distinguished himself at the battle of Brandywine. Colonel Slaughter, also, descended the Ohio, to the Falls with one hundred and fifty Virginia soldiers. This force added to that of Colonel Clark, already stationed there, gave this place the aspect of a regular fortification. The effect, however, was not such as might have been hoped. The people became confident, and careless, in their imagined security. The Indians derived more advantages than the whites from the protection of the Ohio. They could cross that river in their canoes at any point, ravage, plunder, murder, and return before the people could be sufficiently aroused to pursue them; and when once they had the Ohio in their front, and the interminable forests north of it in their rear, it was useless to follow them. Sometimes the soldiers met them and measured back a severe retaliation.

Meanwhile, the British commandant at Detroit, having recovered from the consternation of the blow struck by Colonel Clark, and fearing the effect it might produce upon his Indian allies, prepared to measure back a severer blow than Kentucky had yet felt. He concerted an expedition with the Indian chiefs. Six hundred Indians and Canadians composed it. They were commanded by Colonel Byrd, a British officer. It was appointed with two field pieces, and its first point of destination was Louisville. The summer of 1780, was uncommonly wet; and all the streams were full to overflowing. This circumstance induced the commander to change his original destination, and to ascend the river Licking, which was sufficiently high to afford a water passage to his force and artillery by that route, to the very centre of the country. Colonel Byrd landed his men and munitions on the point at the forks of Licking. His force consisted of one thousand men. He reached Ruddle's station the 22d of June. This was a new stockade station, incapable of any defence against artillery. The excessive rains had driven the wood cutters from their usual business in the woods, to seek shelter under the roofs of the stations. Byrd arrived undiscovered; and the first notice of the people in Ruddle's station of his approach, was announced by the discharge of his cannon. He sent in a flag, demanding an immediate surrender at discretion. This demand Ruddle refused, except on condition that the men surrendered should be the prisoners of the British, and not of the Indians. Colonel Byrd consented to these terms, and immediately the gates were opened to him. The Indians rushed into the fort, and each one laid his savage hands upon the first person that presented. Parents and children, husbands and wives were thus dispersed and separated in a moment. There are few, who can not imagine the wailing, the consternation and agony of children divided from their parents, and parents torn from their children. Ruddle remonstrated against these cruel enormities to no purpose. Colonel Byrd had even some semblance of reason in his apology. He declared his utter inability to control savages so much more numerous than his own troops, and affirmed that he himself was in their power.

After this station was thoroughly plundered, and the possession of the prisoners settled, the savages proposed to march immediately thence to the attack of Martin's station, at the distance of five miles. Colonel Byrd had been so much affected with the barbarity of the savages here, that he peremptorily refused, unless the chiefs would guarantee to him that the prisoners should be entirely in his possession, and that the plunder only should be theirs. They consented. The station was taken without opposition, and the prisoners and plunder were divided according to the terms of their compact. The ease with which these conquests had been made, only stimulated the Indian appetite for more. The savages clamored to be led against Bryant's station, and Lexington. Colonel Byrd declined, and assigned as reasons, that success was improbable; that it was impossible to procure a sufficiency of provisions for the prisoners they already had ; that it would be utterly impracticable to convey their artillery to any point of the Ohio, after the waters should have fallen; and that as there was a prospect of the speedy fall of the waters of Licking, prudence called upon them to avail themselves of their present advantages, and descend the river immediately.

Moved by these reasons, the British and Indians commenced their return march. They descended to their boats, which they had left at the forks, embarked their artillery and munitions on board and began to descend the river. At the forks, the Indians separated from the British, taking with them the prisoners captured at Ruddle's station.

The escape of Hinkston from his savage captors, furnishes an event of interest. He was remarkable for his tact and skill, as a woodsman; and in this escape evinced those powers of reasoning from circumstances, which would have escaped any observation, but one exercised like his; powers, which seem like the mysterious teaching of instinct. The second night of their march, the Indians encamped near the banks of the river. It rained, and the camp fires were not kindled until after the dusk of evening. Part of the savages guarded the prisoners, and part kin-died the fires. While they were so occupied, Hinkston sprang away from them. The alarm was given, and the Indians pursued him in every direction. He ran but a little distance before he laid down behind a great log, in the deep shade of a spreading tree. As soon as he perceived that the uproar occasioned by his escape had subsided, he recommenced his flight as silently as possible. The night was profoundly dark; and even his experience could discern no marks by which to steer. After travelling some time, as he supposed, in the direction of Lexington, he found to his terror, that he had circled back in sight of the camp fires again. There was no mark in the sky. He could not see the moss on the trees; and could think of no clue to the points of the compass. Here he availed himself of his woodland skill. It occurred to him, that although he could not ascertain the direction of the air by his feelings, he might in another way. He dipped his hand in the water. When he raised it, he knew that evaporation and coolness would take place on that side of his hand, from which the wind came. He had observed that the wind was in the west at sunset. Guided by this sure indication, he once more resumed his flight. After travelling for some time, he sat down, exhausted, at the foot of a tree, and fell asleep. Just before day arose a dense fog, in which a man could not be seen at any distance. This saved him when the light of dawn appeared. His ear was assailed with the howl of wolves, the bleating of fawns, the gobbling of turkeys, the hooting of owls, and the cries of the wild animals of the wilderness. He was enough acquainted with savage customs, to be aware that these cries were savage imitations, to entice the animals within the reach of their rifles. They pointed out to him, also, his own danger. He found himself more than once within a few yards of the foe. But he escaped all the dangers and arrived safe at Lexington. He reached there eight days after the capture of Ruddle's station, and brought the first intelligence of that event.

The Indians crossed the Ohio with their plunder and numerous horses, at the mouth of Licking, and there dispersed. The British descended the Licking to the Ohio, and the Ohio to the mouth of the Great Miami, intending to ascend that river, as far as its depth of water would allow the transport of the artillery. The cannon were to be left there, and the forces were to march over land to Detroit.

The panic, occasiono̅d by this severe blow, turned all eyes in Kentucky upon General Clark, whose counsels were received as oracular and imperative. He advised a levy of four-fifths of all the men in the country, capable of bearing arms, to be assembled at the mouth of Licking, on the 7th of July. Colonels Logan, Slaughter, Lynn, Floyd, and Harrod, were to command under him. He ordered the building of a number of transport boats at Louisville. The command of them was given to Colonel Slaughter, and they were ordered up the Ohio to Licking, with provisions and stores. In ascending the Ohio, these boats were compelled to keep near the shore. They were worked up the river in two divisions, one on each shore. It happened that while one of the boats was near the north shore, a party of Indians descended the bank, fired into the boat, and killed and wounded a number of the people, before the other boats could assemble to their assistance. On the way to the place of rendezvous, one of Logan's men deserted, taking with him a valuable horse. It was supposed that he had fled with the horse to Carolina. But on the arrival of the detachment at the mouth of Licking, the horse was found there, and it was ascertaiued that this traitor had gone over to the Indians, and had given them notice of the approaching expedition.

On the 2d day of August, 1780, General Clark, with his troops, took up the line of march from the place where Cincinnati now stands, for the Indian towns. The army marched in two divisions, and consisted of nine hundred and seventy men. The force was arranged according to the most rigid precepts of war; and proceeded, without interruption to the Indian towns, where they arrived the 6th of the month. They found the first town abandoned, and many of the houses burning, having been fired the preceding morning. They cut dowd several hundred acres of corn. At four, in the evening of the next day, they marched for the Piqua towns, distant twelve miles. They had but just commenced their march, when they were drenched by a shower, accompanied with thunder and wind. They encamped in a hollow square, in the unpleasant predicament of being in an enemy's country, and knowing that their guns were all wet. With proper precaution, they fired and reloaded them; and remained on the alert and prepared for action during the night.

At two in the afternoon of the next day, they arrived at Piqua. As they advanced upon the town, they were attacked by the Indians, who concealed themselves among high weeds, that skirted the town. Colonel Logan, with four hundred men, was ordered to file off, and march up the river to the east, and so to post himself as to prevent the escape of the Indians in that direction. Another division, under Colonels Lynn, Floyd, and Harrod were detached, to cross the river and encompass the town on the west side; while General Clark, with the troops of Colonel Slaughter, and those attached to the artillery, advanced upon the town in front. The prairie, where the Indians who commenced the attack were concealed, was about two hundred yards over. The division, who were ordered to encompass the town on the west side, found it necessary to traverse the prairie, in order to avoid the fire of the concealed enemy. The Indians were seen to understand the purposes of the intended attack; and evinced great foresight and skill, in arrangements to defeat it. To prevent being surrounded by the advance of the detachment from the west, they made a powerful effort to turn the left wing. To avoid this, Floyd and Lynn extended their force a mile west of the town; and the engagement was warmly contested on both sides, until five o'clock, when the Indians disappeared, unperceived, and a few only remained in the town. The piece of cannon was brought up, and made to bear upon the houses, which soon dislodged the Indians that were in them. A most unfortunate occurrence took place at the close of the action. A nephew of Colonel Clark, who had been a prisoner among the Indians, escaped from them at this point of the engagement, and was shot by the troops, as supposed to be an Indian. Though mortally wounded, he survived some hours.

On searching the houses, a Frenchman was discovered, concealed in one of the cabins. By him the troops were informed that the Indians had been instructed in all their movements; and had more than once determined to attack them silently in the night, with the knife and the tomahawk. They had intended this attack on the evening after the shower, knowing that the guns were wet, but were prevented by the vigilance of Colonel Clark; and by hearing the firing of the guns, were convinced that the rain had not rendered them useless. The loss was nearly equal on either side, amounting to twenty killed. The Piqua town was built after the manner of the French villages. The houses extended along the margin of the river Miami, more than three miles, and were in many places more than twenty poles apart. Girty, of whom we have so often spoken, had been made a chief among the Mingoes, and was in this action. Remarking the desperation with which Colonel Clark's men exposed themselves to the hottest of the fire, he drew off his three hundred Mingoes, observing that it was useless to fight with fools and mad men. It was estimated that at Chillicothe and Piqua, more than five hundred acres of corn were destroyed, and every thing that related to subsistence, upon which the troops could lay their hands. The policy that required these severe measures was obvious. Apart from the gratification of those feelings of revenge naturally enkindled by the exterminating warfare between them and the savages, when these means of subsistence were destroyed, the Indians were obliged to hunt for food, and of course to suspend their hostilities for a season.

Having completed their work of destruction, the troops commenced their return march. At the mouth of Licking the army dispersed, and each individual selected his own mode and route of return. Seldom have troops been known to encounter the most severe toils and privations more cheerfully. The allowance had been neither more nor less than six quarts of Indian corn, and a quantity of salt for each man a day. And this had been their whole subsistence, except the green corn and vegetables which they found in the Indian villages, and the chance game that

8

offered by the way. But they were fully aware of the emergency of the case, and that if this force was defeated, the Indians would pour in upon the defenceless settlements, and butcher their wives and children in detail. Their purpose, therefore, was to conquer or perish.

A severe action was fought about this time by a small party under Captain Aquilla White. This party followed on the trail of a marauding band of Indians who were retreating to the Falls of Ohio. White supposed that the Indians had already crossed the river, and was preparing to cross it in the pursuit. The Indians were still on the south side, and fired upon his rear. Nine of his party, which consisted of but fifteen, were wounded, one of them mortally. The residue returned to the bank, faced the foe and defeated them.

Soon after this, a station on the present site of Shelbyville was deserted through fear of the Indians. The inhabitants, while on their way to the settlements on Beargrass, and while encumbered with carrying their effects and baggage, and driving their cattle, were fired upon by a large party of Indians. As their wives and children were equally exposed with themselves, the men felt it their duty to disperse, and escape individually if they might. Colonel Floyd learned the predicament of these unfortunate people. He collected twenty-five men and hastened to their relief. He advanced with great caution, but fell, notwithstanding, into an ambuscade, and was defeated with the loss of half his men. The savages were supposed to have been triple in numbers, and nine or ten of them were killed. Colonel Floyd was wounded, and would have fallen into their hands, but for the assistance of Captain Wells, who dismounted, placed him on his horse, and ran by his side to support him. His conduct was the more generous, as the two had been personal enemies. But from this time until their death they were firm friends.

Two men of the name of M'Afee of M'Afee's station, near Harrodsburg, were fired upon. One fell. The other ran for the fort at the distance of a quarter of a mile. An Indian met him. They presented their rifles, the muzzles of which almost touched. The gun of the Indian missed fire, and he fell .dead. Two men came out from the fort on hearing the firing. M'Afee warned them not to advance. One of them not heeding the caution, ran to look at the dead Indian. Concealed Indians intercepted his return. He was now to compete with the Indians in dexterity, and the stake was his life. He sprang from tree to tree pursued by them. His object was to avoid a shot, and their's was to gain it. He reached a fence, one hundred and fifty yards from the fort in safety. As he sprang over the fence, he exposed himself to a shot from one of these staunch hunters. He gained the opposite side of the fence without receiving the shot. His antagonist reached out his head from behind his tree to take aim, and M'Afee shot him in the mouth. He arrived at the fort untouched, experiencing a hair breadth escape. The other man was fired upon by five Indians. He took refuge behind a tree, and four or five more shots were fired upon him. He also escaped them all, and reached the fort in safety. The station was immediately attacked by this same body of Indians. The females moulded and melted bullets for the men. After an attack of two hours, the Indians finding that they produced no effect, killed all the cattle round the station and withdrew.

Forty men under the command of Major M'Gary, hastily assembled at the alarm, and reached the station soon after the retreat of the Indians. They pursued, overtook, defeated, and killed six of them. Of their party one was killed, and one mortally wounded. During the remainder of this season, the attacks of the Indians were in a great measure remitted; and the conviction seemed to be increasing, that something more than these desultory modes of warfare was necessary to expel invaders, who were no longer strangers, wandering over the soil, but men fighting for their families and fire sides. A general confederacy of the Indian nations determined to make one grand effort to effectuate this purpose the succeeding year.

The counties began to wear the form of a regular and orgainzed government. Officers, civil and military, were appointed, and the acts which had hitherto been the spontaneous result of individual wills, assumed the aspect of emanating from the body politic. Among the officers appointed, Daniel Boone received the commission of lieutenant-colonel. The courts of judicature had a qualified jurisdiction in civil and criminal cases. Capital causes of the latter class were tried in Virginia. Justices of the peace, and monthly courts of sessions settled all the smaller civil cases. But the simplicity of manners and habits, the fellowship of suffering and danger, and a distinct perception of their common exposure produced a state of society, little subjected to the evils of litigation. Colonel Clark, with the title of general, had received the chief command of all the military force of Kentucky. His modes of defence were cheap, energetic, and judicious. They consisted in keeping scouts and spies on the frontier, and in causing a row-galley to ply on the Ohio, between the Falls and the mouth of Licking, as a floating battery. The Indians are well known to have almost a superstitious dread of cannon. This galley had some four pounders on board; and the savages seldom crossed the river between the points where it plied. Had a few such been stationed on the Ohio, the Indians of the north-west would have been effectually withheld from crossing. But the militia disliked serving on board of it, and the regular force having melted away, the row-galley was laid up before the end of the year. Many sales of lands were effected in the surveyor's offices, and the tilled land yielded abundant crops. The only considerable Indian attack that we have to record at this period, was one made upon Montgomery station, situated ten or twelve miles from Logan's station, and settled entirely with the relatives of Mrs. Logan. Her father and brother were killed; her sister, her sister-in-law, and four children were taken prisoners.

This disastrous intelligence soon reached Colonel Logan. He collected part of his garrison and hastened to the spot. He was joined by the survivors of the Montgomery family. They marched in pursuit of the Indians. They overtook, attacked, and routed them. Three were killed and one wounded. The captives, except one of the children, threw themselves into the thick brush, and the Indians were too hotly pressed to search for them. The child that remained with them, they killed to prevent its escape. The two women and three children were retaken.

In the spring of 1782, the people, who had experienced a season of repose, began to feel the effects of the savage confederacy, of which we have spoken. Two men were killed at Strode's station. The Indians spread over all the country in small bands, and commenced their customary desultory modes of ambush and murder. This circumstance lulled the apprehensions of the people, and caused them to neglect providing the means of defence against combined and powerful attacks. In May, a party of Wyandotts assaulted Estill's station, south of Kentucky river, and after killing one man, and capturing another, and destroying the cattle, withdrew. Captain Estill raised a party and pursued them. He overtook them on Licking fork near Little mountain. The numbers on each side were nearly equal, and the contest was most obstinately maintained. Captain Estill perceiving that the only issue which could be expected from continuing to fight in this way, would be gradually to weaken and destroy both parties, detached six men under a lieutenant, to fall upon their rear. From some cause, this detachment failed to fulfil the assigned duty. The savages perceiving the diminution of numbers from the proportionate slackening of the fire, pressed more resolutely upon Captain Estill. The party was compelled to retreat. The captain and eight of his men were killed, and four of those who escaped were severely wounded. A county, called Estill, commemorates the intrepidity, name, and misfortunes of this man. The result of this action created great excitement and alarm. Separate from feelings of wounded pride, the people remarked that the Indians had never before been known to manifest so much military skill, and open and manful daring, in what might be called a pitched battle. In several other assaults upon different stations, the savages generally had the advantage.

In August, 1782, a grand assemblage of warriors convened at Chillicothe. The Cherokees, Wyandotts, Tawas, Pottowattomies, and various other tribes bordering on the lakes, were represented in it. They were aided by

8 *

the counsels of Girty and M'Kee. The hands of these wretches were stained with the innocent blood of women and children ; and they added the acquirements of the whites to the instinct and skill of the savages, whose ways they preferred, and whose interests they espoused with even more ferocity than the savages themselves. Girty played the orator on this occasion. His speech is reported to have been admirably calculated to arouse the most malignant feelings of vengeance in the savages. He painted to them the delights of the land of cane, clover, deer, and buffaloes, and the charming valleys of Kentucky, for the possession of which so much blood had been shed. He represented the gradual encroachments of the whites, and the necessity of a determined effort, if they would ever regain possession of that fair domain. He warned them, that if the present order of things continued, the whites would soon leave them no hunting grounds, and no means of procuring rum, with which to warm and cheer their desolate hearts, or blankets to clothe their naked backs. The speech was received with yells of enthusiastic applause.

At the close of this harangue, the savages took up the line of march for Kentucky. Their first point of destination was Bryant's station. It consisted of forty cabins, built in the form of a parallelogram, and the intervals between the houses were filled up with pickets in the customary manner. The four angles were fortified with block houses. The savage force arrived before the place, on the 15th of the month. The garrison had been weakened by the desertion of most of the immigrants from North Carolina, who had returned to their own country in discouragement, occasioned by the death of William Bryant, who had been killed by the Indians at the mouth of Cane run. Fortunately, their loss had been supplied by immigrants from Virginia. Among them was Robert Johnson, Esq., father of the present Colonel R. M. Johnson. This station was more open to the savage attacks than any other in Kentucky. The Miami on the north, and the Licking on the south side of Ohio, were long canals that conducted the savages from their villages directly to this point.

There were but two other stations occupied at this time, north of the Kentucky river. These were M'Gee's and Stroud's.

The savages reached this station by night; and the inhabitants were admonished of their presence in the morning, by being fired upon as they opened their doors. It was providential that the attack was commenced so early in the morning; for the men of the garrison were preparing to march to the aid of the other two stations, the troops of which were reported to have been attacked by the savages. In a couple of hours they would have been on their way, and the men of the fort would have been reduced to a mere handful. The garrison immediately despatched messengers to Lexington, to announce the assault. On arriving there, the messengers found that the male inhabitants had left that place, having marched to the assistance of Holder. The messengers followed on their route, and overtook them at Boone's station. Sixteen mounted men, and thirty on foot, were immediately detached to the assistance of Bryant's station.

In conformity to the common modes of Indian warfare, they attempted to gain the place by stratagem. A party of one hundred commenced the attack upon the south-east angle, with a view to draw the whole attention of the garrison to that point. The great body of the enemy, to the number of five hundred, lay concealed among the weeds upon the opposite side of the station, and within pistol shot of the spring from which it was supplied with water. This stratagem was predicated on the belief, that the people would all crowd to the point where the attack commenced, and leave the opposite one wholly undefended. The garrison, however, comprehended the whole purpose; and instead of returning the fire, instantly commenced repairing the palisades, and putting the station in a condition of defence. Aware that the Indians were concealed near the spring, they were assured that they would not fire until they saw the men repairing to that point. The women in this confidence, ran to the spring and drew water for the supply of the garrison, within shooting distance of the concealed Indians. When a sufficiency of water had been drawn, and the station put in such a state of defence, as such a short notice might furnish, thirteen men were sent out in the direction where the fire commenced. They were fired upon by one hundred Indians, and the ambuscade rushed upon the side of the fort which they deemed was now without defence. Their disappointment may be imagined, when they found every thing prepared for their reception. A well directed fire from the garrison put the savages to flight. Some of the more desperate and daring approached sufficiently near to fire the houses, some of which were consumed. But an easterly wind providentially arose, and drove the flames from the mass of the buildings and the garrison was saved. The enemy withdrew and concealed themselves on the bank of the creek near the spring. They had been in some way informed of the despatch of the two men to Lexington for aid; and they arranged an ambuscade to intercept such forces as might be sent, on their approach to the station. When this reinforcement came in sight, the firing had ceased. No enemy was visible; and they drew near in the confidence that they had come on a false alarm. They rode forward through a lane which was ambuscaded for one hundred yards on either side by Indians. The mounted men created a dense cloud of dust as they moved along. The Indians fired upon them close at hand, but the obscuring dust hindered their aim. The six rode through this close fire unharmed, and without having even a horse wounded. The footmen were less fortunate. They were approaching the garrison through a thick corn field, and in a direction to have reached it unobserved by the savages. But hearing the firing on their mounted companions, they rushed to their aid, and were intercepted by masses of the savages, constantly increasing between them and the station. They would all have fallen, but for the thickness of the corn field. These brave men reached the fort with the loss of two killed and four wounded. The cattle and sheep that came in towards the garrison as usual in the evening, were mostly destroyed.

A little after sunset, the famous Girty covertly approached the garrison, and on a sudden made himself visible on a stump, whence he could be heard by the people within, and demanded a surrender of the place. He managed his proposals with no little art, assigning as a reason for making them, that they were dictated by his humanity; that in case of a surrender he could answer for the security of the prisoners; and that in the event of taking the garrison by storm he could not; that cannon were approaching with a reinforcement, and would arrive that night; in which case they must be sensible that defence of the place would be wholly unavailing. His imposing manner had the more effect in producing consternation, as the garrison knew that the same foes had recently used cannon in the attack of Ruddle's and Martin's stations. In the course of his harangue, Girty demanded of the garrison, if they knew who it was that addressed them? A young man by the name of Reynolds, of whom honorable mention will be made hereafter, observing the depressing effect of this speech, came forward and answered him to this effect—that they did know him well; and that he was held in such detestation and contempt, that he himself had named a worthless dog that he owned *Simon Girty;* that the garrison too, expected reinforcements enough, to give an account of the cowardly wretches that followed him; that he, for his part, held them in so much contempt that he should disdain to discharge fire arms upon them, and that if they broke into the fort, he had prepared a great number of switches, which he had no doubt would be sufficient to drive the naked rascals out of the country.

Girty seemed very little flattered or edified with such an impolite reply, and affecting to deplore their obstinacy and infatuation, speedily retired. During the night a small party was left to keep up occasional firing, and the semblance of siege, but the main body marched hastily away to the lower Blue licks. The Indians and Canadians exceeded six hundred, and the besieged numbered but forty-two. The Indians must have suffered a considerable loss, but the amount is not known.

As the battle of the 'Blue licks' gave this place a melancholy notoriety, it may not be amiss to present the reader a general view of its locality. It is situated forty miles from Lexington, and thirty from Bryant's station. The river Licking at this place, in common stages of the water, is three hundred feet wide. The lick is in an elliptical bend of the river, and the lime stone has been laid bare by the innumerable herds of animals that in the ages past, came here to drink the water, and lick the salt clay. It is intersected by ravines and a ledgy ridge. The summit of the ridge was sterile and almost naked of timber. But the ravines were timbered and skirted with thick brush.

Shortly after the decampment of the Indians from Bryant's station, the soldiers of Lexington, Harrodsburg, and Boonesborough assembled at Bryant's station, to the number of one hundred and sixty, and determined immediately to pursue the Indians. They were commanded by Colonels Todd and Trigg. The odds in point of numbers, was very great between this force and that of Girty. But they were brave and high spirited men, well mounted, provided, and armed. The veteran Boone was among them, and they burned with a desire to chastise the insolent and murderous invaders. Prudence should have induced them to wait for the reinforcement of Colonel Logan, who was known to be collecting forces in the other stations, to join them. They rashly chose to march unaided and by themselves. On their route, they soon came upon the Indian trail. The experienced eye of Boone collected and intuitively comprehended circumstances which convinced him at once, that the savages wished to be pursued, and to conceal their numbers. The first he inferred from the circumstance that they had taken no pains to conceal their trail; the second from the fact, that they marched in single file, treading the one in the steps of the other, so that it was impossible to decypher their numbers, from counting their footsteps.

This gallant force arrived at the lower Blue licks, without having seen a single Indian. On reaching the river at this place, they discovered a few Indians, leisurely retiring over the bald ridge that crowned the upper extremity of the valley. The party halted, and the commanders consulted Colonel Boone, as a man skilled in Indian warfare, and of deep experience in their modes of assault and deception, and as capable of drawing inferences, as to their numbers and purposes, and as also acquainted with the ground. Colonel Boone gave it as his opinion, that the enemy were more than double their number, and were in the ravines in ambush; that if the troops advanced upon them, the Indians had the advantage of position, still more than numbers. He advised, therefore, that their force should be divided into equal parts; that the one part should march up the river, and cross it at Elk creek above the upper ravine, while the other part should take a position, to be able to co-operate with them in another quarter; that in this way the advantage of position would be taken from the Indians and transferred to them; but above all, he cautioned them against crossing the river at all, until they should have sent out spies thoroughly to reconnoitre the position and force of the savages. The officers were disposed to listen to this salutary counsel of wisdom and experience. But Major Hugh M'Gary, remarkable for his impetuosity, exclaimed against the cowardice of delay. 'Let all,' cried he, 'who are not cowards, follow me, and I will show them the enemy.' Saying this, he spurred his horse into the river. As might be expected, the party caught the contagious rashness. The officers were borne along by the mass, as it crowded tumultuously into the river. After the crossing, there was neither order nor arrangement; but every man rushed forward at his own choice, over the bare rocks towards the sheltered ravines, and the wooded ground, where the Indians were concealed in close ambush.

Majors M'Gary and Harland, and Captain M'Bride led the advance. Girty, at the head of a select band of savages rushed upon them with their customary yells. The contest was instantly fierce and sanguinary. The Indians had every advantage both of numbers and position. The disorderly front of the assailants gave them still further superiority. The right wing was soon turned; and a retreat was inevitable, and that too, under the murderous edge of the tomahawk. Colonels Todd and Trigg, and Major Harland fell early in the action. The survivors pressed their retreat for the ford, on foot and on horseback.

But the Indians interposed between them, and intercepted their approach to the ford; thus forcing them to take to the river, where it could only be crossed by swimming. Of course the greatest carnage took place near the ford; and many were tomahawked in the river. A man whose personal courage had been the subject of doubt and question, here nobly proved those doubts unfounded. He halted on the opposite bank, and animated others to follow his example. They faced and commenced a fire upon the pursuers, and checked them for a moment; thereby enabling some exhausted and wounded fugitives to evade the tomahawk, already uplifted to destroy them. The brave and benevolent Reynolds, whose reply to Girty has been reported, relinquished his own horse to Colonel Robert Patterson, who was infirm from former wounds, and was retreating on foot. He thus enabled that veteran to escape. While thus signalizing his disinterested intrepidity, he fell himself into the hands of the Indians. The party that took him, consisted of three. Two whites passed on their retreat. Two of the Indians pursued, leaving him under the guard of the third. His captor stooped to tie his moccasin, and he sprang away from him and escaped. It is supposed that one-fourth of the men engaged in this action were commissioned officers. The whole number engaged was one hundred and seventy-six. Of these, sixty-one were slain, and eight made prisoners. Among the most distinguished names of those who fell, were those of Colonels Todd and Trigg, Majors Harland and Bulger, Captains Gordon and M'Bride, and a son of Daniel Boone. The loss of the savages has never been ascertained. It could not have equalled that of the assailants, though some supposed it greater. This sanguinary affair took place, August 19th, 1782.

Colonel Logan, on arriving at Bryant's station, with a force of three hundred men, found the troops had already marched. He made a rapid advance in hopes to join them, before they should have met with the Indians. He came up with the survivors, on their retreat from their ill-fated contest, not far from Bryant's station. He determined to pursue his march to the battle ground to bury the dead, if he could not avenge their fall. He was joined by many friends of the killed and missing, from Lexington and Bryant's station. They reached the battle ground on the 25th. It presented a heart-rending spectacle. Where so lately had arisen the shout of the robust and intrepid woodsmen, and the sharp yell of the savages, as they closed in the murderous contest, the silence of the wide forest was now unbroken, except by birds of prey, as they screamed and sailed over the carnage. The heat was so excessive, and the bodies were so changed by it, and by the hideous gashes and mangling of the Indian tomahawk and knife, that friends could no longer recognize their dearest relatives. They performed the solemn rites of sepulture, as they might upon the rocky ground.

The Indian forces that had fought at Blue licks, in the exultation of victory and revenge, returned homewards with their scalps. Those from the north, and they constituted the greater numbers, returned quietly. The western bands took their route through Jefferson county, in hopes to add more scalps to the number of their trophies. Colonel Floyd led out a force to protect the country. They marched through the region on Salt river, and saw no traces of Indians. They dispersed on their return. The greater number of them reached their station, and laid down fatigued and exhausted, without any precaution against a foe. The Indians came upon them in this predicament in the night, and killed several women and children. A few escaped under the cover of the darkness. A woman taken prisoner that night, escaped from her savage captors, by throwing herself into the bushes while they passed on. She wandered about the woods eighteen days, subsisting only on wild fruits, and was then found, carried to Lynn's station, and survived the state of extreme exhaustion in which she was found. Another woman taken with four children, at the same time, was carried to Detroit.

The terrible blow which the savages had struck at Blue lick, excited a general and immediate purpose of retaliation through Kentucky. General Clark was appointed commander in chief, and Colonel Logan next under him

in command of the expedition, to be raised for that purpose.
The forces were to rendezvous at Licking. The last of
September, 1782, General Clark with one thousand men
marched from the present site of Cincinnati, for the Indian towns on the Miami. They fell in their route upon the
camp of Simon Girty, who would have been completely
surprised with his Indians, had not a straggling savage
espied the advance, and reported it to them, just in season
to enable them to scatter in every direction. They soon
spread the intelligence that an army from Kentucky was
marching upon their towns.

As the army approached the towns on their route, they
found that the inhabitants had evacuated them, and had
fled into the woods. All the cabins at Chillicothe, Piqua,
and Willis' were burnt. Some skirmishing took place,
however, in which five Indians were killed, and seven made
prisoners, without any loss to the Kentuckians, save the
wounding of one man, which afterwards proved mortal.
One distinguished savage surrendered himself, and was
afterwards inhumanly murdered by one of the troops, to
the deep regret and mortification of General Clark.

A female achievement of heroism, is worthy of record
in this place. A party of Indians in October, of this year,
approached a house near the Crab orchard. A woman
with three children and a negro servant were the occupants.
One of the Indians rushed into the house, and made towards the negro. A little girl instantly shut the door between him and the entering Indians. The negro grap-
pled with the Indian and threw him down. The woman
seized an axe and killed him with a well directed blow on
the head. The Indians on the outside hearing the mortal
affray, attempted to cut down the door with their tomahawks. A body of armed men happened to be passing
that way, and came to the relief of the family, upon which
the Indians fled.

The summer of 1783, was one of repose and respite
from Indian war. Immigrants continued to pour into the
country. The rough and unwrought furniture from the
woods gave place to cabinet furniture. Considerable money circulated, and labor was well rewarded. Cattle and

flocks multiplied; and that rank growth of corn was seen in the fields, which was the presage of the abundance of this state in that article ever since. Wheat began to be raised at first as an experiment. Reading and writing schools were commenced. The pernicious article, whiskey, began to be manufactured. Merchandize was wagoned from Philadelphia to fort Pitt, now Pittsburgh, and was thence conveyed in flat boats to Louisville, where a retail store was opened.

An amusing incident in the administration of the laws, occurred at this time, which may serve also, to give a general idea of the state of things in the country. Thomas Paine had published a book, the substance of which was to prove that Virginia had no right to the Kentucky lands; but that they belonged of right to congress. Two Pennsylvanians who had become converts to this doctrine, descended to Kentucky to proselyte the people there. One went to Louisville, but gained no converts. The other succeeded better at Lexington. He persuaded some people to commence clearing in their neighbors' lands, in the hope, that when these were declared congress lands, they might claim by pre-emption. The occupants of these lands were alarmed, and applied to a justice, to arrest this disciple of Paine's doctrines, as a disturber of the peace. It was necessary to find a law for the purpose; and one was discovered in the Virginia code, which made it penal for any one to be the bearer of false intelligence; and the person convicted was to pay a mulct of tobacco, at the discretion of the court. On this statute the man was arrested and brought up for examination. At the second trial, the man was convicted, as he had not even had the precaution to bring the book with him; and perhaps had a plagiarizing purpose, to pass as the author and inventor of the doctrine. A great concourse of people attended the trial. He was sentenced to pay one thousand pounds of tobacco, or go to prison. There was not that amount of tobacco in the country. While he was sadly ruminating with himself upon the moral turpitude and guilt of circulating false intelligence, preparatory to his imprisonment, it was intimated to him that if he left the country, it would answer the laws as well as if he went to prison. The man made his election and disappeared.

The winter of 1783 and '84, was uncommonly severe. The accumulation of snow and ice did not quite reach that of the hard winter mentioned before. Companies of speculators in Kentucky lands, were formed in Philadelphia, and a mercantile establishment, of which General Wilkinson was at the head. The general came out to Lexington in February, 1784. His appearance, standing, rank, and supposed wealth procured for him such a reception, as might naturally be expected, in such circumstances of the country. The time, within which the British posts on the frontiers should have been evacuated, elapsed without that desirable event taking place. The country north of Licking had been, as yet, unoccupied by the whites, through fear of the northern savages. Surveyors were sent into this country to survey it in March, 1784. They discovered that Indians were among them in the country, and consulted their own safety by returning.

Many of the more thinking and intelligent people in the country, wished to put an end to this long series of murders and retaliations, by inviting the Indians into the settlements, and treating them with kindness, and by inspiring them with confidence, creating in them pacific sentiments. There were others, who in remembrance of murdered friends, had sworn irreconcilable enmity. By a man of such feelings, an Indian was enticed into the woods and murdered. An attempt was made to discover and punish the assassin; but this was found impracticable. The clouds of another Indian war were gathering. It had been suspended for a while. This was one among many circumstances that caused it to burst anew.

In 1784, Simon Kenton re-occupied the settlement near Washington, which he had commenced in 1775. Associated with a number of people, he erected a block house, and made a station here. This became an important point of covering and defence for the interior country. Immigrants felt more confidence in landing at Limestone. To render this confidence more complete, Kenton and his associates built a block house at Limestone. Two men of the name of Tanner had made a small settlemen the year preceding at Blue lick, and were now making salt there. The route from Limestone to Lexington became one of the most general travel for immigrants, and many stations sprung up upon it. Travellers to the country had hitherto been compelled to sleep under the open canopy, exposed to the rains and dews of the night. But cabins were now so common that they might generally repose under a roof, that sheltered them from the weather; and find a bright fire, plenty of food, and with the rustic fare, a most cheerful and cordial welcome. The people of these new regions were hospitable from native inclination. They were hospitable from circumstances. None but those who dwell in a wilderness where the savages roam, and the wolves howl, can understand all the pleasant associations, connected with the sight of a stranger of the same race. The entertainer felt himself stronger from the presence of his guest. His offered food and fare were the spoils of the chase. He heard news from the old settlements, and the great world, and he saw in the accession of every stranger, a new guarantee of the security, wealth, and improvement of the infant country where he had chosen his resting place.

In October, 1785, Mr. M'Clure and family, in company with a number of families, was attacked and defeated on Skegg's creek. Six were killed, and Mrs. M'Clure, her child, and a number of others made prisoners. The attack was made in the night. The circumstances of the capture of Mrs. M'Clure furnishes an affecting incident, illustrating the invincible force of maternal affection. She had secreted herself with her four children among thick brush, which, together with the darkness, screened her from observation. Had she chosen to have left her infant at a distance, she might have escaped. But she held it to her bosom, aware that its shrieks would make known her covert. The Indians, directed by its cries, killed the three larger children, and took her and her infant captives. This unfortunate woman was obliged to accompany their march on an untamed and unbroken horse. Intelligence of this massacre circulated rapidly. Captain Whitley immediately collected twenty-one men from the adjoining stations, overtook, and killed two of them, and retook Mrs. M'Clure, her babe, a negro woman, and the scalps of the six persons, whom the Indians had killed.   Ten days afterwards, another party of immigrants led by Mr. Moore, were attacked, and nine of their number killed.   Captain Whitley pursued the perpetrators of this bloody act, with thirty men.   On the sixth day of pursuit, he came up with twenty mounted Indians, clad in the dresses of those whom they had slain. They dismounted and fled.   Three of them were killed. The pursuers recovered eight scalps, and all the plunder which the Indians had collected at the late massacre.

In consequence of the recommendation to the county-lieutenants, an expedition was got up against the Wabash Indians.   The command was given to General Clark.   It consisted of nearly one thousand men, and marched for the Indian towns from Louisville.   The provisions and munitions proceeded for the Wabash in boats.   The men arrived near the towns befors their provisions.   They became discontented and mutinous in consequence.   Gen. Clark called a council of his officers, and finding it impossible to appease the discontents of the soldiers, marched them back without striking a blow.

Colonel Logan at the same time raised a force to march against the Shawnese Indians who dwelt on the Scioto. He rightly deemed that the Indians there would have their thoughts turned towards General Clark's expedition, so as to leave their own towns unprotected.   It was some time before he was able to collect a sufficient force.   He reached, and surprised an Indian town, killed a number of the warriors, and took most of the women and children prisoners.

In October, 1785, the national government convoked a general meeting of the Indian tribes north of the Ohio, at the mouth of the Great Miami.   The commissioners to meet them were General Butler from Pennsylvania, General Clark from Kentucky, and General Parsons from New-England.   No tribe met them, except the Shawnese, and no beneficial effects resulted from the meeting with them. From the representation of a majority of the commissioners, congress seems to have entertained an impression that at least a part of the cause of these continued hostilities lay at the floor of the Kentuckians, and that in many instances, they had been the aggressors.

In the chronicle of Indian assaults, we ought to record the death of Colonel Christian, who was killed by the Indians on Beargrass, in April, 1785. He was a native of Virginia, and married a sister of Patrick Henry. He had served honorably in Braddock's war, under Lord Dunmore, and during the war of the revolution. He had led an army of one thousand two hundred men from Virginia, with success, against the Cherokees. In 1785, he removed with his family to Kentucky. Colonel Floyd had also recently deceased in this settlement, from the effect of a wound inflicted by the Indians. The fall of Colonel Christian, of distinguished name and influence among the people, increased the dismay occasioned by that event.

The first newspaper printed in Kentucky, was issued August 28th, 1787. It was published on a demi sheet in Lexington, by Mr. John Bradford, and entitled the 'Kentucky Gazette.' No other paper was printed nearer than five hundred miles. The political slander and heart-burnings that had been hitherto transmitted by oral channels, were now concentrated in this gazette. The convention appointed by the legislature of Virginia, met at Danville, and voted that the separation between Virginia and Kentucky should take place, upon the proposed terms of the Virginia act. An address to congress was prepared, requesting the admission of the state into the Union, by the name of Kentucky. The authority of Virginia was to terminate the last day of December, 1788. At the same time they provided for the meeting of another convention to frame a constitution of government for the state. They also requested that one of the Virginia representatives to congress might be chosen from Kentucky. Virginia consented, and in December, Mr. Brown was chosen. This gentleman had acted a very conspicuous part in the affairs of this country for some time past. It was estimated that Kentucky had doubled her population within the last three years.

In February, 1788, General Wilkinson returned from New Orleans. He encouraged the culture of tobacco, by raising and purchasing it, and this may be considered as the era of the origin of that cultivation in this country. In giving these important details of the civil interests of the country, we have a little preceded the order of Indian assaults. For some time past, many individual massacres had occurred. April 11th, 1787, a party of fourteen Indians attacked a family living on Coope's run, in Bourbon county. As this attack may serve as a general sample of the undescribed detail of horrors in most cases of similar assault, and as the circumstances possess a peculiar and intrinsic interest, we will give them in detail. The family consisted of the mother, two sons of mature age, a widowed daughter with an infant in her arms, two grown daughters, and a daughter of ten years. They occupied a double cabin. In one division were the two grown daughters and the smaller girl. In the other the remainder of the family. At evening twilight, a knocking was heard at the door of the latter, asking in good English, and the customary phrase of the country, 'who keeps house?' As the sons were opening the door, the mother forbade, affirming, that there were Indians there. The young men sprang to their guns. The Indians being refused admittance, made an effort at the opposite door. They beat open the door of that room with a rail. They endeavored to take the three girls prisoners. The little girl escaped, and might have evaded danger in the darkness and the woods. But the forlorn child ran towards the other door and cried for help. The brothers wished to fly to her relief, but the mother forbade her door to be opened. The merciless tomahawk soon hushed the cries of the distracted girl by murdering her. While a part of the Indians were murdering this child, and confining the other girl that was made prisoner, the third defended herself with a knife, which she was using at her loom, at the moment of attack. The heroism of this girl was unavailing. She killed one Indian, and was herself killed by another. The Indians in possession of one half of the house, fired it. The persons confined in the other part of the cabin, had now to choose between exposure to the flames, spreading towards them, or the tomahawks of the savages. The latter stationed themselves in the dark angles of the fence, while the bright glare of the flames would expose, as a clear mark, every person who should escape. One son took charge of his aged and infirm mother; and the other of his widowed sister and her infant. The brothers separated with their charge, endeavoring to spring over the fence at different points. The mother was shot dead in attempting to cross. The other brother was killed, gallantly defending' his sister. The widowed sister, her infant and one of the brothers escaped the massacre. These persons alarmed the settlement. Thirty men commanded by Colonel John Edwards, arrived next day to witness the horrid spectacle presented by this scene of murder and ruin. Considerable snow had fallen, and it was easy to pursue the Indians by their trail. In the evening of that day, they came upon the expiring body of the young woman, apparently murdered but a few moments before their arrival. The Indians had been premonished of their pursuit by the barking of a dog that followed them. They overtook and killed two of the Indians who had apparently staid behind as victims to secure the escape of the rest.

CHAPTER VII.

SETTLEMENT OF TENNESSEE.

In 1730, this fine country was all a vast forest. From various causes it had been long deserted by the Indians; and in the fertile bottoms and grassy barrens, game left to increase unmolested, had become abundant. To hunt in this unoccupied and beautiful country had become a lucrative business: Many of the first settlers were drawn here to pursue this object. The ancient maps of the western country enable us to judge of the situation of places at the time that France claimed the whole country south of Canada, between the Mississippi and the Alleghany mountains. French forts are represented on these maps, as standing, one at the mouth of the Kentucky river; one on the south bank of the Ohio; another on the north side of the Ohio, at the mouth of the Wabash; one near the junction of the Ohio with the Mississippi; one at the Chickasaw bluffs; one on the east bank of Red river; and one at the junction of the Coosa and the Tallapoosa, called Alabama, after the name of the river. On the head waters of the Tombeckbee they had also a fort, called *Thoulouse*. Five leagues up the Tennessee they had another. One, situated at the mouth of the Kenhawa was called Shawnee. One, not a great way above the mouth of the Illinois, was called *Creve Cœur;* one, half way up the Illinois is marked by the name French fort, and one on the north-western extremity of lake Michigan. This was part of that famous plan of posts, and connected lines 'of defences by which it was the French policy to hold this vast and fertile country in subjection. In 1755, the Cherokees, at that time a powerful tribe, were in alliance with the French, and of course hostile to the English. In 1756, a treaty was made, both with them and the Catabas, on the condition that the English should build a fort in the country of each tribe; and the motive alleged was, that they would be for the defence of the women and children, when they were absent on their expeditions. With this view, fort Loudon was built for them in 1757. A garrison was placed in this fort; and the Indians offered bounties of land to induce artizans to come and settle in the vicinity. The remembrance of a three year's war was not immediately erased; and the Cherokees still manifested such symptoms of hostility, that Colonel Byrd was sent among them. He built and garrisoned two forts, one of them on the river Holston, opposite the upper end of Long island, in which forts his army wintered in 1758. The fort on the Holston was beautifully situated. At this time there was not another white settlement on that river. But after the building of the fort, the reports which were circulated of the fertility of the soil, and the abundance of game, led some persons to settle between them, before the breaking out of the Cherokee war, which commenced in 1759. The circumstance which gave rise to this war, was the taking some horses by the Indians, which belonged to the new white settlers, to replace those which the savages had lost during the preceding war with France, in which they had joined us. The white settlers seized their horses again; and either killed, or made prisoners of the warriors that had taken the horses. Thus was opened a vast field for the exercise of those terrible acts of ferocity, for which savages are so famous. The frontiers of Virginia and North Carolina were terribly ravaged with the flames and the tomahawk, as is customary in such cases.

Fort Loudon was situated on the north side of Little Tennessee, a mile above the mouth of Tellico, in the centre of the Cherokee country. It had a small garrison. The Indians besieged it; and the garrison was compelled to surrender for want of provisions. They were to be allowed to retreat to the white settlements beyond the Blue ridge. All of them but nine, fell by indiscriminate massacre. Between two and three hundred men, women, and children were slain. This event, so memorable in the first settlement of Tennessee, took place in 1760. In 1761, Colonel Grant led a strong force into their country, and compelled them to sue for peace. A treaty was the result. In consequence of this war, the only settlement which had been made in the vicinity of fort Loudon, was deserted. The treaty renewed the confidence of the immigrants from Pennsylvania and Virginia, who had deserted the country. They, and others associating with them, returned to the country with the purpose of renewing their projects of hunting and settlement. They settled in East Tennessee. These men gave those names to the chief mountains and rivers which have been retained since that time. The names ' Cumberland and Laurel' were given by them in affectionate remembrance of their native mountains. The mass of hunters and adventurers continued to advance step by step, and broaden their circle, setting the example of American settlers in the wilderness, in all subsequent pe-

riods.   They soon penetrated the interior of what is now
called East Tennessee.

In 1764, Daniel Boone, the patriarch of settlements in
the western forests, made an excursion from North Carolina into the woods of Tennessee.   In 1766, Colonel Smith,
with some friends, traversed a great portion of West Tennessee.   They descended to the mouth of Tennessee and
Cumberland rivers, on a trip of discovery.   They saw no
white people in these regions.   In 1768, an exploring party came into this country from Virginia.   They spent
some months traversing it in all directions.   But they found
on their return that the country which had so recently been
a wide wilderness, was no longer so.   Most of the fertile
spots, in eligible situations, had been occupied.   The first
permanent settlements were made in East Tennessee, in
the winters of 1768, and 1769.   The settlers came from
Virginia and North Carolina.   At this time Daniel Boone
joined them.   The settlements continued to increase until
1774, and 1775, when an extensive purchase of land from
the Indians was made by a company.   There was among
these settlers the usual mixture of respectable and worthless people; and they were impelled to form these new establishments by the usual mixture of motives.   But even
those desperate characters that had fled from debt and the
laws, were of use here; for they stationed themselves on
the frontier of this remote and unprotected settlement, and
became a barrier between it and the savages.   The inhabitants who had fixed themselves nearest the limits of Virginia, placed themselves under the government of that
state; and those that were the nearest to Carolina, threw
themselves under the protection of its laws.   But the troubles which were just commencing in the Atlantic country,
prevented the parent region from being able to extend efficient protection to these remote and feeble establishments
in the wilderness.   In 1774, the Shawnese and other con-
federated Indians from the north of the Ohio, made an excursion into that part of this country, which is now called
Sullivan county.   They were met by the people of the
country, aided by a few regular troops, and were attacked
with a spirit which had the effect to put a stop to their in-

cursions, until 1776. The purchase which has been mentioned above, was not agreeable to all the Indians. It was particularly disagreeable to a chief among them, called *Occonnostata.* He made a very animated speech against it. It was not, however, heeded by the Indians.

In 1776, the Indians of these remote regions began to feel the effects of the revolutionary troubles in the Atlantic country; and commenced their customary depredations. The people of Virginia and North Carolina sent such troops as they could spare, who were aided by the people. This force exercised vigilance and unanimity; and in some cases anticipated the attacks of the Indians. At this time it was, that the united settlements sent delegates to the convention that established the district of Washington. The name of Captain John Sevier is one that occurs often in the early history of this state. In 1774, he had held the commission of Captain under Earl Dunmore, governor of Virginia; and in 1777, Governor Caswell, of North Carolina, gave him the commission of lieutenant-colonel of the Washington regiment of militia under Colonel Carter. A battle was fought in June, 1776, between the force of the inhabitants united with the soldiers from Virginia, and the savages, at a place called Long-island flats, which was a great advantage to the settlers; not only because victory declared in their favor without the loss of one man, but as it gave them confidence in themselves, in demonstrating, that they were able to compete with the savages; and by showing to the hostile Cherokees what they might expect, in the issue of a battle, if they continued to practice their hostilities.

Notwithstanding this lesson, the Cherokees not only continued to manifest a hostile spirit, but assaulted the forts; and murdered every person who was so imprudent or so unfortunate as to be found alone. Aroused by the story of burning and murder from these infant settlements, Virginia, notwithstanding her pressure at home, ordered Colonel Christian, with a respectable force, to march into the heart of the Cherokee settlements. His force amounted to one thousand eight hundred men. They found no Indians until they arrived at a town called Tamotlee. The Indians did not dare to look this force in the face; and sued for peace. It was agreed that the Indians should enter into a treaty on the May following. Until that time, it was stipulated that hostilities should cease on both sides, with the exception of two Indian towns, near which a prisoner had been burned. This enormity had been practised upon a young son of Mr. Moore, who had been captured on the Watauga. The excepted towns were burned, and the army returned to quarters. The Indians were awed; but notwithstanding their fears, and the promise of a treaty, they still showed manifest intentions to inflict all the injury they could.

In 1777, an arrangement was brought about between the states of North Carolina, Virginia, and the Indians. A definitive boundary was settled for the country, which is now called Tennessee. It was then supposed to belong to those states. The Indians at this time professed to be in treaty with us; but they frequently murdered the settlers, when they found them unprotected and alone. This year, the district of Washington was made a county. Courts were organized, and a land office opened, in which great quantities of land were entered. That tribe of the Cherokees that lived on the creek called Chicamauga, and that were called by that name, had always been hostile to the whites, and had never entered heartily into the treaties between the settlers and the Indians. By the addition of a number of hostile tribes on the Ohio, their numbers were increased to a thousand warriors. In 1779, they began openly to attack the frontiers from Georgia to Pennsylvania. A force was sent against them from North Carolina and Virginia. This force came upon the Indians by surprise, who fled without giving battle. The soldiers pursued them, burned their villages, and destroyed their crops. This event happened at the same time that the British governor, General Hamilton, was captured by General Clark at Vincennes. These two coincident events restored peace to the western settlements for a time. During this interval of repose and security, such numbers of people settled in Tennessee and Kentucky, that the British and Indians

were never afterwards able to break up the settlements.
Another county was constituted by the name of Sullivan.

In 1779, the Cherokees began to commit outrages again.
The dispute which was now fiercely agitated in the Atlantic country, between the colonies and Great Britain, became, by the instigation of the British, the mean of bringing on a general Indian war. A deep feeling that every
thing was at stake, caused the western people to act with
great energy; and they often inflicted strong and summary acts of justice. From the misfortunes of the American
army in South Carolina, great exertions were required on
the part of the frontier people, to guard against the Indians, who were attacking them in every direction. They
had to exert all their efforts at the same time against the
British, who were triumphantly overrunning the southern
states.

SETTLEMENT OF WEST TENNESSEE.

In 1767, West Tennessee began, as East Tennessee had
been, to be the temporary home of hunters. Even before
this, some French people had settled where Nashville now
stands. They kept a station there for some time. There
was another French station at the same time on the Tennessee, about forty miles above its mouth. There was one
also at fort Massac, on the Ohio. A detachment of these
hunters, in 1769, penetrated as far as the foot of the mountains on *Roaring river.* They there deposited the proceeds of their hunt. They found no signs of human habitancy or cultivation. Some of their number were killed
by southern Indians, who were travelling to the north.
They had traversed a country covered with high grass.
They discovered many of the caves that are so well known
at the present day. By the borders of creeks they found
stones set up, apparently as burial monuments, over grea
masses of human bones.

In the year 1770, some members of this party set out
with the proceeds of their hunt on a trading expedition, intending to advance as far as fort Natchez. As they descended the Cumberland, near the place where Nashville

now is, they discovered the French lick, where they saw great herds of buffaloes, and other kinds of game. They attained the objects of their journey, made a profitable trip, and returned home in safety. In 1776, with a number of others associated with them, they came again to West Tennessee to hunt. Among them was an old man like Boone, passionately fond of hunting, and roving in the woods. He had so far lost the sight of his eyes with age, that the only way in which he could take sight at the buffaloes and deer, was to tie a piece of white paper to the muzzle of his gun. In this way he killed a number of deer. This old man strayed from the encampment, lost himself in the woods, and was absent nineteen days. He survived the extreme cold, hunger, and exhaustion, and perfect helplessness in which he was found. He recovered and killed a number of deer afterwards. Such men of iron, were the pioneers of civilization in the west.

The country was often scoured by hunting parties; but no permanent settlements were yet made. One of a hunting party was killed in 1777, by a wounded buffaloe from a herd, of which he had killed and wounded a great many. A small field of corn was planted in 1778, near Bledsoe's lick; and in 1779, there were a number of families settled permanently there. They built and inhabited stockaded forts. These were formed by arranging connected lines of log cabins into a hollow square. Nashville had its share of these settlers. A number of immigrants embarked in a boat, which they called 'The Adventure,' on the Holston, intending to descend that river and the Tennessee; and then to ascend the Ohio and the Cumberland, to where Nashville now is. They reached this place; but suffered severely on the way. They were frequently fired upon by the Indians, and they endured much from hunger. When they first visited that portion of the country that surrounds Nashville, there were no marks of former habitancy. The country round French lick, which had formerly been called 'the old field,' was a large tract of ground that had been thoroughly trampled by buffaloes, and beaten with numberless paths; as if situated near the resorts of numerous herds of domestic cattle. Though there were no traces of former habitancy on the surface, they found in digging round the springs, great numbers of graves, and the appearance of walls enclosing ancient habitations. Sometimes these walls had entrenchments added to them; and were so capacious as to include ten acres.

In 1780, the settlers were first attacked by the Indians. The attacking party were Delawares. Between 1780 and 1781, was fought the famous action of King's mountain, in which the first settlers of Tennessee and Kentucky had so glorious a share. Lord Cornwallis had overrun the southern states, and all was confusion and dismay in those regions, among the friends of the United States. Major Ferguson, a famous British partisan, marched with a force nearly two thousand strong, upon the mountains, that separate North Carolina from Tennessee. His object was at once to punish the whigs, who had either killed or imprisoned a number of peculiarly obnoxious tories, and to encourage the tories or loyalists, as they were called, by way of courtesy, to come forward and join the king's standard. Colonel Arthur Campbell, Colonel Isaac Shelby, and Colonel Sevier commanded the forces of the mountaineers and backwoodsmen. There had been a number of severe skirmishes between these partisan corps, in which the Americans generally had the advantage.

The American forces commanded by Colonel M'Dowell, were attacked by Major Ferguson who had been strengthened by the addition of a large body of loyalists, and a strong reinforcement of British regulars. The engagement took place near Enoree river. It was severely fought, but in the end the British retreated, leaving a considerable number of dead, and more than two hundred prisoners. The prisoners alone equalled one third of the number of the American forces. This advantage was more than balanced by the general panic and discouragement that ensued upon the defeat of General Gates and Colonel Sumpter, by the British. Major Ferguson was at Gilbertstown, in North Carolina, with two thousand men. In the vicinity were more than five hundred tories ready to join him. In this emergency the mountaineers, animated by the earnest persuasion of Colonel Shelby, to strike on the enemy, while they were within striking distance, determined to attack them, athough they were scarcely half their numbers. The mountaineers pursued Ferguson with nine hundred and ten mounted riflemen. After pursuing him in a drizzling rain for thirty-six hours, without alighting from their horses but once for refreshment in the whole distance, the pursuers came upon him encamped on King's mountain, a table eminence, five or six hundred yards in length, and seventy yards wide. Colonel Sevier commanded the right wing; Colonel Campbell's and Colonel Shelby's regiments composed the centre. The right wing was led to battle by Colonel Sevier and Major Winston; the left, by Colonels Cleveland and Williams. The attack was commenced by the two centre columns, as they were attempting to gain the eastern acclivity of the mountain. The battle at this point was furious and bloody. Columns on each side repeatedly gave way, and were as often cheered again to the contest. Towards the latter part of the action, the enemy made a fierce and gallant charge upon the American troops on the eastern summit of the mountain, and drove them almost to the foot of it. The Americans were again rallied, and returned to the charge; and the enemy in their turn gave way. The enemy was driven down the western declivity of the mountain, and forced into a disorderly mass. Colonel Campbell pressed upon them with his regiment, killing all that came in his way; and pouring in his deadly fire upon the crowded mass. The British rallied again, and came upon the Americans with fixed bayonets. Few actions on record have been more hotly contested. Ferguson formed his troops into columns as a last effort, and attempted to cut his way through the assailants. In the attempt he was shot dead. The fire from the Americans had become so hot and fatal, that the British were no longer able to sustain it. They laid down their arms, and were made prisoners. Colonel Campbell received the highest, and most honorable testimonials of gratitude from the legislature of Virginia. The general assembly of North Carolina voted similar testimonials to Colonel Shelby, and Colonel Sevier; the one a patriarchal soldier and settler of Kentucky, and the other of

Tennessee. In this action the mountaineers and their gallant leaders gained imperishable honors, which their countrymen to the third and fourth generation will not forget. Colonel Williams, from Ninety-six, was the only distinguished officer that was mortally wounded. Fifteen hundred stands of arms were taken. The commander and one hundred and fifty of the enemy fell on the field, and six hundred and ten were made prisoners. Only four hundred and forty escaped. The issue of this most gallant action had an effect far beyond its influence upon the people in the immediate vicinity. The drooping spirits of the people east of the mountains were again animated with the flush of hope. Lord Cornwallis hearing of Ferguson's total defeat by the mountain riflemen, immediately paused in his victorious career, and retreated to Winnsborough, a distance of between seventy and eighty miles.

The effects of this battle upon the whole south-west of the Mississippi valley was highly auspicious to the new settlers. The rumor soon reached the Indians, and effectually awed and repressed them from every incipient effort to favor the tories. The Cherokees and Chickasaws sued for peace. A land office was opened in 1783. But these cheering prospects for settlers were soon overclouded by the renewal of Indian hostilities against the settlers of West Tennessee, which amounted to a war of extermination. The settlers were disheartened, and many of them abandoned their forts, and returned to Kentucky and Illinois. Those who remained were chiefly confined to two forts, suffering much from various causes; but chiefly from want of provisions. These were principally obtained from hunting, to pursue which, parties banded together in the strength and order of battle. The crop had failed from a general inundation of the rivers. Those who survived all these difficulties until 1782, were enabled by a law of that year to claim pre-emption rights. The termination of the war of the revolution soon rendered the Indians less hostile, and immigrants from North Carolina began to fill the forests of West Tennessee.

We should be glad to give a history of the origin and downfall of the republic of Frankland, in Tennessee, but it would be foreign to our purpose. It is sufficient to remark that the inhabitants of Tennessee proposed to erect themselves into an independent state with this name. North Carolina, the parent state, objected; and there were two courts in Frankland, the one acting under the authority of the new state, and the other of North Carolina. Sheriff was at war with sheriff, and court with court. It was the first war, perhaps, in history, in which the chief battles were the wind of words, with a number of fist fights, and but one death, together with a few persons wounded. In 1788, the republic of Frankland ceased to exist. From this time to the period when Tennessee was admitted into the Union in 1796, the progress of population and improvement was rapid. 1791, the first newspaper was published at Rogersville, and was called 'the Knoxville Gazette.' The disastrous defeat of General St. Clair, brought on a renewal of Indian hostilities over all the west. After suffering the usual results of Indian murders and frontier assaults, an assault of the Cherokees with one thousand warriors and one hundred mounted Indians was made upon Tennessee, in 1793. General Sevier was sent against them with a force amounting to nearly one thousand two hundred men. An engagement took place, which has absurdly been called the battle of High tower. The Americans in this skirmish lost but three men. A few Indians were killed, and many wounded. Spanish guns were found in the Indian camp, and clear evidences that the Indians received aid and countenance from that quarter. Our troops marched through the Cherokee country, destroying their towns, and laying waste their resources. A portion of that people were disposed to peace. Incalatanga, or Double Head, one of their most blood-thirsty spirits, who was supposed personally to have shed more blood of the whites, than any other savage in the west, incited them to persevere in hostilities. The Hanging-maw, on the contrary, was for peace, and imputed the late murders to the instigation of the Spaniards. The main body of the tribes professed peaceful intentions; but notwithstanding this, a boat passing down the Tennessee was fired upon. The crew returned the fire, and killed two Indians. The boat was pursued by two hundred and fifty savages to the Muscle Shoals, where it was overtaken, and every person on board killed.   The history of Tennessee at this time is little more than a dreary chronicle of Indian massacres. Many of these narratives, related apart, would possess a harrowing interest.   Grouped together, they occur in such numbers, and with such uniform circumstances of atrocity and barbarity, that they lose their interest in the confusion of the mass.   No less than thirty murders of individuals, or of whole families, occurred within three years after the setting up the federal government.   To a person travelling through this fine and populous country, where there is now no more apprehension from Indians, than in the vicinity of Philadelphia, it seems almost incredible that such scenes should have occurred in the vicinity of Nashville, so late as 1796.

The most conspicuous characters among the Indian chiefs were Double Head, Hanging-maw, Bloody-fellow, Maddog, and other chiefs with equally terrible names; and Bowles, Watts, and M'Gillivray, whites, who had become chiefs among them.   Piomingo, a Chickasaw chief, is often mentioned in the annals of these times, as having been uniformly friendly to the Americans.

The last severe lesson taught these people by the Americans, previous to the inflictions of General Jackson, by which they were completely and finally subdued, was at Nickajack, in 1794.   An expedition was fitted out against this town from Tennessee.   It had been a central point, whence the war parties had proceeded.   The American force was sufficient to look down opposition.   The town was large and populous.   The inhabitants attempted to escape in their canoes across the river, on which their town is built.   The troops opened a deadly fire upon the canoes.   Some were killed, and some leapt into the water and attempting to escape by swimming, were killed before they were out of the reach of the guns.   Some women and children were taken prisoners, fifty-five warriors were slain, and that town and another reduced to ashes. In Nickajack were found fresh scalps taken at Cumberland, and a quantity of powder and lead just received from the Spanish government, and a commission to the Breath, a chief of that town, who was killed in the action. This severe chastisement with other events that soon occurred, broke the spirits of the Cherokees.

Among the murders that still continued to occur, we select the following as a fair sample of the desperate character of the conflicts between the Indians and Americans. We may infer that similar resistance took place in almost every case of the almost numberless assaults and murders in these border wars. On the 27th of January, a party of Indians killed George Mason, on Flat creek, about twelve miles from Knoxville. During the night he heard a noise at his stable, and stepped out to ascertain the cause; and the Indians coming in between him and the door, intercepted his return. He fled, but was fired upon and wounded. He reached a cave a quarter of a mile from his house, out of which, already weltering in his blood, he was dragged and murdered. Having finished this business, they returned to the house to dispatch his wife and children. Mrs. Mason, unconscious of the fate of her husband, heard them talking to each other as they approached the house. At first she was delighted with the hope that her neighbors, aroused by the firing, had come to her assistance. But understanding English and German, the language of her neighbors, and perceiving that the conversation was in neither of these tongues, she instantly inferred that they were savages coming to attack the house. This heroine had that very morning learned how the double trigger of a rifle was set. Fortunately the children were not awakened by the firing; and she took care not to disturb them. She shut the door, and barred it with benches and tables; and took down the well charged rifle of her husband. She placed herself directly opposite the opening which would be made by forcing the door. Her husband came not, and she was but too well aware that he was slain. She was alone in the darkness. The yelling savages were without, pressing upon the house. She took counsel from her own magnanimity, heightened by affection for her children, sleeping unconsciously around her. The Indians pushing with great violence, gradually opened the door sufficiently wide to attempt an entrance. The body of one was thrust into the opening, and just filled it. He was struggling for admittance. Two or three more, directly behind him, were propelling him forward. She set the trigger of the rifle, put the muzzle near the body of the foremost, and in a direction that the ball, after passing through his body, would penetrate those behind. She fired. The first Indian fell. The next one uttered the scream of mortal agony. This intrepid woman saw the necessity of profound silence. She observed it. The Indians in consequence were led to believe that armed men were in the house. They withdrew from the house, took three horses from the stable, and set it on fire. It was after wards ascertained that this highminded woman had saved herself and children from the attack of twenty-five assailants.

CHAPTER VIII.

INCIDENTS OF THE BORDER WARFARE OF WEST PENN-SYLVANIA AND VIRGINIA RESUMED.

In order to give something like a connected view of the incidents attending the first settlement of Kentucky and Tennessee, we have preceded the order of time, and return to narrate some of the more prominent events of Indian hostility in the older settlements of the north-eastern extremity of the valley. A hasty glance at these events is all our limits will enable us to bestow.

After the many bloody assaults of families in West Virginia in 1778, the Indians appeared on Dunkard creek, ambushing the men of the settlement as they were returning from their work in the neighboring fields. Many fell by the first shot; but those who survived it returned their fire, and a severe contest ensued. But borne down by numbers, the few that escaped fled to Straddler's fort, near at hand, leaving eighteen of their companions dead in the road, exposed to the usual process of scalping and mangling. To repel these repeated invasions, and chastise the perpetrators, the veteran and popular commander, General Clark was appointed by Virginia to lead an expedition into the heart of the Indian country. A regiment of infantry and a troop of cavalry were placed under his command, and he descended the Ohio, and marched through the vast wilderness to Kaskaskia, near the Mississippi, in what is now the state of Illinois. He surprised and took the town. The French settlements in what was then called the Illinois, had hitherto preserved a sort of doubtful neutrality between the English and Americans, during the war of the revolution. But they evidently inclined, both from their habits and inclinations, to the party of the English and Indians; and it was deemed by this gallant commander a wise and just precaution to subject them, as natural allies of the savages, to the American government.

At Kaskaskia, General Clark received intelligence that governor Hamilton from Detroit, had arrived at Vincennes, one of the most ancient settlements, which the French had made east of the Mississippi, with a force chiefly composed of Indians, amounting to six hundred men, and destined against the settlements of Pennsylvania and Virginia, west of the mountains. Hamilton was unconscious that General Clark was between him and the Mississippi. He reposed in perfect security at Vincennes; and had detached his Indians in marauding parties among the American settlements on the Ohio, reserving for the defence of the town only one company, and a few cannon. General Clark determined to surprise him, although it was mid-winter and the weather uncommonly severe. He fitted out a barge with two small cannon, and four swivels. The barge was obliged to make her way through floating ice, under circumstances that would have deterred any other man from making the attempt. In February he set out amidst the storms and deep snows, with one hundred and thirty men, to make his way by land to unite with the force that he had sent around by water. The hardships that he endured, and the difficulties he surmounted, can be credible only to those who know the habits of backwoodsmen. In crossing the drowned lands of the Wabash, they were forced to wade five miles through the water and ice, sometimes as high as their breasts. They appeared at length before Vincennes; and as fortune awarded it, almost simultaneously with their barge. Their appearance was so unexpectd, and their array so formidable, that Hamilton, in surprise and consternation, at beholding such an enemy, at such a season, surrendered the garrison prisoners of war, without firing a gun. This commander had been justly detestable for the atrocities practised by the Indians, either by his instigation or permission. General Clark was ordered by the governor of Virginia to detain him and his subordinate instruments and counsellors in these nefarious transactions, close prisoners in irons.

This daring and successful achievement drew after it a train of important consequences. It broke the chain which the British were attempting to form behind our frontiers. It awed the French inhabitants, and gave us the command of the country quite to the Mississippi. It unkennelled the savages from their lurking places, and detached them from their alliances; and it gave us a fair claim in the definitive treaty to the boundary which we obtained to the eastern bank of the Mississippi. A joint invading force of one thousand men was committed by Virginia to General M'-Intosh, to march at the same time with General Clark against the Indians. The force was directed against the Sandusky tribe. It was less efficient and successful than that under General Clark. He found great difficulty in raising, equipping, and organizing so large a force; and it was late in the season before it was ready to march. He penetrated the interior as far as Tuscarawa, and erected fort Lawrens on the banks of that river, leaving a garrison of one hundred and fifty men under Colonel Gibson, and returned with the main body to fort Pitt.

In the depth of winter a body of savages approached the new fort unperceived. Having caught the garrison horses outside the fort, they rode them into the woods. Then ap-

11

proaching the fort, concealing themselves in the high grass, and jingling the bells taken from the horses, they succeeded in beguiling sixteen men to come out from the fort, in the hope of finding their horses. Allured by the sound of the bells, the detachment followed towards the sound until they were led into an ambuscade of the enemy. Fourteen of the sixteen were killed, and the other two made prisoners. The garrison was now besieged by eight hundred and forty-seven warriors, continuing to menace, and propose conditions for six weeks, during which time they became so destitute of provisions, as to be obliged to abandon the siege. After some other skirmishes fatal to parties of the Americans, the garrison itself was evacuated.

One of the desperate conflicts of the settlers with the Indians happened in 1779, at Ricket's fort in West Virginia. Mr. Morgan came in contact with two Indians, and was pursued by them. Being old and infirm, he faltered in his flight, and stepped behind a tree. awaiting his chances for a shot. The Indians, too, slid behind trees to shoot him in safety. One of them was not sufficiently sheltered, and Morgan, watching his opportunity, at length aimed at an exposed part of his body. The shot took effect, and the savage, rolling over in the agony of his wound, stabbed himself in the breast. Morgan having his gun thus unloaded, fled again. The other Indian gained rapidly on him. Seeing his enemy close at hand, and his gun poised, Morgan adroitly dropped aside, and the ball passed by him. Both now pressed to single combat, and the struggle for life. Morgan struck with his gun. The Indian threw his tomahawk, which cut off one finger, and otherwise wounding his hand, at the same time disabling his gun, and knocking it out of his grasp. They closed, and Morgan being an expert wrestler, threw the Indian, but was soon overturned and beneath his powerful foe, who feeling for his knife, uttered the fearful Indian yell of assured victory. A woman's apron, which with savage fondness for our dress, he had bound round his waist, hindered him from coming at his knife. Morgan, too, having got possession of his fingers in his teeth, was able to operate upon the sinew of the red skin with effect. The Indian, after fumbling behind the apron, at length grasped the knife, elate with the confidence of despatching his prostrate foe. But he had seized the handle far towards the blade; and Morgan was enabled to grasp the remainder of the handle. As the Indian drew it from the scabbard, Morgan, crippling another finger with his teeth, causing the hand to relax a little from its force, drew the knife through the hand of the savage, cutting a deep wound in his hand, as he gained the entire possession of it. Both now sprang erect. But Morgan had still a savage finger in his mouth, and the body in his grasp, from which the Indian was struggling to disengage himself. He had now all the advantage, and was soon able to plunge the knife to the hilt in the body of the savage, which sunk from his grasp.

A female exploit on Dunkard's creek ought to be recorded in this place. Two or three families of this settlement had fled for safety to Mr. Boyarth's house. The indians came upon it, when it contained only Mr. Boyarth and two other men. Warned by the children that the 'ugly red men' had come, one of the men ran to the door. He received a shot, and fell. The Indian who had shot him, sprang in after him, and grappling with the other white man, was thrown on a bed. Having no weapon, the white man called Mrs. Boyarth for a knife. Not finding a knife, the heroine seized an axe, and cleft the red man's skull, as he lay under his foe. At this moment another Indian entering shot the victorious white man dead. Mrs. Boyarth brandished her axe upon him, as soon as he had shot, and by a well directed blow at his body, laid him yelling on the floor. Others continuing to enter, she levelled the first one by a blow on the head. The Indian behind drew out his yelling companion, and leaving the door way clear, she closed it on the rest, and made it fast. The men within had been wounded, but not so as to prevent their aiding the heroine to maintain possession of the house, until they were relieved by a party from a neighboring settlement. All the children in the yard were slain, and the whole transaction scarcely occupied three minutes, during which Mrs. Boyarth killed three Indians, and saved the remainder of the family.

An Indian expedition about this time, advancing from Wheeling to Washington, had made many prisoners.—Learning that a strong force was embodying against them, they determined to massacre all their prisoners, and retrace their steps across the Ohio.   Dreadfully did they carry their savage purpose into effect.   The members of families were pinioned, and bound to trees in sight of each other.   Parents, children, husbands, and wives were all slowly despatched in each others' view.   Their tormentors, the while, exulting in this spectacle of ineffable horror.

Another similar massacre occurred.   A party of Indians assailed the settlements near Booth's creek, on the upper waters of the Monongahela.   They came upon the house of Captain Thomas, a religious man.   In the midst of his family of seven children, himself and wife had just risen from prayers, and were singing the first line of the hymn 'Go worship at Immanuel's feet,' when a gun was fired at him, and he fell.   The mother implored mercy for herself and her children in vain.   The mother and six children were stricken with the merciless tomahawk.   The seventh child was taken captive.   A neighbor who was with this unfortunate family, engaged in prayer with the rest, crept under the bed, when the first gun was fired, and escaped the observation of the savages through all this scene of horror.   The savages plundered every thing, and firing the house, left it.   The neighbor, drawn from concealment by the flames, found Mrs. Thomas still alive, though she soon after expired.

Some prisoners at this time were rescued from the savages by a party of relatives, who pursued and fired upon them.   As soon as the fire of the whites was opened on the red men, five of them fell dead.   The remainder fled, abandoning a mass of plunder.   Unhappily, one of the prisoners, Alexander Rony, was killed by the fire of his own people.   His mother escaping from them, and ignorant that her son was among the slain, frantic in the exultation of deliverance, exclaimed, as she reached the rescuing party, 'I am Alexander Rony's wife, of the valley, and a pretty little woman too, if I was well dressed.'   An Irishman, also, was delivered, who benumbed, dressed like an

Indian, and from his broad dialect, scarcely able to make himself understood, had well nigh been sacrificed as an Indian. Terror unloosed his organs of speech, and he exclaimed in his own broad dialect. 'Lord Jesus! am I to be killed by white people at last?' These exclamations saved his life. Impartiality requires us to add that our own people sometimes proved savage, and acted after the worst examples of their foe. The only mitigation of the horrible massacre of the Moravian Indian settlements must be found in the exasperated state of the public mind, goaded to almost unendurable revenge by a series of Indian assaults and murders, which had been accumulating in the public memory for half a century.

These converted savages were settled on the Muskingum. They had been converted through the agency of the Moravians, had received either German or Bible names, and had made no inconsiderable progress in civilization and christianity. Situated intermediate between the hostile savages and the frontier whites, allied to the one people by blood, and to the other by the ties of a common faith, striving to do good to both, and be friends to each, they shared the common fate of mediation between fierce, jealous, and hostile opponents. They were suspected by both, and trusted by neither. The whites were planning their destruction, because of their supposed co-operation with the savages. Their own race charged them with conveying information to the whites, discouraging their allies, and frustrating their vengeance. Their number amounted to between three and four hundred. Jealousies, rumors, suspicions, criminations had been gathering force against them for years. At length a private expedition was fitted out against them, commanded by Colonel Williams. The professed object was to destroy their crops, that the hostile savages coming through their country, might not avail themselves of this resource for supplies, and to remove the Indian converts to fort Pitt. The village was surrounded with the same precautions, as though the invading force expected to be attacked. In fact, the infuriated whites, on some pretext, real or supposed, began to fire upon the Indians, and three or four of the converts were

11 *

killed. The rest surrendered. Their brethren were collected from the neighboring villages. All showed an entire readiness to be conducted to fort Pitt, and gave up their arms. Colonel Williams had been censured for using too much lenity towards this people on a former expedition against them. An accursed thirst for popularity, reckless of justice, has been one of the vilest traits of the American people from the beginning. A council was held in regard to the fate of this hapless people. Alas! all the fiercer passions had sealed their doom. But a few were found sufficiently independent and just to incline to the side of mercy. The victims were forewarned that they must die. Imprisoned, unarmed, they fell into each others' arms, wept, prayed, confessed, forgave, soothed, and encouraged each other. Their comforting words were all about a happy meeting, 'where the wicked trouble not, and the weary are at rest.' Being asked if they were ready to die, they answered, 'Yes. We have commended our souls to God, and are ready to die.' Thus fell ninety-six Moravian Indians, of each sex and every age, from the hoary head to the infant on its mother's breast. The black transaction stands recorded to repress national boastfulness, and an impressive memento to teach the people to listen to the voice of truth and mercy, rather than the brute suggestions of the passions. This expedition was conducted by inhabitants of West Pennsylvania.

This dreadful success drew numbers around the standard of this expedition, until the force amounted to five hundred. Under the command of Colonel Crawford it moved against the Moravians, near the Upper Sandusky. When arrived at these villages, they found them utterly deserted; and the expedition weary, misguided, and dispirited, commenced a return march. They were attacked on their return, by a large body of Indians, and after some loss, were glad to divide in small parties, and retreat in the night. The Indians fell upon these parties in detail, harassing them, killing, and making prisoners on all their return march. Crawford himself with nine others were made prisoners, and marched off towards the Indian towns. They soon came upon the bodies of four of the captives, and arrived in time to see five more put to death by squaws and boys, who were immediately engaged in kicking about the bloody heads in sport. Soon after, they met Simon Girty and several Indians on horse back. Colonel Crawford, meanwhile, was stripped naked, pinioned, and fastened to a post by a cord, which allowed him to sit down, and walk once or twice around it. A fire burnt briskly close by. The doomed sufferer looked at Girty, as one of his own race, and asked him if he had been spared the tomahawk only to die by a slow fire. 'Yes,' observed the monster with composure, 'you must be burned, Colonel.' 'Dreadful!' replied the sufferer. 'But I will endeavor to bear it patiently.' All the sickening inflictions of torture which savage ingenuity could invent, were applied. In the midst of this long agony, he begged Girty to shoot him. The wretch replied, ironically laughing heartily the while, 'How can I? You see I have no gun.' The scene lasted more than three hours.

Dr. Knight, who had been taken with him, witnessed this revolting spectacle, and was told by Girty that he must be led to the Shawnese towns to afford the inhabitants the same gratifying show. The distance was forty miles. Having been conducted twenty-five under the guard of a young warrior, and stopping to encamp, the Indian unpinioned him, to enable him to make a fire to drive away the mosquitoes. Watching his opportunity, he gave the savage a blow which stunned him. He seized the gun of his captor, who, seeing his position, fled with a yell of terror. He drew the cock of the Indian's gun, with so much force, in his eagerness to fire, as to break it, and the Indian escaped. After wandering twenty-one days in the woods, subsisting on berries, nettles, and raw tarrapins, and food of that kind, he arrived in a famished state at fort M'Intosh.

The massacre of the family of the Rev. John Corbly, on Muddy creek in West Pennsylvania, from obvious circumstances, excited a strong sympathy at the time. The father, his wife, and five children were on their way to the church where he officiated. He happened to be a little way in the rear. His wife, assailed first by the Indians, warned him to fly. He fled to raise assistance. They

began with the infant in its mother's arms. The tomahawk fell in succession upon each, and last upon the hapless mother. When the father returned, two of his daughters manifested signs of life, and were recovered.

An amusing incident which occurred in a second Indian
expedition against Wheeling, serves to break the gloomy
uniformity of these chronicles. The house of Colonel
Zane, outside of the fort, contained a supply of ammunition,
and was garrisoned by seven or eight persons, male and
female, beside his own family. He was determined to
maintain it. The savage army approached, and before firing upon the fort, demanded the surrender of the house.
A brief and well directed fire was the reply. The women,
as usual, moulded bullets, charged the guns, and handed
them to the men, enabling them to fire with so much vivacity, as to cause the assailants to recoil. By night, they
attempted to fire the house. A savage crawled to the
kitchen, and while waving a brand in the air, to kindle the
fire so as to communicate it, received a shot from a black
man, which sent him yelling away. An incident which
promised the savages success in the end, operated in favor
of the besieged. A small boat from fort Pitt, bound to the
Falls of the Ohio, loaded with cannon balls, put to shore
at Wheeling. It was steered by one man, who, though
slightly wounded, reached the fort. The boat of course
fell into the hands of the savages. They had balls in a-
bundance, and a single cannon would have enabled them
to batter down the pallisade. Necessity with the red as
the white race is the mother of invention. A hollow log
was procured with a cavity of calibre as nearly fitting the
balls, as they could find. To render the new piece of ordnance safe, they adopted the ingenious expedient of apply-
ing chains obtained from a blacksmith's shop hard by, and
strongly twisted them around either end of the wooden cannon. It was then heavily charged, and pointed towards
the pallisade. Their imaginations presenting the walls
battered down, and themselves entering to apply the tomahawk and scalping knife, they applied fire. Like the o-
vercharged gun of Hudibras, the wooden mischief blew
into a thousand fragments, killed a number, wounded more,

and left the survivors staring in mute astonishment at the folly of meddling with the inventions of the white men.

Exasperated to frenzy, they returned from the discomfiture of the log cannon to the assault of the house. A deadly fire again compelled them to retire. Meanwhile, the ammunition was failing, and unless a supply could be obtained, the house must yield. It was proposed that some one should make a sally among the savages, and bring from the fort a keg of powder. Though the enterprise was forlorn, volunteers offered to assume it. A young sister of Colonel Zane, who had just returned from a boarding school in Philadelphia, was of the number. When reminded of the advantage of fleetness and force, which a man would have over her, the heroine replied 'that the loss of a woman would be less felt.' Arranging her dress for the purpose, she bounded towards the fort. The besiegers under their native impulses, stood wrapt in admiration, and only exclaimed, 'a squaw! a squaw!!' When arrived at the fort, Colonel Silas Zane, who commanded the fort, filled a table cloth with the contents of a keg of powder, bound it round her waist, and sent forth his fair and admirable kinswoman on her glorious errand. The Indians discovering the object of her mission, were no longer chained into inaction by the daring of the fair squaw! But she escaped untouched through a whole volley of balls, and reached the fort in safety. A party soon after relieved the fort, and raised the siege.

An achievement of Mr. Adam Poe, about this time would be worthy the narration of Sir Walter Scott. A party of savage marauders were out between Wheeling and fort Pitt. Eight men pursued them. Among these were two brothers of the name of Poe, remarkable for gigantic size and strength. Adam Poe fearing an ambuscade, left the rest, crossed the Ohio, and under high weeds crawled down the bank, searching for the enemy. A Wyandott chief, a large and powerful man, and a small Indian were on the shore, and so intent upon their own espionage, as not to have noticed him. Poe's gun missed, and the noise of the lock betrayed him. Too near to retreat, he grasped the large Indian by the breast with one arm, and the small one round the neck with the other, and threw both on the shelving bank. The small Indian cleared himself from his grasp, and aimed his tomahawk at his head. A kick opportunely applied, staggered him, and shook the tomahawk from his hand. Recovering it in a moment, the nimble Indian flourished some exulting blows over his head, as preludes to the intended fatal one. Waiting for that, Poe threw up his arm, and averted it from his head by a wound in his wrist. Extricating himself from the clutches of the chief, who was attempting the while to throw him to the earth, he snatched his fallen gun, and shot the little Indian dead. By this time the large chief was erect, and seizing Poe by the leg and shoulder at the same moment, prostrated him. Poe bounded on his feet in an instant, and both closed in a struggle, which plunged both in the Ohio. A contest ensued between these great and fierce combatants, the object of which was to drown each other. First one and then the other was thrust under the water by alternate successful efforts. Poe at length seized the long, black club of hair on the crown of the chief, skewered up in Indian fashion, and held the red man under the water, until he thought he had consigned him to the empire of the fishes. But he mistook. The savage was again erect in the water, and grappling again, each was carried beyond his depth, and obliged to swim. Both aimed for shore, each straining to reach it first, in order to seize one of the guns lying there, and dispatch the other. The Indian proved the better swimmer; and Poe perceiving it, made for the middle of the stream in the hope to avoid the shot of his foe by diving. Fortunately, the chief first took the gun of the other Indian which had been discharged, and Poe gained time and was thus enabled to get farther into the river. Two of the whites came up at this moment, and mistaking Poe for a wounded Indian, fired and wounded him in the shoulder. He turned and swam bleeding towards the shore, and recognized his brother, called on him to shoot the big Indian between him and the shore. The brother shot the Indian, and then plunged in the water to aid his brother to get to shore. Meanwhile, the wounded Indian, to escape being scalped, plunged into the deep water, and sunk to rise no more.

In 1784, general horror was excited by the result of an expedition of the savages to Clinch river, in which, among many murders, and the taking of many prisoners, Mrs. Moore, and her daughter Jane, an interesting girl of sixteen, were burnt to death with all the aggravated circumstances of Indian torture.

A remarkable instance of female heroism is recorded in the case of Mrs. Merill, of Nelson county, in 1791. The house was assaulted by savages. Mr. Merill opened the door to ascertain the cause of the barking of the dogs. He was fired at, and fell wounded into the room. The savages attempted to rush in after him, but Mrs. Merill and her daughter effectually closed the door. The assailants began to hew a passage through it with their tomahawks; and having made a breach, began to squeeze through into the room. Undismayed by the cries and groans within, and the exulting yells without, the courageous wife seized an axe, gave the entering ruffian a fatal blow, and dragged him through the opening in the door. Another and another pressed in, supposing their precursors were safely engaged in the work of death within, until four were slain. The silence within induced one of those without to explore the interior, through the crevice of the door. Discovering the fate of his companions within, after some counsel with those without, two mounted the house, and began to descend the broad wooden chimney. Aware from the noise of the climbers what was in agitation, Mrs. Merill promptly met that danger. Her little son was ordered to cut open a feather bed, and throw the contents in the fire. The two lodgers in the funnel, scorched and suffocated by the burning feathers, tumbled down in a half insensibility far from enviable. Mr. Merill so far recovered from his wound as to aid his heroic wife, helped to dispatch them, while she continued to guard the door with her uplifted axe. Another savage attempted to enter, but was saluted with such a blow, as drove him howling away. Thus the whole party were either killed or wounded by female intrepidity without a parallel. A prisoner heard this incident related by the survivor in his own town. Being asked as usual, 'what news?' he answered 'bad news! The squaw fight worse than the Long knives.'

We select but one incident more from these border horrors. Two boys living on Short creek, on the west bank of the Ohio, were at play at a distance from their house. They were taken captive by two Indians, and led away four miles into the wilderness, where their captors, after giving them food, laid down for the night, each holding one of the captives in his arms. The elder endeavored to comfort his brother with the hope of escape. The younger wept bitterly on finding himself in the power of those terrible red men, with the dread of whom his mother had often hushed him to sleep. But the trembling one soon fell asleep in the muscular arms of his master. The other slept not; and finding his keeper in sound sleep, he arose, and to try the soundness of the sleep of his captors, renewed the fire with such movements as required noise, and would yet seem allowable to the Indians, should they awaken. Their sleep remained profound. He walked to his brother, gently awakened him, and whispered in his ear, 'we had better go home now.' The younger replied, 'they will follow and catch us.' 'Never fear,' said the elder, 'we will take care for that.' It was not without difficulty that the elder prevailed on the younger to aid him in killing their captors. The Indians had but one gun between them, and near it lay their tomahawks. The elder placed the gun levelled on a log near the ear of one of the Indians, and stationed his brother with his finger on the trigger to pull it at his signal. He bestrode the other savage with tomahawk in hand. Brandishing it as the signal for pulling the trigger, the gun was discharged and the tomahawk fell together.' Lay on,' exclaimed the younger, 'I have done it for mine.' The first blow of the tomahawk was not fatal; but it was plied anew with so much force, that the Indian, who upon the first blow had risen to his feet, was brought down again. Leaving their captors dead, the young heroes set off for home, where they arrived at early dawn, and heard, as they came to the door, the plaintive voice of their mother, exclaiming 'poor little fellows, they are killed or taken prisoners.' 'No,' they responded from without, 'we are here safe.'

CHAPTER IX.

SETTLEMENT OF OHIO.

PREVIOUS to entering upon the annals of the Indian wars incident to the settlement of this great state, it becomes necessary to dwell a moment upon some events of greater and more general moment to the interest of the whole valley, and to the settlement of Ohio, than these chronicles of skirmishes, and the assaults and massacres of detached settlements. The battles of General Harmar, General St. Clair, and General Wayne were fought by considerable bodies of regular troops, raised by the general government, with great masses of Indians. The consequences of these battles were felt over all the West, and through the Union. We return to the order of events in the West, immediately subsequent to the close of the revolutionary war.

The savages had generally taken part with Britain in this war. That power still held posts within our ceded limits, whence her traders issued the means of influence and corruption among them. These posts were central points from which they marched upon our incipient settlements on the frontier, armed with the tomahawk and the scalping knife. One of the earliest objects of the attention of our government after the war, was either to pacify the Indians, or restrain and punish their cruelties. The Creeks, a powerful nation in the centre of the southern country, were in a position to be excited to enmity, both by Britain and Spain. They were headed at this time by M'Gillivray, a man who united in his character the strong points, both of the savage and the civilized life. He was at first refractory and indisposed to terms. A second effort with him was more successful. Colonel Willet, who was charged with the negotiation, induced M'Gillivray to repair to New York; and a treaty was signed which bears his name along with that of Washington.

12

Attempts to pacify the Indians of the Wabash and the Miami were not equally successful. The measures of Washington were soon taken. When he saw that the ordinary motives would have no effect in bringing them to terms, policy and humanity alike called for strong measures. An expedition against the hostile tribes north-west of the Ohio, was planned. The object was to bring the Indians to a general engagement; or if that might not be, to destroy their establishments on the waters of the Scioto and the Wabash. General Harmar was appointed to the command of this expedition. Major Hamtranck, with a detachment, was to make a diversion in his favor up the Wabash.

On the 13th of September, 1791, General Harmar marched from fort Washington, the present site of Cincinnati, with three hundred and twenty regulars, and effected a junction with the militia of Pennsylvania and Kentucky, which had advanced twenty-five miles in front. The whole force amounted to one thousand four hundred and fifty-three men. Colonel Hardin, who commanded the Kentucky militia, was detached with six hundred men, chiefly militia, to reconnoitre. On his approach to the Indian settlements, the Indians set fire to their villages and fled. In order, if possible, to overtake them, he was detached with a smaller force that could be moved more rapidly. It consisted of two hundred and ten men. A small party of Indians met, and attacked them; and the greater part of the militia behaved badly,—leaving a few brave men who would not fly, to their fate. Twenty-three of the party fell, and seven only made their escape, and rejoined the army. Notwithstanding this check, the army succeeded so far as to reduce the remaining towns to ashes, and destroy their provisions.

On their return to fort Washington, General Harmar was desirous of wiping off in another action, the disgrace which public opinion had impressed upon his arms. He halted eight miles from Chillicothe; and late at night, detached Colonel Hardin, with orders to find the enemy, and bring them to an engagement. Early in the morning this detachment reached the enemy, and a severe engagement

ensued. The savages fought with desperation. Some of
the American troops shrunk; but the officers conducted
with great gallantry. Most of them fell, bravely discharging their duty. More than fifty regulars and one hundred
militia, including the brave officers, Fontaine, Willys, and
Frothingham, were slain.

Harmar, in his official account of this affair, claimed the
victory, although the Americans seem clearly to have had
the worst of it. At his request, he was tried by a court
martial, and honorably acquitted. The enemy had suffered so severely, that they allowed him to return unmolested
to fort Washington.

The terrors and the annoyance of Indian hostilities still
hung over the western settlements. The call was loud and
general from the frontiers, for ample and efficient protection. Congress placed the means in the hands of the executive. Major General Arthur St. Clair was appointed
commander in chief of the forces to be employed in the
meditated expedition. The objects of it were, to destroy
the Indian settlements between the Miamies, to expel them
from the country, and establish a chain of posts, which
should prevent their return during the war. This army
was late in assembling in the vicinity of fort Washington.
They marched directly towards the chief establishments of
the enemy, building and garrisoning in their way the two
intermediate forts, Hamilton and Jefferson. After the detachments had been made for these garrisons, the effective
force that remained amounted to something less than two
thousand men. To open a road for their march was a slow
and tedious business. Small parties of Indians were often seen hovering about their march; and some unimpor-
tant skirmishes took place. As the army approached the
enemy's country, sixty of the militia deserted in a body.
To prevent the influence of such an example, Major Hamtranck was detached with a regiment in pursuit of the deserters. The army now consisting of one thousand four
hundred men, continued its march. On the 3d of November, 1792, it encamped fifteen miles south of the Miami
villages. Having been rejoined by Major Hamtranck,
General St. Clair proposed to march immediately against
them.

Half an hour before sunrise, the militia was attacked by the savages, and fled in the utmost confusion. They burst through the formed line of the regulars into the camp. Great efforts were made by the officers, to restore order; but not with the desired success. The Indians pressed upon the heels of the flying militia, and engaged General Butler with great intrepidity. The action became warm and general; and the fire of the assailants passing round both flanks of the first line, in a few minutes was poured with equal fury upon the rear. The artillerists in the centre were mowed down; and the fire was the more galling, as it was directed by an invisible enemy, crouching on the ground, or concealed behind trees. In this manner they advanced towards the very mouths of the cannon ; and fought with the infuriated fierceness with which success always animates savages. Some of the soldiers exhibited military fearlessness, and fought with great bravery. Others were timid and disposed to fly. With a self-devotion, which the occasion required, the officers generally exposed themselves to the hottest of the contest, and fell in great numbers in desperate efforts to restore the battle. The commanding general, though he had been for some time enfeebled with severe disease, acted with personal bravery, and delivered his orders with judgment and self-possession. A charge was made upon the savages with the bayonet; and they were driven from their covert with some loss, a distance of four hundred yards. But as soon as the charge was suspended they returned to the attack. General Butler was mortally wounded; the left of the right wing broken, and the artillerists killed almost to a man. The guns were seized, and the camp penetrated by the enemy. A desperate charge was headed by Colonel Butler, although he was severely wounded; and the Indians were again driven from the camp, and the artillery recovered. Several charges were repeated with partial success. The enemy only retreated, to return to the charge, flushed with new ardor. The ranks of the troops were broken, and the men pressed together in crowds, and were shot down without resistance. A retreat was all that remained, to save the remnant of the army. Colonel Darke was ordered to charge a body of savages that intercepted their retreat. Major Clark, with his battalion, was directed to cover the rear. These orders were carried into effect; and a most disorderly flight commenced. A pursuit was kept up four miles, when fortunately for the surviving Americans, the natural greediness of the savage appetite for plunder called back the victorious Indians to the camp, to divide the spoils. The routed troops continued their flight to fort Jefferson, throwing away their arms on the road. The wounded were left here, and the army retired upon fort Washington.

In this fatal battle fell thirty-eight commissioned officers, and five hundred and ninety-three non-commissioned officers and privates. Twenty-one commissioned officers, many of whom afterwards died of their wounds, and two hundred and forty-two non-commissioned officers and privates were wounded.

The savage force in this fatal engagement was led by a Mississago chief, who had been trained to war under the British, during the revolution. So superior was his knowledge of tactics, that the Indian chiefs, though extremely jealous of him, yielded the entire command to him; and he arranged and fought the battle with great combination of military skill. Their force amounted to four thousand, and they stated the Americans killed, at six hundred and twenty, and their own at sixty-five; but it was undoubtedly much greater. They took seven pieces of cannon, two hundred oxen, and many horses. The chief, at the close of the battle, bade the Indians forbear the pursuit of the Americans, as he said they had killed enough.

General Scott with one thousand mounted volunteers from Kentucky, soon after marched against a party of the victors, at St. Clair's fatal field. He found the Indians rioting in their plunder, riding the oxen in the glee of triumph, and acting as if the whole body was intoxicated. General Scott immediately attacked them. The contest was short, but decisive. The Indians had two hundred killed on the spot. The cannon and military stores remaining were retaken, and the savages completely routed. The loss of the Kentuckians was inconsiderable.

The reputation of the government was now committed in the fortunes of the war. Three additional regiments were directed to be raised. On the mo ion in congress for raising these regiments, there was an animated, and even a bitter debate. It was urged on one hand, that the expense of such a force would involve the necessity of severe taxation; that too much power was thrown into the hands of the president; that the war had been badly managed, and ought to have been entrusted to the militia of the West, under their own officers; and with more force they urged that no success could be of any avail, so long as the British held those posts within our acknowledged limits, from which the savages were supplied with protection, shelter, arms, advice, and instigation to the war. On the other hand, the justice of the cause, as a war of defence, and not of conquest, was unquestionable. It was proved that between 1783 and 1790, no less than one thousand five hundred people of Kentucky had been massacred by the savages, or dragged into a horrid captivity; and that the frontiers of Pennsylvania and Virginia had suffered a loss not much less. It was proved that every effort had been made to pacify the savages without effect. They showed that in 1790, when a treaty was proposed to the savages at the Miami, they first refused to treat, and then asked thirty days for deliberation. It was granted. In the interim, they stated that not less than one hundred and twenty persons had been killed and captured, and several prisoners roasted alive; at the term of which horrors, they refused any answer at all to the proposition to treat. Various other remarks were made in defence of the bill. It tried the strength of parties in congress, and was finally carried.

General St. Clair resigned, and Major General Anthony Wayne was appointed to succeed him. This officer commanded the confidence of the western people, who confided in that reckless bravery, which had long before procured him the appellation of 'Mad Anthony.' There was a powerful party, who still affected to consider this war unnecessary; and every impediment was placed in the way of its success, which that party could devise. To prove to them that the government was still disposed to peace, two excellent officers and valuable men, Colonel Hardin and Major Truman were severally despatched with propositions of peace. They were both murdered by the savages. These unsuccessful attempts at negotiation, and the difficulties and delays naturally incident to the preparation of such a force, together with the attempts that had been made in congress, to render the war unpopular, had worn away so much time that the season for operations for the year had almost elapsed. But as soon as the negotiations had wholly failed, the campaign was opened with as much vigor as the nature of the case would admit. The general was able, however, to do no more this autumn, than to advance into the forest towards the country of the savages, six miles in advance of fort Jefferson. He took possession of the ground on which the fatal defeat of St. Clair had taken place, in 1791. He here erected a fortification, with the appropriate name of fort Recovery. His principal camp was called Greenville. In Kentucky, meanwhile, many of the people clamored against these measures, and loudly insisted that the war ought to be carried on by militia, to be commanded by an officer taken from their state. It was believed, too, by the executive, that the British government, by retaining their posts within our limits, and by various other measures, at least countenanced the Indians in their hostilities. That government took a more decisive measure early in the spring. A British detachment from Detroit advanced near fifty miles south of that place, and fortified themselves on the Miami of the lakes. In one of the numerous skirmishes which took place between the savages and the advance of General Wayne, it was affirmed, that the British were mingled with the Indians.

On the 8th of August, General Wayne reached the confluence of the Au Glaize, and the Miami of the lakes. The richest and most extensive settlements of the western Indians were at this place. It was distant only about thirty miles from the post on the Miami, which the British had recently occupied. The whole strength of the enemy, amounting to nearly two thousand warriors, was collected in the vicinity of that post. The regulars of Gen. Wayne were not much inferior in numbers. A reinforcement of one thousand one hundred mounted Kentucky militia, commanded by General Scott, gave a decided superiority to the American force. The general was well aware that the enemy were ready to give him battle, and he ardently desired it. But in pursurnce of the settled policy of the United States, another effort was made for the attainment of peace, without the shedding of blood. The savages were exhorted by those who were sent to them, no longer to follow the counsels of the bad men at the foot of the Rapids, who urged them on to the war, but had neither the power nor the inclination to protect them; that to listen to the propositions of the government of the United States, would restore them to their homes, and rescue them from famine. To these propositions they returned only an evasive answer.

On the 20th of August, the army of General Wayne marched in columns. A select battalion under Maj. Price, moved as a reconnoitering force in front. After marching five miles, he received so heavy a fire from the savages, concealed as usual, that he was compelled to retreat. The savages had chosen their ground with great judgment. They had moved into a thick wood, in advance of the British works, and had taken a position behind fallen timber, prostrated by a tornado. This rendered their position almost inaccessible to horse. They were formed in three regular lines, according to the Indian custom, very much extended in front. Their first effort was to turn the left flank of the American army.

The American legion was ordered to advance with trailed arms, and rouse the enemy from his covert at the point of the bayonet, and then deliver its fire. The cavalry led by Captain Campbell, was ordered to advance between the Indians and the river, where the wood admitted them to penetrate, and charge their left flank. General Scott, at the head of the mounted volunteers, was commanded to make a considerable circuit and turn their right. These, and all the complicated orders of General Wayne, were promptly executed. But such was the impetuosity of the charge made by the first line of infantry, so entirely was the enemy broken by it, and so rapid was the pursuit, that only a small part of the second line, and of the mounted volunteers could take any part in the action. In the course of an hour, the savages were driven more than two miles, and within gun shot of the British fort.

General Wayne remained three days on the field of battle, reducing the houses and corn fields, above and below the fort, and some of them within pistol shot of it, to ashes. The houses and stores of Colonel M'Kee, an English trader, whose great influence among the savages had been uniformly exerted for the continuance of the war, was burned among the rest. Correspondence on these points took place between General Wayne and Major Campbell, who commanded the British fort. That of General Wayne was sufficiently firm; and it manifested that the latter only avoided hostilities with him, by acquiescing in the destruction of British property within the range of his guns.

On the 28th, the army returned to Au Glaize, destroying all the villages and corn within fifty miles of the river. In this decisive battle, the American loss in killed and wounded amounted to one hundred and seven, including officers. Among those that fell, were Captain Campbell and Lieutenant Towles. The general bestowed great and merited praise for their bravery and promptitude in this affair, to all his troops.

The hostility of the Indians still continuing, their whole country was laid waste; and forts were erected in the heart of their settlements to prevent their return. This seasonable victory, and this determined conduct on the part of the United States, rescued them from a general war with all the nations north-west of the Ohio. The Six Nations had manifested resentments, which were only appeased for the moment, by the suspension of a settlement, which Pennsylvania was making at Presqu' Isle, within their alleged limits. The issue of this battle dissipated the clouds at once which had been thickening in that quarter. Its influence was undoubtedly felt far to the south. The Indian inhabitants of Georgia, and still farther to the south had been apparently on the verge of a war, and had been hardly restrained from hostility by the feeble authority of that state.

No incidents of great importance occurred in this quarter, until August 3d, of the next year; when a definitive treaty was concluded by General Wayne, with the hostile Indians north-west of the Ohio. By this treaty, the destructive war which had so long desolated that frontier, was ended in a manner acceptable to the United States. An accommodation was also brought about with the southern Indians, notwithstanding the intrigues of their Spanish neighbors. The regions of the Mississippi valley were opened on all sides to immigration, and rescued from the dread of Indian hostilities.

The progress of the great state of Ohio has no parallel in the history of colonies. No records can be found of equal advancement of population, national wealth, strength and improvement of every sort, by the unforced progress of immigration and natural increase. But little more than thirty years ago, it was all possessed by ruthless savages; and we now see cities and towns, more than an hundred thousand militia, a million inhabitants, two canals, the one nearly seventy, and the other three hundred miles in length, a great number of flourishing villages, handsome farm houses, and every indication of comfort and abundance, and the whole scene has at first view the aspect of fable and enchantment. We see one respectable and rapidly advancing town; and a mass of farmers spread over the greater portion of the surface of the state, not rich in money, but rich in rural abundance, in simplicity of manners, and the materials of genuine independence. The people are as well fed and clothed, and as contented and happy, perhaps, as the same number of people any where on the globe. There are schools, colleges, manufactories, national works and improvements, of which any state, or any order of society, howsoever advanced, might be proud. This colony, which has flourished by its own innate principle of vigor, without factitious support from speculation, or any forcing from opulence and power, still sees the original trees standing in its fields.

We should be glad to trace the origin and progress of every town and settlement in the state from Marietta, Cincinnati, a d Galliopolis, the oldest towns in the country, to the most recent establishment on lake Erie. It would be pleasant to trace the gradual advance of the settlement from these central points and the shores of the Ohio, along the two Miamies, over the heights which separate the waters of the Ohio from those of lake Erie. The history, also, of the settlement of the Connecticut Reserve, is an interesting one. We there find a large and compact settlement, distinct from the other divisions of the Ohio population, in the equal dispersion of farms over the surface, in the disposition to support schools and public worship, exceedingly like the parent people from whom they sprung. But they who achieved these great works, thought little of transmitting the remembrance of their works to posterity. Their minds were pleasantly occupied with other views, and those copious, exact and satisfactory materials, necessary for a detailed history of the progress of Ohio, will, probably, perish with the living depositories of them. Many of the founders of this great state still exist; but they are too intently occupied, in laying up the superstructure of their recent establishments, to think of furnishing such materials. Besides, the details of such a work would fill volumes. Neither our limits or materials allow any more than some very abbreviated sketches.

The first effective settlement of Ohio, was by purchasers under the 'Ohio Company' in 1788. The writer of this distinctly remembers the wagon that carried out a number of adventurers from the counties of Essex and Middlesex, in Massachusetts, on the second emigration to the woods of Ohio. He remembers the black canvass covering of the wagon; the white and large lettering in capitals 'To Marietta on the Ohio.' He remembers the food which even then the thought of such a distant expedition furnished to his imagination. Some twenty emigrants accompanied this wagon. The Rev. Dr. Manasseh Cutler, he thinks, had the direction of this band of emigrants. General-Putnam seems to have been the only one who preceded him in claims to be considered the patriarch of the Marietta settlement. Dr. Cutler, at the time of his being engaged in the speculation of the Ohio Company's purchase, had a feud,—it is not remembered whether literary, political, or religious,—with the late learned and eccentric Dr. Bently of Salem, Massachusetts. Dr. Bently was then chief contributor to a paper which he afterwards edited. The writer still remembers, and can repeat doggerel verses by Dr. Bently upon the departure of Dr. Cutler on his first trip to explore his purchase on the Ohio.

The first travellers to explore Ohio, availed themselves of the full extent of the traveller's privilege in regard to the wonders of this new land of promise, and the unparalleled fertility of the soil. These extravagant representations of the grandeur of the vegetation, and the fertility of the land, at first excited a great desire to emigrate to this new and wonderful region. But some returned with different accounts, in discouragement; and the hostilities of the savages were painted in the most appalling colors. A reaction took place in the public mind. The wags of the day exercised their wit, in circulating caricatured and exaggerated editions of the stories of the first adventurers, that there were springs of brandy, flax, that bore little pieces of cloth on the stems, enormous pumpkins and melons, and the like. Accounts the most horrible were added of hoop snakes of such deadly malignity that a sting, which they bore in their tails, when it punctured the bark of a green tree, instantly caused its leaves to become sear, and the tree to die. Stories of Indian massacres and barbarities were related in all their horrors. The country was admitted to be fertile; but was pronounced excessively sickly, and poorly balancing by that advantage all these counterpoises of sickness, Indians, *copper headed and hoop snakes*, bears, wolves, and panthers.

The tendency of the New England mind to enterprise and emigration, thus early began to develope. For all these horrors portrayed in all their darkness, and with all the dreadful imaginings connected with the thought of such a remote and boundless wilderness, did not hinder the departure of great numbers of the people following in the footsteps of General Putnam and Dr. Cutler. They were both men of established character, whose words and opinions wrought confidence. Dr. Cutler was a man of extensive and various learning. He was particularly devoted to the study of natural history; and was among the first who began scientifically to explore the botany of our country. He had great efficiency in founding the upper settlement on Ohio; and his descendants are among the most respectable inhabitants of the country at present.

General Rufus Putnam had been a reputable and unblemished officer in the war of the revolution. He emigrated from Leicester, in the county of Worcester, Massachusetts. He was, probably, the member of the Ohio Company who had the greatest influence in imparting confidence to emigration from New England to Ohio. When he moved there, it was one compact and boundless forest. He saw that forest fall on all sides under the axe; and in the progress of improvement, comfortable, and then large, commodious and splendid dwellings rise around him. He saw his favorite settlement sustain an inundation of the Ohio, which drowned the cattle, wafted away the dwellings, and in some instances the inhabitants in them. He saw the settlement survive the accumulated horrors of an Indian war. He saw its exhaustless fertility, and its natural advantages triumph over all. He saw Marietta making advances towards an union of interest with the gulf of Mexico, by floating down to its bosom a number of sea vessels, built at that place. He saw such a prodigious increase of navigation on the Ohio, as to number an hundred large boats passing his dwelling in a few hours. He heard the first tumult of steam boats as they began to be borne down between the forests. He had surrounded his republican mansion with orchards bending with fruit. In the midst of rural abundance and endeared friends, who had grown up around him, far from the display of wealth, the bustle of ambition and intrigue, the father of a colony, hospitable and kind without ostentation and without effort, he displayed in these remote regions, the grandeur, real and intrinsic, of those immortal men who achieved our revolution. He has passed away. But the memory of really great and good men, like General Putnam, will remain as long as plenty, independence, and comfort, shall prevail on the shores of the Ohio.

The next settlement in Ohio, in the order of time, and

really the most efficient and important of all others, and which may be clearly considered the nucleus of the population, was that between the two Miamies. Of this settlement Judge Symmes may fairly be considered the founder. He was a civilian, a lawyer, and an inhabitant of New Jersey. He was a member of congress when he first contemplated the idea of emigrating to the western country. He was the representative and agent of the company which made the first purchase between the two Miamies. It comprehended a million of acres. He was afterwards a judge under the territorial government. His name is identified with all the subsequent sales, locations, establishments of the sites of towns, and similar transactions, until Ohio became a state. Had his speculation been followed with the success which ought to have resulted from the foresight with which it was made, and the vigor with which it was carried into effect, it must have secured an immense fortune for his posterity. But the issues of such great and combined operations are often determined by elements, beyond the reach of human foresight. Clear as his vision was into the future, he little foresaw the future value and consequence of these lands. Purchasers, with a ken still more limited, had not the courage nor forecast to make him sufficient payments to meet the great expenses of his speculations. He was unquestionably fitted in a high degree to become the foster father to a new colony. He possessed a sound understanding, great firmness of purpose, and was a man of industrious habits, and devoted to business; and had not the slightest touch of the hunter and *coureur du bois*, which so strongly marked the first settlers of Kentucky and Tennessee, in his character. He was a zealous patron of the industrious and enterprising; and all that was necessary to secure the countenance and support of Judge Symmes, was to convince him that the man was sober, industrious, and disposed to exert himself. It was an honorable trait in his character, that he was a real and efficient friend of the poor. Many amiable eccentricities belonged to his character; and among other traits that might seem most foreign to his industrious, calculating, and municipal habits was, that he was a writer of verses, of which very copious proofs, as well as honorable to his muse, remain. The names of his chief associates in the settlement of the Miami country will naturally be interwoven in these annals. Among them was Colonel Israel Ludlow, one of the first settlers, a man of great amiability of character, and whose early decease was considered a deep loss to the country.

Exploring parties had made temporary residences on the north shore of the Ohio, previous to the establishment of any permanent settlement, and boats, ascending and descending the river, had had rencontres with the Indians, in which many of those thrilling and terrible adventures, which we have already related to repetition, were common. We read of the occurrence of one in the autumn of 1776, as related by Mr. Patterson, who was ascending the Ohio in a boat, with six or seven companions, and who was fired upon by the Indians. A part of the company were killed, and the remainder wounded. They were an hundred miles from settlements or relief, lying in their wounds and blood, exposed to the rain and elements. One only was able to travel, and he was wounded. He proceeded up the river to the nearest settlement, procured help, and carried off his wounded companions, who recovered. The narrative of the sufferings of this company is one of harrowing interest. Nothing that human nature can suffer was wanting to their misery; and their case furnishes an impressive proof, through how much misery and suffering man can survive. We could easily fill up copious annals of these desperate rencontres, and hair breadth escapes, and recoveries from wounds, which would be deemed utterly hopeless in the view of the best surgical aid, and all the palliations of the comfort and aid of society. But, however impressive these narratives, the brevity of our plan excludes them, and we commence these annals with the first permanent settlement of Ohio.

This commenced at Marietta, April 7th, 1788, under General Rufus Putnam, as agent for the Ohio Company. The company that came with him consisted of 47 persons, and were from Massachusetts, Rhode Island, and Connecticut. Their first business was to build a stockade fort of sufficient strength to secure them against any desultory attacks of the savages. These were all laborious men, who thought much more of the plough and hoe than the rifle and game. They were delighted with the appearance of the rich alluvion, and the immense trees and grape vines that rose from it; and treated themselves to the jests which had been circulated in their native regions, respecting pumpkin vines that ran across the Ohio, and bore pumpkins of a size to furnish space in which sows might litter. The exuberant grandeur of the wild vegetation might well justify extravagant expectations from the fertility of the soil. They deadened the trees, and planted fifty acres of corn. In the autumn twenty more families joined them. They were chiefly revolutionary soldiers, who had been used to face dangers and hardships of all sorts, and to give and receive blows. Their vigilance and boldness of countenance appear to have awed the Indians, so that they molested them very little. While these prudent and laborious men tilled their grounds, they had always some one of their number stationed upon a high stump, or elevated point of ground, to forewarn them of the approach of the foe. Game of all sorts abounded in the woods, and fish in the rivers. The fields yielded the most ample abundance of return for whatever they had planted; so that abundant subsistence was obtained with the greatest ease.

Six years afterwards, in 1794, the settlements of Bellepre and Newbury, the one fifteen miles, and the other twenty miles below, on the river, were commenced. In each of these places stockade forts, to which the people could retreat in case of alarm from the savages, were built, according to the invariable custom in all the new western settlements. The strongest of these received the appropriate name of the 'Farmer's Castle.'

In 1791, Indian hostilities commenced upon these settlements. The Ohio Company organized, and kept in constant employment, a small company of spies, whose duty it was to perambulate the settlement. When these rangers discovered footsteps, or other indications of the contiguity of the savages, they were to give verbal notice; or if the emergency of alarm was urgent, to fire signal guns. On receiving these signals, it was the duty of the settlers immediately to retreat to their stockades, and the soldiers to repair to their post of defence. The unsleeping and untiring vigilance of these settlers did not at all match with Indian notions of attack, who always seize the moments of carelessness and the unguarded point of weakness for the hour of assault. That this settlement suffered so much less than those that preceded it, under the same circumstances, in the western country, may be solely attributed to that habitual watchfulness and unremitting posture of defence.

Between 1791 and 1795, Major Goodall, a most valuable member of the settlement, and three others were killed. To have right estimates of this comparatively small amount of suffering from Indian warfare, it must be remembered, that this settlement stood alone on the north shore of the Ohio; was a frontier to the most numerous and powerful Indian villages in the western country, and the object of their bitterest enmity and most concentered efforts. In addition to the men, mentioned above, one woman and her two children were slain. Another infant in her arms was tomahawked, but was rescued by the inhabitants, and recovered from its wounds.

In 1790, a settlement was commenced at the forks of Duck creek, twenty miles up the Muskingum, at the site of the present town of Waterford; and another fifteen miles higher on the same river at Big Bottom, and a third at Wolf creek, near the forks. These settlements were on a tract of one hundred thousand acres of land, laid off into farms of one hundred acres each, called 'donation lots,' which were gratuitously assigned to actual settlers. At the close of 1790, these settlements contained 447 men, of whom 107 had families; a striking demonstration of the rapid increase of population even amidst the dangers of an Indian war.

The settlement at Big Bottom was destroyed by the Indians, January 2d, 1791. Fourteen persons were killed, and five taken prisoners. This fatal assault was made by the Indians with their usual guile and treachery. They had kept up a show of frankness and friendship towards

13*

these people, which had lulled them to a ruinous security. Unperceived by the people, the Indians watched the settlement from the summit of an adjacent hill. The inhabitants were returning from their labors at evening twilight to their supper. The Indians, preceded by a huge Mohawk, rushed in upon the garrison and inflicted an unresisted massacre. One woman only contended, and she inflicted a wonnd upon the Mohawk, before she was killed. A boy was spared, and carried captive to Detroit.

The settlement at Wolf creek was warned of its impending danger by two men of the name of Bullard, who escaped from the massacre of Big Bottom. Next morning the Indians arrived to the assault of this place; but finding the inhabitants apprised of their attack, and in readiness for them, they decamped without any serious attempts upon it. Some murders were committed at Waterford and Little Wolf creek, in 1794, and 1795. Although Marietta, from its vigilance and preparation, was considered by the savages impregnable, the cows of the settlement often came in with arrows sticking in their bodies, as proofs of the good will of the Indians to injure them, were it in their power.

The escape of the late R. J. Meigs, Esq. afterwards governor of Ohio, and Postmaster General, from various circumstances, merits a relation. He was returning at night from the labors of the field, in company with Mr. Symonds and a black boy. The Indians fired upon Symonds and wounded him. He escaped them by reaching the river and swimming. The black boy was scalped. An Indian, armed only with a tomahawk, motioned Mr. Meigs to surrender. Instead of surrendering, he advanced upon the savage with his gun presented, but which happened not to be loaded. As they came in contact, the one struck with his gun and the other with his tomahawk. Mr. Meigs was stunned by the blow; but recovering, he fled from the Indian, who pursued without being able to overtake him. Seeing his victim like to escape him, he fired his tomahawk upon him, which narrowly missed his head. The Indian raised his customary war cry, and gave up the pursuit.

In all this time the people of this settlement were not known to have killed but two Indians. One had mounted on the roof of a cabin, in an abandoned settlement at Duck creek. With the customary disposition to pry into the concerns of the whites, he was looking down the large wooden chimney. Some spies happened to have occupied the cabin for the night. They discovered him, and killed him on his perch. The spies had a shot at another Indian in company, who was amusing himself in turning a large grindstone; but he escaped. The other was killed by one of the spies on the Little Muskingum. At this period the country contiguous to this settlement abounded with game, such as buffaloe, deer, and wild turkeys. The deer were killed for their hides and tallow, and the turkeys afforded a game too common to be prized as a luxury.

We return from these annals of the first settlement in Ohio, in the order of time, to contemplate the progress of that between the two Miamies, the first in the order of importance. This country was explored by Colonel Bowman, in 1779, at the head of ninety men, marching against the Indian village at Little Pickaway. The town was destroyed; but the returning party suffered severely from the Indians, and lost ten of their number. He gained, however, an accurate knowledge of this fertile and interesting country, and the position and force of the Indian towns contiguous to it.

Between the years 1780 and 1782, General Clark conducted a larger force against the Indians of that region, in which Old and New Pickaway villages were burned. In 1784, our government effected a treaty with them, in which, by certain mutual stipulations, they ceded to the United States the country lying upon the Muskingum, Scioto, and Little and Great Miami.

The 'Ohio Company' was organized at Boston, March 1st, 1786. It was composed of revolutionary officers and soldiers, to whom Congress assigned a military grant of land north-west of the Ohio. The grant consisted of a million and a half of acres. General Putnam made the settlement, which we have just been contemplating, under this grant; and this was the germ from which has grown up this great and populous community.   In 1788, congress passed an ordinance, establishing a territorial government over the North-western Territory.   Arthur St. Clair was appointed Governor.   In September, 1788, the first judicial court was holden in the territory.   The first political object with the governor was to establish a peace with the various hostile tribes, contiguous to the territory.   The chiefs met at fort Harmar, at the mouth of the Muskingum, and agreed upon a former treaty, which had been settled at fort M'Intosh, in 1785, and which was now renewed in 1790.

In the winter of 1786, Mr. Stites, of Redstone, now Brownsville, on the Monongahela, presented himself before congress, then sitting in New York, with a view to purchase a tract of country for settlement between the two Miamies.   He was introduced to John Cleves Symmes, then a member of congress, whose aid he solicited, in order to enable him to make the purchase in question.   Mr. Symmes was so much impressed with the project, as to make a journey to the country, wisely thinking it best to judge of the country by personal inspection.   He journeyed to the Ohio, and descended it to Louisville.   He was pleased with the country, and on his return, a purchase of one million of acres lying on the Ohio, and between the two Miamies, was made in his name.

Mr. Symmes soon afterwards sold to Matthias Denman that part of his purchase which now forms the site of Cincinnati.   The first settlers were from New York and New Jersey.   Mr. Stites added several families from Redstone. Mr. Filson, in exploring the country, was killed by the Indians.   Lieutenant Kersey and Ensign Luse, with nearly forty soldiers, were ordered to join Mr. Symmes' party, as a corps of defence for the contemplated settlement. Major Stites, with the necessary preparation for commencing a settlement, descended to the mouth of the little Miami.   In November 16th, 1789, they commenced to the number of twenty-six, the erection of a block house on the position where Columbia is now situated.   With the requisite precaution against the Indians, a part stood guard, while the rest labored in the erection of the block house.

A square stockade fort was soon after formed by the erection of three other block houses. This was the germ of the second settlement in Ohio, and the first between the two Miamies. Mr. Symmes soon after joined them with a small sergeant's guard of six soldiers, and they erected a small block house below those at the mouth of the Little Miami.

About the commencement of the year 1790, Israel Ludlow, who, after the death of Mr. Filson, became a joint partner with Mr. Denman and Patterson of the site of Cincinnati, left Limestone with a company of nearly twenty persons, to commence the settlement of their purchase. The town was first named Losantiville. As town making became afterwards, in the progress of the western country in population, a regular business, and the invention and coining of names for towns no mean study, it will be amusing to consider the ingenuity of this far fetched name. The town was commenced opposite Licking river in Kentucky. The name of the town took the initial of that river for its first letter. It borrowed *os*, the mouth, from the Latin; *anti*, opposite, from the Greek, and *ville*, a city, from the French. Hence we have Losantiville, *a city opposite the mouth of Licking*. In a newspaper printed at Lexington in Kentucky, the type, appearance, and printing of which smacks strongly of the simplicity and coarseness of the olden time, is now to be seen the original advertisement of the sale of the lots in this city, then covered with a heavy growth of timber. The newspaper is shown as a curiosity in Mr. Letton's museum in Cincinnati. Mr. Ludlow on his arrival with his party commenced clearing near the present corner of Front and Main streets. Three or four log cabins were built on what is now Main street. Mr. Ludlow surveyed and laid out the town during the winter. The courses of the streets were marked on the trees of the heavy and dense forest. The abundance of game and fish left little difficulty of subsistence, and even the Indians, though hostile, did not annoy them.

Mr. Symmes, with the small force at his disposal, in February, 1789, descended the river fifteen miles to North

Bend, which he deemed the best situation for a town. But neither that place, nor Columbia, above Cincinnati, have yet reached the size of even considerable villages; a clear proof that the wisest human foresight sometimes falls short in such calculations. In the following spring, Indian hostility manifested itself in the customary way of annoyance to the incipient settlements, by stealing horses, killing the cattle, and murdering the inhabitants. Several persons of a surveying party, and five or six soldiers were killed.

June 1st, 1789, Major Doughty arrived at Losantiville with one hundred and forty men, who built four block houses opposite the mouth of Licking. On a lot of fifteen acres, sloping from the upper bank to the river, a little east of the present position of Broadway, was erected fort Washington. At the close of 1789, General Harmar arrived with three hundred men, and took command of the fort, preparatory to his expedition against the hostile Indians. The population, besides the soldiers, consisted of eleven families and twenty-four unmarried men. They inhabited 20 small log cabins, chiefly on the lower bank. But a very small part of the present area of the town was cleared; nor were the logs removed for some years afterwards. Darius Orcutt and Miss M'Henry, and Daniel Shoemaker and Miss Alice Ross were the first couples legally married in Losantiville, and the first child born, in what is now called Cincinnati, was John Cummins. Columbia still exceeded this place in population. The inhabitants at that place had the advantage of tilling fields, which had been made by the Indians, and so productive were these fields in maize, that captain Benjamin Davis measured one hundred and fourteen bushels of corn from a single acre.

In January, 1790, governor St. Clair and the judges of the supreme court descended to Losantiville, where the first judicial court was organized in the Miami country. The governor, in honor of the military society of Cincinnati, changed the name of Losantiville to its present name. In the following spring, Mr. Dunlap and associates laid out the station of Colerain on the Great Miami, seventeen miles north-west of Cincinnati, and Ludlow's, Garrard's, Covalt's, White's, and Round Bottom stations were commenced. At each of these points general Harmar stationed a small number of regulars for defence; and whoever rashly ventured beyond this line of defence was exposed to be murdered, or at least to receive a shot from the hostile Indians, who were constantly prowling round.

Forty families were added to Cincinnati this year. As many cabins and the first two frame houses were erected. Seven mechanics were numbered among the inhabitants. Fifteen or twenty of the new settlers were murdered by the Indians, and Mr. Spencer, at present a distinguished citizen of the place, then a boy, was carried into captivity. On the application of his father, he was ransomed by the governor of Upper Canada, for the sum of one hundred and twenty dollars. The issue of the unfortunate campaign of general Harmar, which took place about this time, has been related in another place.

Twenty acres were planted with corn in different parts of town. The grinding was with hand mills. Flour and bacon, now in such abundance, were then imported from the older settlements. The tables were of split planks, and the dishes were of wood. The men wore hunting shirts of domestic fabric. This dress was bound with a belt, or a girdle, in which were a knife and a tomahawk. The lower part of this dress was deer skin, and after the Indian fashion; in fact the dress of the backwoods people in Illinois and Missouri at the present day. The women, too, were as yet content with dresses of their own fabric. The old inhabitants at times, who still survive, look back from the squares and streets, the opulence, pride, coldness, and competition of the present day, to those primitive times of log cabins, love, amity, and affection, cemented by common wants and dangers, as the golden age of Cincinnati.

January 8th, 1791, a party of four persons, who were exploring the country west of the Great Miami, were attacked by the Indians. One was killed, one taken, and the other two escaped to Colerain station. The station consisted of fourteen inhabitants, and was defended by eighteen soldiers. Two days after the attack upon the exploring party, the Indians came upon this station to the number of three hundred. They demanded a surrender, which was met by a prompt refusal. A fire was instantly commenced from the garrison, and returned by the Indians. An express was sent to Cincinnati for a reinforcement, and sixty-three soldiers arrived next morning. But the Indians had decamped before their arrival. During the attack, lead failed for bullets. The women of the garrison supplied the deficiency, by melting their pewter vessels and moulding balls. Near the garrison was found the body of a prisoner, whom the Indians had slain in the disappointment of their defeat. He appeared to have been horribly mangled, and to have expired from the consuming fire of a burning brand applied to his bowels.

An instance of the keenness of Indian ingenuity, in the invention of original modes of torture is given at this time. The Indians captured a young man of the name of Moses Hewitt, who lived on the Little Hockhocking, and was a member of the Marietta settlement. He was remarkable for the suppleness of his limbs, and the swiftness of his running. The Indians tested him with their champion racers, and, although he could not have run with much spirit, under his depressing circumstances, he easily vanquished them all in swiftness. They affected to be pleased, but their envy was piqued. They were destitute of provisions, and wished to secure their swift-footed prisoner, while they were occupied in their hunt. With this view, and probably to torture him at the same time, they fastened his wrists by crossing them, and binding them firmly with a cord. They then tied his arms to a stake, so as partly to raise the upper part of his body. They fastened his legs in the same way, and partly cut off a young sapling, bending it down, so that the weight of the lower part of his body would be a counterpoise to the elastic force of the curved tree. Thus was he partially raised by his hands and feet, in a way most horribly painful; and yet in a position where death would be slow in arriving to his release. It was like the torture of killing by dropping water on the head. Fortunately the young man had remarkably slender wrist bones. When left alone to meditate upon his terrible situation, he contrived, not without disengaging the skin and flesh from his wrists, to disentangle his arms from their manacles and finally his legs. He picked up a little of the scraps of jerked meat, which the Indians had left. To baffle their pursuit and that of their dogs, he ran on the bodies of fallen trees, and meandered his course in every direction. Such was the adroitness of his management, that he put them completely at fault, escaped them, and came in to the settlement of Marietta, wounded, his flesh torn and mangled, and emaciated to a skeleton—a living proof how much man can survive before he suffers the mortal pang. He had been absent fourteen days.

In the disastrous campaign of General St. Clair, the issue of which has been related in another place, a great number of the inhabitants of Cincinnati were killed. The event of the campaign had a discouraging effect upon the fortunes of the settlement. Several of the inhabitants removed to Kentucky for greater security from savage assault. So fresh was the settlement, that the establishment of a horse mill, for grinding, is recorded as an era in its history.

But notwithstanding the fury and disastrous character of the Indian war, between forty and fifty immigrants arrived at Cincinnati, in 1792. A Presbyterian church was built, not far from the site of the present First Presbyterian church. It was occupied by the congregation of the Rev. James Kemper. The first school was opened this year in town, and consisted of thirty scholars. The next year, 1793, was distinguished by the prevalence of small pox among the soldiers and inhabitants of Cincinnati, which swept off nearly a third of their number. The glorious campaign of General Wayne succeeded; the events of which we have already narrated. The severe chastisement which the Indians received in this campaign, inspired them with sincere dispositions for peace. An end was put to their unprovoked and sanguinary hostility, by the treaty of Fort Greenville, signed August 3d, 1795. It may be imagined with what joy this event was hailed by all the dwellers in the Ohio valley. Now, that they

14

considered the dangers of savage assault or ambush at an end, they issued forth from their straightened and uncomfortable positions, in their forts and block houses, selected the spots of their choice, and the blows of the axe, and the baying dogs of the settlers began to echo through the forest. As soon as the news of peace and security passed the mountains to the Atlantic country, the fame of the western country for fertility revived the natural propensity of the American people to wander. On all the great roads to the western country, flocks of emigrants were seen directing their course to cross the Alleghanies. From the Alleghany and the Monongahela, boats crowded with adventurers were still floating down. Connecticut Reserve was rapidly filled with people, chiefly from Connecticut. The settlements broadened and diverged from the Marietta settlement on the one hand, and Cincinnati on the other, gradually advancing from the shores of the Ohio towards the height of land between the waters of the Ohio and the lakes. The extraordinary fertility of the country on the Scioto caused the banks of that river early to be settled with a compact population. The country on the Great Miami, from Dayton along the courses of Mad River, soon became populous. The extent of the immigration could only be imagined by the innkeepers who lived on the great roads to the western country, or by the agents of the land office, or by the astonishing results of a census. For the rest, the settlers quietly dropped into their forest nests, and the next intelligence of them was by the passing traveller, who spoke of their wheat fields, and commencing improvements. Never was transformation from the silence of the forest to the results of population, towns, villages, farms, and all the accompaniments of civilization and municipal life more silent and imperceptible, and at the same time more sudden.

In four years from the treaty of Greenville, to wit, in 1799, the territory passed to what has since been called the second grade or territorial government. The legislative power, which in the first grade belonged to the Governor and Judges, was transferred to a house of representatives elected by the people, and a legislative council, ap-

pointed by congress. A delegate was chosen to represent
the territory in the national legislature. In 1795, Cincinnati contained 500 inhabitants; in 1800, 750; in 1805,
960; in 1820, 10,000; in 1830, 27,100; in 1831, 30,000.

CHAPTER X.

INCIDENTS ATTENDING THE SETTLEMENT OF LOUISIANA
RESUMED.

WE have already noticed that portion of the annals of
the settlement of Illinois and Louisiana, that fell within
our limits and our object, to the period of the settling of
New Orleans.

This progress of the French in Louisiana could not but
alarm the jealousy of the Spaniards, whose settlements in
New Mexico had now advanced to the immediate vicinity
of the French on Red River.

The French, with their customary felicity of ingratia-
ting themselves with the Indians, had already secured the
friendship of the Indians far up the Missouri, particularly
of the powerful tribe of the Missouries, from whom that
river derives its name. That tribe was engaged in a war
with the Pawnees, still farther up the river. The policy
of the Spaniards was to add their force to that of the Pawnees, and destroy the Missouries, the allies of the French,
as a preliminary to gaining the ascendancy on the Missouri. A Spanish expedition was dispatched from Santa Fe,
so well known for its present extensive trade with St. Louis.
Their destination was the Pawnee towns. But mistaking
their way, they unconsciously reached the chief town of
the Missouries, thinking it was that of the Pawnees. The
mistake was the more natural as the Spaniards knew little
about these remote tribes. Beside, the two tribes spoke the
same language. They communicated their plan to destroy
the Missouries to themselves, requesting their co-operation

in their own destruction. Dissimulation is natural to the reserved and silent savages, who instantly penetrated the mistake of their foe, and affected to come into the plan, craftily enacting the part of the Pawnees. Retaining their customary unchangeable gravity of manners and countenance, they betrayed not the slightest surprise. They only requested time to call in their warriors and consult them upon the proposition. At the end of forty-eight hours they had assembled two thousand warriors, and fell upon the unsuspecting Spaniards, not only reposing in a sense of the most perfect security, but meditating the destruction of these very Indians. The whole expedition was slain with the exception of the accompanying priest, who escaped by the fleetness of his horse to tell the story.

One of the most memorable events in the early history of Louisiana, is the massacre of the French among the Natchez by that tribe, and its final extinction by the French. The history of this interesting tribe has been given us by their destroyers. We may therefore presume that at least all the amiable traits allowed them were their due. Compared with the other tribes of this valley they were a polished people. Their traditions imported that their forefathers had emigrated from some region far to the south-west, probably Mexico. They had laws, subordination of classes, and various municipal institutions, and were considerably acquainted with the application of many of their medicinal simples. They had an established worship, and a temple dedicated to the Great Spirit, on the altar of which they preserved a perpetual fire. Their chiefs, like the Incas of Peru, pretended to derive their origin from the sun. Some barbarous customs were adopted by them, proving that however mild and amiable in other respects, they were the victims of a gloomy superstition. They offered human sacrifices on their altars; and when their chiefs were condemned to death, such was the blind veneration of their subjects that numbers were always ready to offer as voluntary substitutes for them. They were a numerous people, commanding respect and giving the law far up and down the Mississippi. Amidst the ancient forests of these fertile hills, in peace, content with the simple gifts of nature, the admission of white men among them was the era of their doom.

The French both courted and dreaded this formidable people; and of all their allies they had been most perseveringly faithful. They had aided them in all their projects; and more than once, by the supplies which they had furnished the French, had saved them from famine. The outrage that is now to be related, is the more memorable from the circumstance that the French were generally noted for being lenient, faithful, and just in their intercourse with the savages. No doubt that these were the true secrets of their general ascendancy among them.

The cause of the quarrel that ensued between the French and Natchez was of the most trivial character. A soldier of the garrison of fort Rosalie, alleged that an old Natchez warrior owed him corn, and demanded immediate payment. The Indian replied, that the corn was yet green in the fields, and that as soon as it was sufficiently ripe, he should be paid. The soldier persisted to demand prompt payment, threatening him with a beating if he refused. Even the threat of being struck is ever insupportable to an Indian. The old man sprang incensed from the fort, and challenged the soldier to single combat. The soldier, alarmed by the rage of the Indian, cried murder! The warrior on this, and seeing a crowd collecting, retired slowly towards his village. One of the guard fired upon him, and he was mortally wounded. No enquiry was made, or at least no punishment inflicted upon him who had committed the outrage. All the revengeful feelings natural to savages, were called up on the occasion. The Natchez flew to arms, and the French were assailed on every side, and many of them fell. The 'Stung Serpent,' an influential chief, interposed his authority, and the slaughter ceased. A new treaty of peace was the result of the discussion that ensued, and the whole affair seemed to be buried in oblivion.

Soon after this, in the year 1723, under different pretexts, several hundred soldiers were secretly introduced into the settlements, and the defenceless and unsuspecting Natchez were slaughtered in their huts. The head of the

14 *

first chief was demanded as the price of peace, and the wretched Natchez were obliged to yield to the demand. The slaughter had continued four days before peace was granted them. This was a deed of course never to be forgotten, nor forgiven by the savages. They saw at once that there now remained no alternative between their own destruction or that of their enemies. They were moody, pensive, timid, and slow; but they were sure in devising the means of vengeance.

Things remained in this situation until 1729. At this time, M. de Chopart, who had been the chief agent in these transactions, and who was excessively obnoxious to the savages, had been ordered to New Orleans, to meet an investigation of his conduct, touching this affair. The joy of the savages was great; for they hoped, at least to be delivered from his enmity and oppression. To their despair they learned that he was justified, and reinstated in his authority. He seemed on his return more vindictive than ever. To manifest his ill feelings he determined to build a town, two miles below the present site of Natchez, on ground occupied by a large and ancient village of the Indians. Accordingly he sent for the Sun chief, and ordered him to have the huts cleared away and the savages dispersed. The chief replied, 'that their ancestors had dwelt there for ages; and that it was good that their descendants should dwell there after them.' The order was repeated with a threat of destruction, if not obeyed.

The Indians dissembled; and remarking 'that the corn had just come out of the ground, and that their hens were laying their eggs, and that to abandon their villages at that time would bring famine both on them and the French,' requested delay. All that they could obtain of the haughty commandant, was to delay until autumn, on condition that each should bring a basket of corn, and a fowl, as a tribute for this forbearance. The savages met, and held councils in private; and the unanimous result was, to make one final effort to preserve their independence and the tombs of their ancestors inviolate. The Chickasaws, the allies of the English, and the natural enemies of the French, were invited to take a part with them in their meditated vengeance upon the French. The Chickasaws eagerly consented; but by the treachery of one of their women, probably in the interest of the French, were deceived as to the day, and did not arrive until after the blow was struck. The massacre of the French was arranged to take place on the time when the Natchez should be admitted among them, to pay their tribute of corn and fowls. M. de Chopart was warned by a woman, probably attached to some Frenchman, of their approaching doom. But the evil star of the French prevailed, and the commandant, instead of arousing to caution, punished the informer.

The fatal period for the breaking forth of the smothered vengeance of the savages came. The last day of November, 1729, the Grand Sun, with his warriors, repaired to the fort, with the promised tribute of corn and fowls. The soldiers were abroad in perfect security. The savages seized the gate, and other passages, by which the soldiers were excluded from their arms. The garrison was filled with warriors. The houses in the country were occupied, by previous concert, at the same time. It was a general massacre. None were spared but the slaves, and some of the women and children. Such was the horror and contempt of M. de Chopart, that the chiefs would not kill him, and he was slain by one of the meanest of the Indians. Of seven hundred people, scarcely enough survived to carry the tidings of destruction to the capital. All the forts, settlements, and inhabitants on the Yazoo and Washita shared the common fate of massacre and the flames.

Consternation at first pervaded the capital. But the French soon put every engine into operation, to retaliate. The Chickasaws, thinking themselves mocked by the Natchez, in being deceived as to the time when the blow was struck on the French, in resentment for not being at the massacre of the French, were ready to join the latter, to extirpate the Natchez. Fifteen hundred Chickasaws joined themselves to a detachment of French troops aided by cannon. The Natchez had fortified themselves; but on

the appearance of this formidable force, and the discharge
of the cannon, they humbled themselves to sue for peace.
They offered to restore the French prisoners in their possession, and forsake their country forever. M. de Lubois,
anxious to save the prisoners, consented to put off the attack until the next day, provided that the prisoners were
given up. The following night they deserted the fort, in
a silence so profound as not to disturb their enemies. They
crossed the Mississippi, and ascended Red River to a point
not far from where Natchitoches is now situated. The
French pursued them, headed by M. de Perrier, with cannon. They had fortified themselves; and in their last
fastnesses they fought with the desperation of men who
were ready to die. They sallied out, attempted to cut
their way through the besieging force in vain. It was
useless to contend with the strength that surrounded them.
The women and children were enslaved at home; and the
males were sent as slaves to St. Domingo. Thus utterly
perished the once powerful tribe of the Natchez.

The Spaniards had been long in the habit of using multitudes of Indians of the islands, as slaves. The practice
had been far from being common among the French, in
regard to the Indians of Canada and Louisiana. For some
time even the Spaniards had desisted from the practice.
The benevolent Las Casas had labored with the Spanish
monarch and the priests, until his reasonings or his elo-
quence had convinced them, contrary to their pre-concei-
ved opinions, that the Indians had souls. Millions of these
persecuted beings had been slain, and other millions reduced to bondage, before the Spanish government acted
upon this conviction. The planters and cultivators, in the
sultry climates of the Spanish colonies, conceived that
they must have slaves. The guardian and patron of the
Indians had caused the practice to be suspended, in relation to them. The consequence was that the curse fell
upon another race, equally unoffending, in another hemisphere; and the blacks were torn from Africa, to sweat, not
for themselves, in these burning climates. Yet horrible
as this traffic is, it is a striking fact that it had its origin
in perverted and misapplied humanity. Las Casas preach-

ed humanity to the Indians; and the fetters were knocked off from one race only to be rivetted on another. This detestable traffic was started, indeed, by the Spanish. We find their evil example soon followed by the French. Even our own ancestors, pious and humane as we esteem them, were no way behind their Catholic examples, in their readiness to introduce black slaves into our hemisphere.

Meanwhile the Chickasaws, whose country bounded on the English settlements in Carolina, and who had been steadily attached to their interests, had been long obnoxious to the French, who were waiting for an opportunity to make them feel the weight of their resentment. A double motive stimulated them to this wish. The one was to drive the English from among them, and to secure their trade. The other, to abridge the concurrent influence of the English and the Chickasaws among the other tribes in their vicinity. A pretext offered, and the French seized it with avidity. A few of the Natchez Indians, who had escaped the general massacre, had fled to the protection of the Chickasaws, and were incorporated with that tribe. These Indians, in 1736, were demanded by Bienville, and, as he foresaw, the demand was refused. He marched up the Mobile against them with a very considerable force. It came to a battle, and the French had the worst of the conflict, and were obliged to make a disgraceful retreat. At the same time, the Chickasaws had been assailed on their northern borders by the French from the Illinois, to make a diversion in favor of Bienville. These, also, were compelled to fly. It is related as a ludicrous circumstance, that the Illinois French, when they marched up to fight the Chickasaws, suspended wool sacks in front of their bodies, as a shield against the arrows and balls of the Chickasaws. The circumstance excited great glee among the English and Indians, who fired at the legs of these pastoral people, who evinced their value of legs, and the uselessness of wool sacks, by running with their best speed.

Bienville undertook another campaign against them, with a still greater force. It was as unsuccessful as the former. It is said that his force on this occasion was the largest, and best appointed, which had ever been seen in Louisiana. So completely was it reduced, chiefly by famine and desertion, that he was compelled to sue for peace. He obtained a tolerable one only through the ignorance of the enemy of his weakness.

From this peace to the commencement of the war between France and England, in 1754, few events occurred in Louisiana, that properly belong to these annals. The French government had become sufficiently aware of the value of the fertile soil and mild climate of upper Louisiana. With the exception of a few ruptures with the Indians, the colonists were enabled to extend their settlements without interruption. The French fixed their villages in the shade of deep forests, on the fertile prairies, the banks of streams, or at spring sources, as best suited their fancies. The wilderness and the prairies presented a boundless choice. They negotiated marriages or temporary connexions with the young women of their red brethren; and the mixed races which we now see in their settlements were the fruit. Their ambition was gratified by managing their influence, so as to keep up a balance of power among the savage tribes, of such a kind that their weight in the opposite scale was sufficient to make it preponderate. Unlike the English cultivators, who generally preferred range, or a wide space in the wilderness, the French commonly established themselves in compact settlements, with such narrow and huddled streets, that they could carry on their nimble conversations across them. The grand business of the young men was to navigate the almost interminable rivers, to hunt small adventures, trade and consort with the Indians to procure furs. They were mostly clad in skins. Their houses were furnished, their couches made, and their tables supplied from the spoils of the chase. Their evenings, on their return, were spent in dancing, in intercourse with the savages, and in relating long stories of their voyages, adventures, and exploits. Such is a brief outline of the modes of existence in Kaskaskia, Cahokia, Vincennes, St. Genevieve, the post of Arkansas, Natchitoches on Red River, and Natchez on the Mississippi. At the capital there were always a certain number of people of family and education. There was a kind of court, a theatre, and the semblance of amusements of a higher order. The people contemplated their rural countrymen in the woods about at the same distance, and with the same estimation with which themselves were contemplated by the circles of Paris.

Many of the immigrants had been gentlemen, and most of them had been military characters. Some of them were of noble origin. The first settlers were probably of better family, as that matter was then rated, than those of any other colony in North America, save the colonists of Mexico. It is, perhaps, a fortunate trait in the French character—certainly it is an amiable one—that such men could so readily associate with savages, and make themselves so gay and happy in these remote and unpeopled deserts, where they only heard from France once or twice in a year. They had their packs of dogs, their guns, their Indian beauties, and the range of an unexplored world, to fill their desires and their imaginations. Their descendants speak of these ancient 'residenters,' as a superior race of mortals, and of these times as a kind of golden age.

An expedition was started from Michilimackinack, in 1780, against Upper Louisiana. It was composed of hordes of savages, amounting to one thousand five hundred, and one or two companies of English. It was chiefly destined against St. Louis; and is still remembered with shuddering recollections by the peaceful French inhabitants of that country, under the name of '*l'annee du coup*.' Sixty of the inhabitants had been slain, and thirty made prisoners, when the gallant American General Clark appeared on the opposite shore of the Mississippi, with a considerable force. The view of this respectable armament of Americans struck the Indians with astonishment. They had no idea of meeting, or fighting, any people but the French; and they charged their allies with deception, in thus leading them to combat with a people, who spoke the same language with the English. In terrors, lest the jealous savages would turn upon them, the English secretly abandoned them, and both parties made the best of their way to their homes. Unfortunate projects are apt to be disavowed. The British government disavowed the expedition, and the private property of the commander was seized to defray the expenses of it.

CHAPTER XI.

INCIDENTS OF THE LATE WAR WITH GREAT BRITAIN, THAT OCCURRED IN THE WEST.

FROM the severe defeat of the savages by General Wayne, until the late war with Great Britain, few sustained assaults of Indian warfare occurred in the west. At the close of the year 1811, instead of confining themselves to solitary depredations and individual murders, as had been their custom for a considerable time past, they began to harass the frontier settlements in the west with incessant incursions, and the murder of whole families. The several tribes seemed to emulate each other in deeds of horror and blood. These incursions were either countenanced or instigated by the usual influence and arts of the British traders, as had been the case in former days. It was ascertained too, on a solemn investigation, that the savages were thoroughly armed, and equipped with new guns. The influence of a savage called the 'Shawanese prophet,' had been particularly efficacious, in stirring up the tribes of the lakes and the Wabash against the United States. General Harrison, governor of Indiana territory, and General Boyd, commanding a regiment of United States' Infantry in that quarter, were ordered to march to the prophet's town, high on the Wabash, to demand reparation for the past, and security for the future.

In November, 1811, after a long march of more than thirty days, these troops encamped in the vicinity of the prophet's town. General Harrison, anxious to prevent the effusion of blood, made various unsuccessful efforts

at negotiation.   An officer who was despatched to them
with terms, narrowly escaped from them with his life.
The troops were ordered slowly to approach the town in order of battle.   They were met by a deputation of Indians,
with the usual crafty protestations of friendship, and enquiries respecting the object of his march into their country.   They promised to hold a council next day, to dis-
cuss and settle all grounds of complaint.   The prophet by
night consulted his 'grand medicine,' and pronounced
'that the enemy was now in their power, fast asleep, and
should never wake.'

Happily for the result of this battle, little reliance had
been placed upon the avowal of pacific intentions by the
savages.   The troops had been ordered to lie upon their
arms, to be ready at a moment's warning.   The prophet's
forces have been differently estimated from four hundred
to six hundred warriors.   The American force amounted
to about eight hundred men.

The 7th of November, before four in the morning, the
Indians attacked the American camp with a general discharge, and the most horrid yells.   Favored by the profound darkness, they had broken into the camp.   At the
clear and distinct voice of General Harrison the troops
rallied, and a fierce engagement of man with man commenced, amidst the confusion of darkness, and the horrid
yells of the Indian war whoop.   The militia at first recoiled; but the exertions of Colonel Geiger rallied them to
the charge.   During the darkness, it is obvious, under
such circumstances, that the savages would have the advantage.   The troops were soon formed in a parallelogram.
The militia poured upon them a sheet of flame.   As soon
as it was possible to see their position, the fourth regiment
charged them with the bayonet, with all the precision and
effect of their admirable discipline.   They were immediately cleared from the camp and field, and fled.   The
mounted men cut down many of them on the retreat.   It
was a bloody victory, obtained by the loss of one hundred
and eighty-eight men killed and wounded.   Of the Indians,
fifty-three were found dead in and about the camp; and
their whole loss was calculated nearly to equal that of

15

the Americans. General Harrison narrowly escaped, having had the hair of his head cut with a ball. He was distinguished for his exertions and gallantry on the occasion. The officers in this affair merited and received the highest praise. Some of the bravest of them fell. In short, officers and men gained the meed of having done their duty.

Immediately after the battle, the town was deserted by the Indians. In the precipitancy of their flight, they left their provisions, and almost every thing they possessed, behind them. An incontestible proof that they had been supplied with arms by the British, appeared in our finding a great many guns here, which had never been removed from the cases in which they had been imported, and a quantity of fine English-glazed gunpowder. A number of the northern tribes, consisting of the Puttowattomies, Miamies, Shawanese, and Winnebagees, had sent their warriors to this place. They were headed by Stone Eater, White Loon, Winnemac, and Ellskwatawa, commonly called 'the prophet,' and brother of Tecumseh. That celebrated warrior, who makes so conspicuous a figure in the subsequent battles, was absent on this occasion.

After the army retired from the field, the savages, infuriated by their losses, dug up the dead bodies of the officers, scalped and otherwise mutilated them; and they left a small force to hover on the rear of the Americans, to scalp those who fell behind, or died of their wounds.

On the 18th of June, 1812, war was declared by the United States against Great Britain. A small army, consisting of the fourth regiment of the United States' infantry, and three regiments of Ohio volunteers, under the command of General Hull, governor of the Michigan territory, was ordered to march for the protection of the frontiers, against the incursions of the savages. After a long and tedious march of thirty-five days, followed by British and Indians, who constantly hung upon their flanks, these troops arrived at Detroit. They amounted to two thousand five hundred. The British immediately began to defend their opposite shore. Their works were easily destroyed; and General Hull crossed his troops over the river to the Canada side, and with much menace in vaporing proclamations, proposed to invade the country. The fall of Michillimackinack was the first in a series of disgraces and misfortunes that befel the American arms in this quarter, at the commencement of the war. We can only go into these unpleasant details, as far as the troops and the great local interests of the west were immediately concerned.

After a series of skirmishes, in which Colonel Cass, commanding the third regiment of Ohio volunteers, and Colonel M'Arthur, commanding another regiment of volunteers from Ohio, were most honorably engaged, and a series of mismanagements or misfortunes on the part of General Hull, there was a considerable skirmish at Magagua. The American force was commanded by Colonel Miller. Against great odds, the Americans obtained an undisputed victory, in which many Indians and some British were slain.

At the same time that this slight success was obtained, Captain Heald, who commanded at Chicago, at the head of Lake Michigan, received orders to march immediately from that place, and proceed with his command to Detroit by land. He commenced his march, accompanied by fifty-four regulars and twelve militia, escorted by Captain Wells, of Fort Wayne, and a few friendly Indians of the Miami tribe. The inhabitants in that quarter, chiefly women and children, accompanied them, through terror of the savages. They were attacked on their way by five hundred Indians. Twenty-six of the regulars, and the militia to a man, were killed. Among the officers slain were Captain Wells and Ensign Roman, both of them officers of great gallantry. Two women and twelve children were also killed. The rest were made prisoners. Captain Heald and his lady escaped alive to a British post, and were kindly received. Mrs. Heald was wounded by six shot, and the captain by two; but they both survived.

General Hull made a quick return from Canada; and things on his part were soon so far from invasion, that he was summoned by General Brock to surrender. In the most disgraceful manner, and almost without fighting, he did surrender. The men who had conducted so nobly at Brownstown, the heroes of the fourth regiment, the brave volunteers at Raisin, the whole territory, and every thing appertaining to it, were surrrendered with Detroit. Ohio had many brave officers and troops there. They had suffered severely in the skirmishing that preceded this disastrous and disgraceful event. Never was astonishment and humiliation more extreme, than in the case of these surrendered troops. The British and Indians to whom General Hull surrendered, amounted to nearly one thousand four hundred. The force that surrendered to them amounted to about one thousand eight hundred. No event had ever occurred, that produced such a burning sense of shame and disgrace in the west. Many of the bravest of that region were feelingly alive to the honor of their country, and ambitious of returning to their secluded homes, covered with glory. They were dishonored captives in a far distant country. An immense territory was surrendered; and a horde of infuriated savages, flushed with success, was ready to pour upon the western frontier, now left without any shelter.

This disastrous intelligence was distributed by the northern Indian runners, quite to the southern extremity of the Union, with great celerity. The southern Indians were invited to take up the hatchet, in combination with those of the north. The Creeks and Seminoles soon became parties in the war; and not a few of the other tribes either joined them, or evidently wished well to their cause. The whole frontier from Tennessee to the bay of Mobile was laid open to their incursions. The British sent implements and munitions of war to Florida; and they were put into their hands by the Spaniards. To meet these formidable aspects of danger, the people of the contiguous states made great and patriotic exertions. The Seminoles, uniting with stolen or fugitive negroes, made incursions into Georgia; and they commenced their accustomed course of cruelty and murder.

A most brave and desperate exploit was performed against them by Colonel Newman, of the Georgia volunteers, with one hundred and seventeen men. He was on his march for the Lotchway towns, and was met by one hundred and fifty hostile mounted Indians. The meeting was unexpected on both sides. Seldom has a more desperate struggle been recorded. The Indians retreated, and were reinforced to nearly double the number of the whites, and returned to the assault. They were beaten again, retreated a little distance, and entrenched themselves around this little gallant band, to make sure of them. They preserved a profound silence, and the Indians thinking them fled, approached their camp with confidence. They received a deadly fire, which killed and wounded thirty warriors. They were now allowed to retreat unmolested. The Indians lost three of their principal chiefs. Their young leader, and Bow-legs, their second in command, were slain.

In 1812, the famous Tecumseh arrived among the Creek Indians, availing himself of the superstitions of the savages, and the predictions of his brother, the prophet, calculated at once to exasperate, and give confidence to them. The Creeks soon began to perpetrate a series of outrages along the Alabama frontier. The crafty Tecumseh had enjoined secrecy, as regarded the predictions and movements. But the smothered thirst for vengeance was too strong among these savages, rendered confident by these prophecies, to be long concealed. The red war-clubs were soon seen in every part of the nation. Their first fury spent itself on those of their own people, who were desirous of peace with the United States. These were obliged to fly for their lives to the forts and settlements of the whites.

Infatuated by the prophets, with the persuasion that the 'Great Spirit' was on their side, and that they should be found invincible, they made their first assault upon fort Mimms, situated in the Tensaw settlement, in Mississippi; and here they terribly signalized their cruelty and vengeance. It was crowded with women and children, who had fled to it, from terror of the savages, as a place of protection. It was garrisoned by one hundred and fifty men under the command of Major Beasly. The savages obtained their ammunition and supplies from the Spanish at Pensacola; and in 1813, to the number of six or seven hundred, commenced their attack upon the fort. They were fatally successful, and carried it by storm. About three hundred persons, more than half of them women and children, were massacred. Never was savage character more fully developed. The mother and the child were slain with the same stroke of the tomahawk. But seventeen of the multitude that had crowded into the supposed protection of the fort, escaped to relate the catastrophe. The abominable cruelties of the savages, previous to this, mere merged at once in the excitement created by this monstrous and most unprovoked atrocity. As soon as the news reached the adjoining states, a just spirit of resentment was aroused. A campaign had been already planned by the governor of Tennessee, in conformity to instructions from the secretary of war, against them. The feelings universally excited on this occasion, naturally accelerated these operations. General Jackson was selected by public sentiment as the commander in this campaign.

General Jackson, though suffering from a severe wound which he had received in a private rencontre, accepted the command. Colonel Coffee, in whom, also, the Tennesseeans reposed great confidence, commanded under him; and in case the general government should not see fit to adopt the expedition, and defray its expense, the state voted three hundred thousand dollars for its support. In preparing for this campaign, and in marching to the scene of action, General Jackson encountered every difficulty and delay, that could arise from the opinions of opposing factions, from false alarm and intelligence, from the refractory spirit of men generally unused to control, and much more so to the stern control of a camp; and more than all from hunger, and an uncertain supply of provisions. He seemed precisely the man to meet and obviate all these difficulties. Uniting in an uncommon degree perseverance with promptitude, no opposition stood in his way, but that which in the nature of things was insurmountable. He soon marched with such as these circumstances allowed him to collect.

In the vicinity of the Creek settlements, Colonel Dyer was detached to attack Littafutchee-town, one of their villages. He destroyed the village, and returned with a considerable number of its inhabitants prisoners. General Jackson had been for sometime anxiously waiting the arrival of General Cocke from East Tennessee, with reinforcements and provisions. Learning that a considerable body of the enemy had posted themselves on the Tallushatchee, on the south side of the Coosa, thirteen miles distant, he detached General Coffee, with nine hundred men, to attack and disperse them.

General Coffee was so fortunate as to find a fordable point of the Coosa, and there crossed his troops, directing them to encircle the town, and unite their fronts beyond it. The enemy announced their preparation for action, by beating their drums, and the customary yells and war-whoops. The Indians in the first instance assailed an advance party with great fury. The action soon became general, and the savages retreated to their houses. Here they fought to desperation as long as they could stand or sit; neither evincing fear nor asking for quarter. Their loss was one hundred and eighty-six killed; among whom, unfortunately, and in the accidental fury of the conflict, were some women and children. Of the prisoners, eighty-four were women and children, who were treated with the utmost humanity. Of the Americans, five were killed, and forty one wounded. Two were killed with arrows. Most of the warriors had quivers filled with arrows, which they used after the first fire, until they could reload.

On the northern frontier, the effect of the fall of Michilimackinack, Chicago, and more than all, Detroit, was appalling through the Union. It had an electric effect upon the west. An offer was made to receive volunteers for the organization of a new army; and there has not often been on record an instance of an army formed, equipped, and ready to march, with more celerity. From Pennsylvania, two thousand volunteers, under Brigadier General Crooks, General Tupper's brigade of Ohio volunteers, and the 17th regiment under Colonel Wells, were soon on their march, and at their place of rendezvous. The command was assigned to General Harrison, who was highly popular among the troops, and under him in command was General Payne, of Kentucky.

Immediately after the disasters of Detroit, the prophet's Indians marched to invest forts Harrison and Wayne, which were garrisoned only by a few regulars and volunteers. They murdered, burned, and destroyed every thing in the vicinity of these forts. They fired fort Harrison; and the shrieks of women and children, contemplating on one hand the sheet of flame rolling towards them, and on the other hearing the horrid yells of the merciless savages, afford us one of those scenes that were so common during the war. Both of these places were defended with desperate bravery, until they were relieved; the one by a considerable force of mounted volunteers from Illinois, and the other by the forces of General Harrison. He divided his force, in the first instance, into scouting parties, and made these merciless and deluded beings feel, by retaliation, something of the horrors which themselves had perpetrated. Those Indian tribes that had remained faithful to the United States, and whose wish to join our standard had been hitherto refused, by an arrangement with the executive, were permitted to take a part in the war. Logan, a warrior of distinguished reputation, joined General Harrison with seven hundred warriors. Volunteers, more than were demanded by the expedition, poured in from all quarters. The zeal and patriotism of the western states were manifested by the most active exertions, and by sacrifices of every sort, such as the occasion required—sacrifices of endurance, treasure, and blood. Few were more conspicuous in the manifestation of this spirit, than Return J. Meigs, then Governor of Ohio.

A separate command had been assigned to General Winchester, as it appears, to the dissatisfaction of the troops confided to him. The troops of General Payne and Colonel Wells, by this arrangement, were placed at his disposal. He was directed to push forward in a parallel advance, at some distance from General Harrison, and in concert with him, regain the country occupied by the Indians, retake the lost posts, and if possible capture Malden, and all the places near our frontiers, that were central coverts for the Indians. General Winchester advanced, until he found himself in front of an enemy of superior numbers. The advance of his force under Captain Ballard, had already had severe skirmishing with them. A few brave and inexperienced young volunteers, who had rashly ventured beyond the main body under Ensign Liggit, were slain, and caused deep regret at their untimely fall. General Winchester immediately sent despatches to General Harrison, requesting aid. General Tupper, with his mounted men, directly commenced his march to yield the required assistance.

There was some severe skirmishing of the enemy with the advance of General Winchester's force, in which Logan, the friendly chief, after conducting with great personal bravery, was mortally wounded. Colonel Campbell was detached by General Harrison, with a considerable force, against the Missisineway towns. In an attack upon one of these towns, a severe engagement ensued, in which the Indians were defeated, and that and some other towns destroyed. Next morning the Indians were reinforced and attacked him. They were again defeated; but a number of brave officers fell in the charge. The detachment behaved with great coolness and fortitude; and what was still bettter, with humanity to the wounded, and those who fell into their power. Colonel Campbell, having accomplished his object, commenced his march for Greenville. The terrible Tecumseh was reported to be lurking in the vicinity, with five hundred warriors. The weather was severe, and nearly the half of his men were disqualified from duty, by being frozen in some part of their limbs. The men expected an attack, and would probably have been destroyed. Their exemption from attack has been by some attributed to the absence of the prophet, who is supposed to have been slain in the attack upon Colonel Campbell.

A brigade of Kentuckians, under General Hopkins, had been sent into Indiana territory against the savages of the Wabash and Illinois. They destroyed a number of towns, and had some skirmishing with the enemy. A company of cavalry belonging to this detachment, advanced to bury one of their slain companions, and fell into an Indian ambuscade. Eighteen of their number were killed and wounded, and among them were several promising young officers.

Exasperated by these repeated successes of the American troops against the different Indian posts and villages, the enemy resolved to advance with their combined arms to Frenchtown, to intercept the American forces marching upon Detroit. The inhabitants of that village expected to be massacred; and they implored the protection of General Winchester. This expedition appears to have been undertaken without any concert with General Harrison. General Winchester, according to their request, marched to their aid, with six hundred men. After some hard skirmishing, in which the Americans were victorious, the concentrated forces of General Winchester, amounting to about seven hundred and fifty men, found themselves in the vicinity of the British General Proctor, and Tecumseh, with two thousand men. These forces attacked the American camp, and were bravely repulsed, though with severe loss. In a second attack, General Winchester, Colonel Lewis, and some other persons, by some unaccountable inadvertence, were made prisoners. The American force deprived thus of its chief officers, repelled every attack with the bravery of desperation, until a flag from the enemy promised quarters and protection if they would surrender; at the same time menacing the town with conflagration, and the inhabitants with the uncontrolled fury of the savages, if they refused these terms. Twenty-two officers, and two hundred and seventy-five non-commissioned officers and privates had already been slain or wounded. Thirty-five officers, and four hundred and eighty-seven non-commissioned officers and privates surrendered on the faith of General Proctor. The enemy's loss had probably been not much inferior to that of the Americans.

The events that followed, have lost something of their dark coloring by the effect of time, that extinguishes revenge, and softens the remembrance of injuries. But the infamous name of Proctor will never be forgotten in the West. Fathers still repair to the empty monuments of their high spirited and promising sons, who fell in the dastardly treachery of that surrender. Many officers of the first respectability, and young men of the best families and the highest promise, were massacred by the savages, after they had surrendered. The deportment of the British was little short of that of the savages, in regard to the prisoners in their possession. General Proctor, when charged with these enormities, did not attempt to deny them. He only affirmed, that no promise of protection had been given, and no obligation to control the savages incurred. These transactions are commonly known in the West by the name of the 'massacre of the Raisin.'

General Harrison, though his plans were wholly disconcerted by these disasters of General Winchester's troops, set himself immediately to organizing them anew. In this he was strongly aided by the indefatigable Meigs, who promptly forwarded two regiments of Ohio militia, as reinforcements, and by the troops generally, who burned to avenge the loss of their brave brethren in arms. He again advanced to the Rapids, and built a fort, which has since been famous under the name of fort Meigs. He then set out on his return to Ohio, to consult with the governor, and to accelerate the march of the recruits. The fort was besieged in his absence by the enemy. He was soon apprised of the circumstance, and returned. Great exertions were made, alike in the attack and the defence. The British and Indians manifested extreme rancor, and were unsparing in their labors and assaults. The roar of cannon and bombs discharged upon the fort was continual. The defence was gallant and determined, and a number of men were slain in it.

At length a despatch arrived with forty-seven men, from General Clay's brigade, informing that he was at hand, with one thousand one hundred Kentuckians. The besiegers were attacked by him. Their batteries were carried, and their cannon spiked. In the ardor of pursuit, Colonel Dudley was led into an ambuscade, and an attack commenced upon the brave but indiscreet Kentuckians, which terminated in the death or capture of almost the whole detachment. The barbarities of the river Raisin were here acted over again, though not to the same extent. The Indians massacred forty-five of the prisoners, and the gallant Colonel Dudley among them. He is said to have killed one of the assailing Indians, after he was himself mortally wounded. In the meantime, there was a sortie from the fort, which was intended to have been simultaneous with the assault of Colonel Dudley. The troops that composed it experienced hard fighting. They were assailed by four times their number, and would have been cut off had not Lieutenant Gwynne, at the critical moment come to their aid, and gallantly charged the Indians. On the 6th of the month, hostilities seemed suspended, as if by mutual consent. Terms, in relation to the prisoners and wounded, were mutually settled between besiegers and besieged.

On the 9th, the enemy abandoned his works, and the siege, which had lasted thirteen days, and in which he had exhausted his efforts, was raised.

Proctor had vaunted to his Indian allies, that he would capture the garrison, and deliver it over to them, no doubt to share the fate of those who had before fallen into their hands. In the course of the siege, one thousand eight hundred shells and balls had been fired upon the fort, and a continual discharge of small arms been kept up. The American loss in the siege and sortie was two hundred and seventy killed and wounded. Kentucky here, as elsewhere, suffered most severely. The gallant but indiscreet impetuosity of her sons led them to select the points of peril.

In the month of June, the Seneca Indians offered their services to General Harrison, and they were accepted. The incursions of the hostile savages upon our frontiers were frequent and bloody. Many of the inhabitants were killed, or made captives, and the remainder were of course in a state of continual alarm. In one of these assaults, Colonel Ball, with a small detachment, was attacked from an ambush, There were about twenty in each party. In the hottest of the fight, Colonel Ball, whose horse had been shot down, was engaged in personal contest with an Indian of great strength and prowess. He was relieved by an officer of his party, who shot the Indian. The savages then made a desperate onset with the usual yell, indicating that they would neither take nor give quarter. The band of savages was destroyed to a man.

In his general orders after the raising the siege of fort Meigs, General Harrison spoke in the highest terms of the conduct of his men during the siege. To Majors Todd, Ball, Lodwick, Ritzer, and Johnson, he made the public expression of his warmest satisfaction. In speaking of the Kentuckians, he said—'It rarely happened that a general had to complain of the excessive ardor of his troops; but that this seemed to be generally the case when the Kentuckians were engaged; and that they appeared to think that valor alone could accomplish every thing.' Of the conduct of the General himself, it appears to be generally conceded that he merited entire praise. During the seventh day of the siege of which we have just spoken, he received from General Proctor a summons to surrender the fort, making much parade of his own force, and avowing the usual desire to prevent the effusion of blood. The proper answer was returned, and the summons was not repeated.

After the raising the siege of fort Meigs, General Harrison transferred his head quarters to Seneca town, on the Lower Sandusky. It was now generally supposed that General Proctor would unite his forces with those of the main Canadian army, engaged in another quarter. General Harrison better understood his purposes. Fort Meigs had been placed in an excellent state of defence. Great exertions were made to fortify fort Stephenson, as it appears, against the counsels of General Harrison. During the month of July, the congregated tribes of savages under Tecumseh, who was reported to have received the rank and emoluments of Brigadier General under General Proctor, together with a considerable force of regulars, proceeded on an expedition, the object of which was the capture of forts Meigs and Stephenson. Tecumseh was

despatched with two thousand warriors, to make a diversion favorable to the British, while they advanced to the
attack of fort Stephenson.   Proctor made a feint, meanwhile, to keep the attention of General Harrison occupied
with fort Meigs.   Proctor immediately appeared before
fort Stephenson, with seven hundred Indians under Dixon,
and five hundred regulars.   A number of gun boats had
been brought round to bear upon the fort.   Major Croghan
was in it with no more than one hundred and sixty men.
He had already disobeyed the orders of his commander in
chief, in not destroying the works, and abandoning the
place, as indefensible.   It was immediately invested with
a force of such immense superiority, as left him but a dark
prospect of being able to maintain a siege, and little hope
of relief, but by the desperate expedient of cutting his
way to the enemy.   He chose to defend it.   He hastily
cut a deep ditch, and raised a stockade round it.

General Proctor attempted to gain the place by artifice.
He sent a flag, accompanied with the noted renegado,
Colonel Elliott, well remembered for his conduct towards
the Americans at the river Raisin.   Parade, artifice, and
menace, were alike unavailing to procure the surrender.
The steady answer of Major Croghan was, ' that he should
never surrender the place as long as there were any men
in it, to defend it.'   General Proctor then opened batteries
upon his works, and commenced a furious cannonade.
This was continued a long time without much effect.   Colonel Short, of the besiegers, then led up a force of three
hundred and fifty regulars, in close column, to storm the
fort.   The fire which the besieged opened upon them threw
them into confusion, and induced a hasty retreat.   Colonel
Short rallied them, and they advanced so far the second
time as to gain the ditch.   They leapt into it, and filled
it.   A concealed six pounder had been so placed as to rake
the ditch in a line.   It was charged with slugs, and discharged upon them.   The front of this column was only
thirty yards from the piece.   Colonel Short, and almost
every man in the ditch, was killed.   A volley of musketry
at the same time was fired with fatal execution, upon those
who were standing upon the outer edge of the ditch.   The

officer who succeeded Colonel Short, rallied the broken column, and led it again into the ditch. A second discharge of the fatal six pounder was made with the same effect as the first; and the volley of musketry that followed, completed the confusion. A retreat ensued, and an army retired from a garrison that contained not a tenth part of their numbers, and which, at the commencement of the siege, had taken counsel only from their despair. No inconsiderable quantity of baggage and arms was left by the besiegers; and their loss was reported to have been not less than one hundred and fifty men. That of the garrison was only one killed and seven wounded. Major Croghan gained and received imperishable honors. Captain Hunter, Lieutenants Johnson, Bayle, Meeks, and Ensigns Shipp, and Duncan, acquired great and deserved praise.

The brilliant and complete victory of lake Erie, by the fleet under the gallant Perry, followed. The result of this splendid action, placed the whole lake under the American control. Then first the masts of a captured British fleet were seen among the trees on the shores of Ohio. These foresters of the shores of Erie gazed on the impressive array of ships, which is usually seen only on the ocean. Six hundred British prisoners were conducted to Chillicothe. The flush of success and the animation of hope were infused into the country. Governor Meigs made an appeal to the militia of Ohio for volunteers, and fifteen thousand were soon under arms. Their original object was the relief of fort Stephenson; but they now entertained other hopes. The governor of Kentucky, Colonel Isaac Shelby, arrived with four thousand mounted volunteers. The greater part of the garrison of fort Meigs, under General M'Arthur joined him. General Harrison immediately determined upon invading the enemy's shores. The troops were received on board the victorious fleet of Commodore Perry, increased by the captured ships of the enemy. From sixteen vessels of war and one hundred boats they were landed, in perfect order, a league below Malden. It must have been a voyage as novel and impressive as it was cheering to these sons of the west.

General Proctor immediately abandoned Malden; and having first set fire to the fort, and destroyed the public property, he retreated with his Indians towards the Thames. The American army entered Amherstburgh, amidst the smoke of the conflagration of the public works. The women of the place came out in a body, and begged that protection which Americans could never refuse. The place was, indeed, in many respects obnoxious to every feeling of retaliation and vengeance. Here the savages had been fostered. Here they had held their horrid orgies of exultation, on their return from successful expeditions. Hence, loaded with presents and munitions of war, they had marched to plunder, massacre, and destroy. Scarcely a volunteer who entered this odious place, but had suffered in his person, property, relations, or friends, by the outrages and massacres, which had been spirited and instigated from this place. But it was determined that the British and Indians should see the difference between the American troops, and those who had enacted the bloody tragedy of the river Raisin. Even the house of the renegado, Colonel Elliott, was spared.

General Proctor and his army made all speed to Sandwich. They were followed by the American army by land, and the fleet through the river Detroit. General Harrison directed General M'Arthur to remain, with most of the regular troops, to occupy Detroit, and to watch the motions of the celebrated chief 'Split-log,' who had retired with a great body of savages to the woods, near the Huron of lake St. Clair. He continued the pursuit of Proctor up the Thames. He was joined by the regiment of Colonel Johnson, part of Colonel Ball's regiment of dragoons, and the whole of Governor Shelby's volunteers. General Cass and Commodore Perry acted as his aids. The fortunate capture of a British Lieutenant of dragoons and eleven privates, who had been left to destroy the bridges, enabled him to save a bridge, and to learn that the enemy had had no certain advices of his destination up the Thames. During this rapid pursuit, the American army captured a quantity of clothing, two thousand stands of arms, and a number of cannon. They easily dispersed the Indians from their path. In a skirmish, the rear of the enemy suffered a considerable loss. Two gun boats, and several barges loaded with provisions, were taken.

On the 5th of the month, the pursuit was eagerly renewed, and intelligence was brought that the enemy was waiting for them, in order of battle, at four miles' distance. Their position was well chosen. On one side was a swamp, and on the other a river. Between the swamp and the river was a level plain, the approach to which was defended by a thick wood. The British were posted in a line across this plain. Their left rested upon the river, and was supported by most of their artillery. Their centre was protected by two heavy pieces of cannon. Their force numbered about one thousand two hundred Indians, and six hundred regulars. The arrangments of General Harrison for the several corps of his army were formed with great judgment. They were entrusted to Lieutenant Colonel James Johnson, Colonel Paul, and Colonel R. M. Johnson, Major Thompson, and Captain Stricker. A division was commanded by General Desha. The American troops moved to the attack, and received the fire of the British. In a moment, the line of the enemy was broken by one thousand horsemen, who dashed through the centre, and either cut or trampled down all that opposed them. The shock was irresistible. There was an immediate surrender of four hundred and seventy-two men, with their officers. General Proctor was aware of his deserts and escaped with all possible speed.

The Indians contested the battle with much more pertinacity than their British allies. Tecumseh put forth all his courage and prowess in this battle. He awaited the shock of the American cavalry, and dealt it a prodigious fire as it advanced. The first effort, although a desperate one, to break the Indian line, failed. Colonel Johnson then ordered his men to dismount, and fight the Indians after their own fashion. The fight was fierce and obstinate. Part of the American line faltered; but at that critical moment Colonel Shelby came up with a reinforcement and turned the scale. A personal contest ensued between Colonel Johnson and Tecumseh. The former had been

16*

wounded five times, was covered with blood, and was smarting with the agony of his wounds. He had been mounted on a beautiful white charger through the action, which rendered him a conspicuous mark for the direction of the savage shots. He had received a shower of bullets, which pierced every part of his dress and accoutrements. His horse was wounded, and in staggering back exposed him to the tomahawk of his savage antagonist. It missed him. He drew his pistol, shot his enemy in the head, and they both fell together. This version of the mode of Tecumseh's death is now questioned. Major Thompson, on whom the command devolved, after the fall of Colonel Johnson, continued to direct the fight. It was long and obstinate. The savages finally fled, and numbers of them were cut down by the cavalry in their flight.

Among the singular trophies of this victory were several pieces of brass cannon, which had been taken from Burgoyne at Saratoga, surrendered by General Hull with Detroit, and now returned again to the Americans. The victory was complete, and the result was all that could be expected, or desired from it. Michigan was recovered. The British force in Upper Canada was broken down. The savages that had depended upon the British there, were intimidated, and their connexion with them broken up and destroyed. The prophet, a most powerful and inveterate enemy of the United States—Tecumseh, the remorseless and intrepid leader, whose hostility had wrought so much mischief to us—these chiefs no longer in being to lead them to battle, the confidence of the Indians sunk at once, and most of them made terms with the conquering General. The general result to the west was, that the frontier people were relieved from their well founded apprehensions. They no longer mistook by night the howl of the wild beasts for that of the savages. They returned in peace to their habitations, their confidence, and accustomed pursuits.

While these events were occurring on the northern frontier, the Indians of the west and of the upper Mississippi were not idle. There can seldom be a movement of the savages in one quarter, without exciting a simultaneous movement of them in another quarter. The incursions of the northern and western Indians were so severe upon the frontiers of Illinois and Missouri, that many of the incipient settlements in both those territories were broken up. The Indians often extended their ravages to the central villages of those regions. A band of Sacs, Foxes, and Pottawattomies, ranged through Missouri, and committed a great number of the most atrocious murders. In some instances, whole families were destroyed, and their accustomed fury was let loose upon women and children. A considerable force of mounted rangers was raised in the two territories. They were active and vigilant in scouring the frontiers, and in repressing the savage incursions.

Meanwhile the war with the Creeks still raged in the south. After the battle of Tallushatchee, General Jackson was still waiting in the Indian country for the junction of the troops from East Tennessee. Intelligence was despatched to him, that the hostile Indians had arrived before Talladega, a fort or town of friendly Indians. These Indians had incurred their peril by their fidelity to the United States. Honor and policy alike forbade that they should be sacrificed. General Jackson, although painfully disappointed in his expectations of the junction of forces from East Tennessee, marched directly to the aid of the friendly Indians. The force of the Americans was not far from one thousand eight hundred.

On the 8th of December, 1813, at one in the morning, the army began crossing the river, behind which the Indians were posted. It was here six hundred yards wide, and of course to cross it was a work of difficulty, as well as time. The next day at four in the morning the army was again in motion. The infantry proceeded in three columns; the cavalry in the same order. The advance, consisting of a company of artillerists, with muskets, two companies of riflemen, and one of spies, marched about four hundred yards in front, under the command of Colonel Carroll, with orders, after commencing the action, to fall back on the centre, and draw the enemy after them. Lieutenant Colonel Dyer was placed in the centre, with two hundred and fifty cavalry, as a corps of reserve. The remainder of the mounted troops were directed to advance on the right and left, after encircling the enemy, by uniting the fronts of their columns, and keeping their rear rested on the infantry, to face and press towards the centre, so as to leave the savages no possibility of escape. The remainder of the army advanced by heads of companies, General Hall's brigade occupying the right, and General Roberts' the left.

At eight in the morning, the advance, within eighty yards of the enemy, received a severe fire from them, concealed as they were, behind a thick shrubbery. They returned it, and according to their instructions, fell back upon the centre. The enemy, with their customary yells and whoops, rushed upon General Roberts' brigade, a few companies of which recoiled in alarm, and fled at the first fire. To fill the chasm created by this desertion, the commanding general directed a volunteer regiment of Colonel Bradley, which appeared to linger, to advance and occupy the vacant space. This order was not executed by Bradley. Owing to this failure, it became necessary to dismount the reserve, which met the rapid approach of the enemy with great firmness. This example inspirited the retreating militia, who rallied, and assisted in checking the advance of the savages. On the left they were met and repulsed by the mounted riflemen. But, owing to the dilatory movements of the volunteer regiment, and the too extensive circuit made by Colonel Allcorn, who commanded the cavalry of that wing, the intended circle was not so closed but that a number of the enemy escaped in the interval.

The savages fought with determined spirit for some time, and then retreated for the adjacent hills. Many of them fell in this retreat, and the slaughter did not cease until they were sheltered among the hills, at the distance of three miles. General Jackson, in his report, bestowed the highest commendations on the officers and soldiers generally. He mentioned Colonel Carroll and Lieutenant Colonel Dyer in terms of high praise for the spirited gallantry with which they met and repulsed the enemy; stating that both officers and privates had answered his highest expectations, and merited the gratitude of their country.

The enemy brought one thousand and eighty to this battle, of whom two hundred and ninety-three were killed on the field. It is supposed that many were killed in the flight. Few escaped unwounded. Their whole loss, as since stated by themselves, was about six hundred. The American force lost fifteen killed, and eighty wounded, of whom many afterwards died.

A scene ensued this victory that would be difficult to describe. The friendly Indians had been besieged closely for several days. They were a handful surrounded by infuriated enemies. Torture and the most horrible death were in reserve for them, as the certain consequence of surrender. In their siege, they endured every privation, particularly the dreadful one of water. They were relieved on the very day when an assault was to have been made upon them, which would almost inevitably have resulted in the destruction of every one of them. Their deliverance was one of the few occasions that melts even the savage heart to tenderness and joy. The manifestations were affecting. Famished as they had been, they sold their provisions for the supply of the famished troops of General Jackson.

Imagination can scarcely conjure up more difficulties than those which the General had to encounter in this campaign. General Cocke, who commanded the troops from East Tennessee, was, like General Jackson, a Major General, having apparently a separate and independent command, and charged with precisely the same objects— to avenge the injuries of the country, and punish the savage foe. He seems to have been equally hearty in the cause. His reasons for attempting a separate campaign were, that on joining his troops to those of General Jackson, adding the number of so many mouths to be filled, would cause the famine that already prevailed in his camp, to press still more heavily on the troops of both Generals; and that in an united command the former would gain all the laurels.

Looking in vain for aid from that quarter, suffering

personally from famine at his own table, and still more from witnessing the privations of the camp, and the mutinous and complaining spirit of insubordination, so natural to men, situated as were the troops from Tennessee, the General was obliged to turn his back upon all the advantages already gained, and to retreat under the aspect of defeat, rather than of victory.

All these difficulties were increased by the arts of some officers among his troops, who believing that the campaign was about to break up, wished to be the first to return home, and render themselves popular by being the heralds of their own exploits, and by taking part in the complaints of the soldiers. The officers and soldiers of the militia, collecting in their tents, and talking over their grievances, finally determined to abandon the camp, and return home. The general had immediate warning of their purpose, and was determined at every hazard to prevent it. At the moment when they had determined to carry their intentions into effect, they beheld the volunteers, with the General at their head, in front of them, with positive commands to prevent their advancing, and to compel them to return to their camp. This decision and energy overawed them, and they returned to their camp, not only without murmuring, but extolling the unalterable firmness of their General.

The next day presented a different spectacle. The volunteers, who had been the day before the instruments of compelling the militia to return to their duty, particpating with them in the same discontents, and secretly wishing well to the cause, began in turn to mutiny themselves. Knowing the disaffection of the militia, they deemed that when their discontents were manifest, there would be no power in the hands of the General to prevent their carrying their plans into effect. To their surprise, they found the militia disposed to return the good offices which they had received; and when they had made all their arrangements to move off, they found the militia between them and their purposes, manifesting a fixed determination to obey the orders of their general. They fell in with the example which had been placed before them the day before, and moved back in quietness to their quarters.

Part of these amusing results may be ascribed to pique, and the gratification which the parties alternately felt, in being able to thwart the views of those who had so lately crossed their own. Added to this, they were conscious that they had complained beyond their causes for complaint. They were anxious, from a great and mixed variety of motives, to return to their homes. But the militia appear to have stopped short in their mutinous spirit sooner than the volunteers. To the latter there seemed no alternative between carrying their point and dishonor. They were anxious that their cause should prosper, that it might seem to be founded in justice. The wishes of the cavalry to return had such a just foundation, from the impossibility of procuring forage, that on a solemn pledge by their platoon and field officers, that they would return as soon as their horses were recruited, and themselves furnished with winter clothing, General Jackson granted their request, and they immediately set out on their return.

The discontent was smothered for the moment, but it was not quenched; and the General was aware that on a favorable occasion it would be sure to burst forth again. His prospects of supply were brightened by letters, just received from the contractors, that provisions for the army were then on the road, and would shortly arrive in the camp. Under these circumstances he assembled his troops, and addressed them in the most energetic and animating terms, imploring them by every consideration to follow up the blow they had struck; promising them, that if supplies did not arrive in two days, he would himself march back with them; requesting them to reflect seriously upon the subject during the following night, and let him know the result of their intentions on the succeeding morning. On retiring to their tents, and deliberating on the measures proper to be adopted on this emergency, the officers of the volunteers concluded that nothing short of marching the army immediately back to the settlements could prevent the disgrace which must attend a forcible desertion of the camp by the soldiers. The officers of the militia determined differently, and were willing to remain until it could be ascertained whether a supply of provisions could be had. 'If it can,' said they, 'let us proceed with the campaign. If not, let us be marched back where it can be procured.' The General, who greatly preferred the latter opinion, was nevertheless disposed to gratify those who appeared unwilling to submit to further hardships, and he ordered General Hall to march his brigade to fort Deposit, where a supply of provisions was collected, and after satisfying their own wants, to return, as an escort to the provisions. The second regiment, however, unwilling to be outdone by the militia, consented to remain, and the first proceeded alone. On this occasion the General could not forbear to remark, 'that men, for whom he had cherished so warm an affection, and for whom at all times he would have been willing to make any sacrifice, desiring to abandon him at a moment when their presence was so particularly necessary, filled him with emotions which language was too feeble to express.'

The two days had elapsed since the departure of the volunteers, and no supplies had arrived. The militia demanded, that the pledge which had been given them, that they should be marched back, should be redeemed. The pledge had been given under the confident expectation that the provisions would arrive within the two days. Nothing now remained, however, but to redeem the pledge. It was a moment of deep dejection to the General. All the objects on which his heart had been so earnestly fixed, were apparently about to escape him, if his men should abandon him, and he be compelled to relinquish his conquests to the possession of the enemy. While indulging these gloomy meditations, he exclaimed earnestly and aloud, 'If only two men will remain with me, I will never abandon this post.' Captain Gordon, of the spies, facetiously replied, 'You have one, General. Let us see, if we cannot find another;' and immediately, with a zeal suited to the occasion, he undertook with some of the general staff to raise volunteers, and in a little while succeeded in procuring one hundred and nine, who pledged themselves to remain and protect the post. The General, delighted with the idea that he should not be compelled to abandon his position, marched towards fort Deposit with the remainder of the army, with the distinct understanding, that on meeting supplies, they were to return and prosecute the campaign. They had not marched more than twelve miles, when they met one hundred and fifty beeves. A sight which gave the General so much delight, was to the discontented equally unwelcome. Their faces were towards home, and the prospect of returning back to the war was hateful. As soon as their devouring appetites were appeased, they were ordered to return to their encampment. Low murmurings ran along the lines, and presently broke out into open mutiny. One company was already moving off in a direction towards home. As soon as the General was informed of this, he pursued them with a part of his staff, and a few soldiers with General Coffee, who had halted a quarter of a mile in advance. He ordered them immediately to form across the road, and to fire on the mutineers, if they attempted to proceed. Snatching up their arms, these faithful adherents presented a front which awed the deserters, and caused them to retreat precipitately on the main body. But the example of mutiny was contagious. He soon ascertained that a whole brigade was in the attitude of marching back by force. In this crisis, having taken his ground, he determined to triumph or perish. Seizing a musket, and resting it on the neck of his horse, for he was disabled by a wound from the use of his left arm, he threw himself in front of the mutinous column, and declared that he would shoot the first man who should venture to advance. In this situation he was found by Major Reid and General Coffee, who, judging from the length of his absence, that some disturbance had arisen, hastened to his side, and waited the result of his perilous determination, in the anxious suspense of expectation. For many minutes the column preserved a sullen, yet hesitating attitude, at once fearing to proceed, and reluctant to retreat. In the mean time, those who remained faithful to their duty, amounting to about two companies, were collected and formed in rear of the General, and in advance of the troops, with positive orders · to imitate his example in firing, if they attempted to advance. The timidity, resulting from the consciousness of

17

a bad cause, prevailed. They returned quietly to their posts. This firmness, at this critical moment, undoubtedly saved the campaign, and perhaps determined the issue of the war. There are but few men who could have adopted such a course with safety.

Shortly after the battle of Talladega, the Hillabee tribes, who had suffered most severely on that occasion, sued for peace. General Jackson sternly demanded the proper reparation and submission, assuring them that fort Mimms should long be remembered by them in bitterness and tears, but informing them, that on manifestation of sincerity in their desires for peace, he was not disposed to make war on those who were willing to become our friends.

But before this answer arrived among them, General White had attacked and destroyed their town, killing sixty, and making two hundred and fifty-six prisoners. This unfortunate circumstance contributed to the desperation with which the Creeks afterwards fought. They had asked for peace on the General's own terms. Finding themselves attacked under such circumstances, it produced among them the false conviction, that no submission would avail them, and they considered it as a war of extermination. There is no instance afterwards of their asking for quarter, or manifesting a disposition to receive it.

We have been thus particular in giving the details of the first difficulties and mutinies which General Jackson had to encounter at the commencement of the Creek war, as they serve as accurate samples of all his subsequent difficulties in bringing this war to a successful termination.

They remind us of the trials which Washington had to endure, in prosecuting the war of the revolution. His soldiers were little accustomed to any, even the most necessary control. They were full fed, and much accustomed to spend their time at their own discretion at home. Their enlistments were for periods too limited. The arrangements of the contractors for supplies were grossly mismanaged. Some of the officers were no letter than partisans. So formidable were the difficulties in the way of prosecuting the campaign, that even the Governor advised its abandonment. The troops were not certain whether they were to look to the general government, or that of their state, for their pay; or whether they might not ultimately fail of being paid by either. On the 12th of December, General Cocke arrived with one thousand five hundred men; but it was found that they were not brought into the field under the requisition of the President of the United States; that the term of service of a great part of them would expire in a few days, and the whole in a few weeks. Mutiny succeeded to mutiny, and such was the general gloom of the prospect, that a man of any other temperament and character than that of General Jackson would have yielded to the advice of Governor Blount, and wearied and disgusted with quelling mutiny in one form to-day, only to see it renewed in another to-morrow, would have abandoned the enterprise forever.

Not so General Jackson. He harangued his troops.— He appealed to every motive that can influence the human heart—their honor, their patriotism, their avarice, and their fears in turn. The more obstacles and impediments arose before him, the more firmly he attached himself to the cause. In one instance, he ordered the arrest of a mutinous officer, Lieutenant Kearly, and demanded his sword. His reply was, 'that he was a free man, not subject to the orders of General Jackson, or any other person;' declaring, at the same time, that his sword should protect him on his way to Tennessee. The guards, who were ordered to arrest him, cocked their guns. Lieutenant Kearly and his men did the same. The General hastened to the scene, and demanded Kearly's sword in person, which he persisted to refuse. The General snatched a pistol from his holster, and was levelling it at the breast of Kearly, when friends interposed, and he was induced to surrender his sword. During the crisis, both parties were prepared to fire, and a scene of bloodshed was narrowly escaped. Under these discouragements, and the departure of the troops from East Tennessee, for their homes, and the scattering away of his forces, he was far from being induced to despond, and he was determined to

prosecute the campaign, with the feeble force still remaining with him.

On the 2d of January, 1814, Colonel Carroll and Mr.
Blackburn arrived at head quarters, reporting the approach
of eight hundred and fifty volunteers. These men had
scarcely arrived, and chosen Colonels Perkins and Higgins to command them, when these officers refused to
march their regiments to head quarters under command of
General Coffee. There was no small difficulty in quelling
this mutiny, and it was not until the 13th of the month, that
these officers arrived at head quarters with their regiments.
The whole effective force at this time consisted, according
to the report, of only nine hundred men, and was in reali-
ty short of that number.

On the 15th, the troops commenced their march, and
moved to Wehogee creek, three miles from fort Strother.
At Talladega he was joined by two hundred friendly Indians, badly armed, and discouraged at the weakness of
the united force. A thousand men, under such circumstances, were led into the heart of an enemy's country,
with no possible hope of escape, but from victory. To
march seemed now the only alternative, although it was
a course so full of peril. To march was necessary, to
afford a diversion favorable to General Floyd, who was
advancing from Georgia with an army against the Creeks.
Another reason rendered this course indispensable. The
officer commanding at fort Armstrong, had received intelligence, on which the utmost reliance was placed, that the
warriors from fourteen or fifteen towns on the Tallapoosa
were about to combine their forces, and attack that place.
For the want of a sufficient garrison, it was in a defenceless condition. On reaching Talladega, the General received a letter from the commander at fort Armstrong,
confirming the report, that this depot was about to be
attacked. He was also informed, by an express from
General Pinckney, that General Floyd was moving on the
Creek country, and would shortly be at Tuckabatcha.
The express desired him, for various reasons, to advance
upon such of the Creek towns as might be within striking
distance from him.

Had he hesitated before, these advices would have decided him. It was understood, that the hostile force was collected in a bend of the Tallapoosa, near the mouth of a creek, called Emuckfaw. On that point he marched by the shortest route. As he advanced, he became more and more sensible of the ignorance of his guides, and the inexperience and insubordination, both of his officers and troops. But they were in high spirits, and anxious to meet the enemy. On the 21st, the General encamped his small force on the eminences, that overlooked Emuckfaw, and made every preparation against an attack. At midnight, spies reported that they had discovered a large encampment of Indians, at three miles distance, yelling and dancing in a manner to indicate that they were apprised of his arrival. At the dawn of the next morning, the alarm guns of the sentinels, succeeded by shrieks and savage yells, announced the attack of the enemy. Their first assault was on the left flank, commanded by Colonel Higgins. It was met, and opposed with great firmness. General Coffee and Colonels Carroll and Sitler instantly repaired to the point of attack, and by example and exhortation encouraged the men to their duty. The action raged for half an hour. The brunt of it being against the left wing, it had become considerably weakened. The first part of the action had taken place during the dimness of twilight. The clear light of the morning, showing the position of the enemy, and Captain Ferril's company having reinforced the left wing, General Coffee directed a charge, and a rout immediately ensued. The enemy were pursued two miles.

The General immediately detached General Coffee, with the friendly Indians and four hundred men, to storm the enemy's encampment, unless it should be found too strongly fortified, in which case he proposed to bring up the artillery. Coffee, having reconnoitered the position, and found it too strongly fortified to be assailed with his force, returned to camp. He had not returned more than half an hour, when a fire was opened on the piquets on the right, accompanied with the usual savage yells. General Coffee volunteered his services to move upon the left flank

17*

of the assailants. His detachment was taken from different corps. He placed himself at their head, and moved rapidly upon the foe. While he was thus occupied, the rear of his force had an opportunity to slip away unperceived, until the whole number did not exceed fifty men. He found the enemy occupying a ridge of open pine timber, covered with low underbrush, which afforded them every opportunity for concealment. To drive them from their lurking places, General Coffee ordered his men to dismount, and charge them. In carrying this order into execution, the General was wounded through the body, and his aid, Major Donelson, killed.

This was followed by a violent onset on the line of the left. General Jackson repaired in person to the point of attack. The battle was maintained by the assailants by quick and irregular firing from behind logs, trees, shrubbery, and whatever could afford concealment. Behind these, they prostrated themselves, after firing, to reload, and rise, and fire again. After sustaining this fire for some time, a brilliant and steady charge, under Colonel Carroll, broke their array, threw them into confusion, and caused them to fly. Their loss, though it was certainly considerable, was not exactly known.

On the right, General Coffee had not been able to drive them from their fastnesses to his wish; and with a view to draw them from their retreat, he affected to retire towards the place where he had first dismounted. This stratagem had the desired effect. They forsook their hiding places, and advanced rapidly upon him. The fight was renewed again on equal terms. A severe contest ensued, which lasted almost an hour, with nearly the same loss on each side. At this crisis, when several of the detachment had been killed, many wounded, and the whole was exhausted with fatigue, a timely reinforcement from General Jackson made its appearance on the enemy's left flank, and put an end to the contest. General Coffee, although severely wounded, instantly ordered a charge, from which the enemy fled in consternation, and were pursued with great slaughter. At this place, few, if any, escaped. It was a day of almost continual hard fighting.

The night, that drew on after such a day, amid the gloom of the forest, would naturally be dispiriting to troops, most of whom had never before seen an enemy, or formed a distinct idea of the horrors of a battle. The spirits of the men were observed visibly to flag, as the darkness increased. During the night, at even the least noise, the sentinels would fire their alarm guns, and retreat upon the main body. General Jackson, having accomplished the main objects of the expedition, a diversion in favor of General Floyd, and the relief of fort Armstrong, began to think of returning to his former station at the Ten Islands. The impossibility of subsistence for men and horses, where they were, rendered this measure indispensable. The appearance of a retreat, too, would probably draw the savages from their strong holds, where they could not be attacked with his present force, with any prospect of success. Every arrangement for the comfort and conveyance of his wounded being made, he began his retreat, at ten the next morning. He marched without interruption, until nearly night, and encamped on the south side of Enotichopco creek.

The next day, various circumstances instructed the General that he was pursued. The delay of an attack led him to fear that he was marching into an ambuscade. The necessary crossing of a deep ravine between two hills, sheltered with thick shrubbery and brown sedge, affording a most favorable concealment for savage attack, exposed him to an ambuscade. A few pioneers were despatched to find another crossing place. At this place, the front guards, and part of the columns, had passed, and the artillery was crossing. The company of Captain Russell, who marched in the rear, was suddenly attacked by greatly superior numbers. The General had made all possible arrangements for the emergency of an attack in this place, and calculated on a certain victory. Great was his astonishment, when he beheld the right and left columns of the rear guard, after a feeble resistance, giving way, carrying confusion and dismay with them, and obstructing the passage over which the principal strength of the army was to be recrossed. This timid deportment was well nigh being followed with the most fatal consequences, which were only prevented by the determined bravery of a few men. Nearly the whole of the centre column had followed the example of the other two. Not more than twenty men remained to oppose the torrent of assault. The artillery company, commanded by Lieutenant Armstrong, and composed of young men of the first families, who had volunteered their services at the commencement of the campaign, formed with their muskets before their piece of ordnance, and hastily dragged it from the creek to an eminence, whence they could discharge it on the enemy to advantage. This piece they defended with the most desperate bravery, against an enemy five times their number, and checked the advance of a foe, already animated from beholding the consternation which his first shock had produced. The brave Armstrong fell beside his piece, exclaiming as he fell, 'Some of you must perish; but do not abandon the gun.' By his side fell, mortally wounded, his associate and friend, Bird Evans, and the gallant Captain Hamilton. In the meantime, General Jackson and his staff, by the greatest exertions, were enabled to restore something like order. The enemy, perceiving a strong force advancing upon them, and being warmly assailed on their left flank by Captain Gordon, at the head of his spies, in their turn were stricken with alarm, and fled, throwing away whatever retarded their flight. They were pursued two miles; many were destroyed, and the remainder wholly dispersed.

The highest praise was due, and was given to General Coffee. In consequence of the wound he had received at Emuckfaw, he was carried only the day before on a litter. He was this day on horseback, and commanded with his usual calm and deliberate firmness. On this crisis, all etiquette was thrown aside, and officers and men each fought in the place where his services seemed to be neeessary. The hospital surgeon, Dr. Shelby, rendered important services in the battle. Captain Gordon, by his opportune sally on the left flank of the savages, essentially contributed to restore the fight. The Adjutant General, Sitler, displayed the greatest firmness. Of General Jackson, it is but justice to remark, that but for him, rout and ruin mus have ensued. Firm, energetic and self-possessed, he was alike the rallying point for the timid and the brave. Amidst showers of balls, he calmly performed the duties of subordinate officers, rallying the wavering, arresting their flight, restoring order to his columns, and inspiriting them by his example. An army retreating in dismay was thus rescued from the inevitable destruction that must have ensued from a rout. The American loss was twenty killed and seventy-five wounded, some of whom afterwards died. The loss of the enemy could not be accurately ascertained. Scattered on the heights and hollows, many of the wounded escaped, and many of the killed were not found. Their prisoners estimated their loss at considerable over two hundred, although they endeavored to conceal the extent of it among themselves, by representing that many of the slain were gone on an expedition, that they might thus account for their absence.

The army returned without accident to fort Strother. Fort Armstrong was relieved, and such a diversion had been made in favor of General Floyd, from Georgia, that he had been enabled to gain a victory over the savages at Autossee, where, but for this movement, he would have been outnumbered by the enemy, and would, probably, have experienced a defeat. The army returned triumphant, and experience has proved how easily the ranks of a victorious army are filled.

This army, whose term of service had nearly expired, was discharged. The spirit of the people was roused, and a new army was speedily collected, with a longer period of enlistment. A renewal of the difficulties of supplies and of insubordination was experienced, though in a less degree than at the commencement of the former campaign. These evils, in a greater or less degree, are inevitably incidental to the calling into service inexperienced militia, whose submission and duties are not settled by prescription, who are subjected to conflicting authorities, the limits of which are not well defined, and who constantly experience in the camp the most earnest longings to return home.

The severe example of the execution of a mutinous private, John Woods, had a most salutary effect in checking the incipient spirit of mutiny, and probably prevented a second edition of the original difficulties from that quarter. But there remained anxieties enough to leave little repose or quietness to the General. The East Tennessee brigade, under the command of General Doherty, manifested, also, symptoms of disaffection, and was hardly restrained from returning immediately home. One hundred and eighty men deserted in a body. To put an end to this order of things, General Jackson issued an order to General Doherty, to arrest and send to fort Strother, under guard, any officer, of whatever rank he might be, who should be found in his camp, attempting to incite the soldiers to mutiny.

About this time, Colonel Dyer was detached with six hundred men to the head of the Black Warrior, to ascertain if there were any Indians embodied in that quarter, and if there were, to disperse them, and prevent their coming on in the rear of the army. This detachment marched eight days along the ridges of the Cahaba, and fell in with a trail of the enemy passing eastwardly; but being able to gain no certain information of them, they desisted from the pursuit, and returned to camp.

On the 14th of March, 1814, General Jackson had made such arrangements, and obtained such supplies, as enabled him to commence his march for the enemy. At the mouth of Cedar creek, he established fort Williams. On the 24th, leaving a sufficient force for the protection of the fort, under Brigadier General Johnson, he set out for the Tallapoosa, by the way of Emuckfaw. His whole effective force was something less than three thousand men. At ten in the morning of the 27th, after a march of fifty-two miles, he reached the village of Tohopeka. The enemy had collected here in considerable numbers, to give him battle. The warriors from Oakfusky, Hillabee, Eufalee, and New Youcka, amounting to nearly one thousand two hundred, were at this place waiting his approach. They had selected an admirable place for defence. Situated in a bend of the river, which almost surrounded it, it was accessible only by a narrow neck of land. This they had used great exertions to render impregnable, by placing large timbers and trunks of trees horizontally on each other, leaving but a single place for entrance. From a double row of port holes, they were enabled to fire in perfect security behind it. General Coffee, with mounted infantry and friendly Indians, had been despatched early in the morning, to encircle the bend, and manœuvre in such a way as to divert the savages from the real point of attack. He was particularly directed to prevent their escape to the opposite shore in their canoes, with which, it was represented, the whole shore was lined. The General posted the rest of his army in front of the breastwork. He began to batter their breastworks with his cannon. Muskets and rifles were used, as the Indians occasionally showed themselves. The signals, which were to announce that General Coffee had gained his destination, were given. The soldiers hailed it with acclamations, and advanced with the intrepidity of veterans. The 39th regiment, led on by their skillful commander, Colonel Williams, and the brave but ill-fated Major Montgomery, and the militia, amidst a sheet of fire that poured upon them, rushed forward to the rampart. Here an obstinate and destructive conflict ensued. In firing through the port holes on either side, many of the enemy's balls were welded between the muskets and bayonets of our soldiers. At this moment, Major Montgomery, leaping on the rampart, called to his men to follow him. Scarcely had he spoken, when he was shot through the head, and fell. Our troops had now scaled the ramparts, and the savages fled before them, concealing themselves under the brush and timber, which abounded in the peninsula, whence they still continued a galling fire. Here they were charged, and dislodged. Their next alternative was their canoes; but they perceived that a part of the army lined the opposite shore, and precluded escape on that quarter. They that still survived the conflict, leaped down the banks, and took shelter behind the trees which had been felled from their margin. A flag, with an interpreter, was here sent them, to propose a surrender. They fired upon the party,

and wounded-one of them. Ascertaining their desperation, orders were given to dislodge them. The brush and
trees about them were set on fire by lighted torches, sent
down among them, and the blaze drove them from their
hiding places, and brought them to view. The slaughter
continued, until night concealed the combatants from each
other. A few of the misguided savages, who had avoided
the havoc of the day, made their escape under the covert
of the darkness. The friendly Indians contributed not a
little to the completeness of this victory. Several of the
Cherokees, and Russell's spies, in the heat of the action,
swam across the river, and fired the Indian town in the
rear of the foe. Thus they found themselves assailed on
every side, and vulnerable on a quarter from which they
had not expected an attack.

This battle gave a death blow to their hopes; nor did
they afterwards venture to make any decided stand. Here
they had strongly fortified themselves. Here their prophets had led them to believe, that they were secure of the
aid of the 'Great Spirit,' and invincible. They had never
met with so severe a loss, in any previous engagement.
Their best and their bravest warriors fell. Few escaped
the carnage. Many were thrown into the river, while the
battle raged. Many were destroyed by Coffee's brigade
in endeavoring to cross it, and five hundred and fifty-seven
were found dead on the field. Among the slain, were
three of the prophets. These miserable impostors, with
the fantastic and magic finery of 'medicine men,' danced,
and howled, and prophesied, and kept up the delusive confidence of the savages to the last. Monohoe, one of the
chief of them, fell, with a cannon shot in the mouth, at the
very moment when uttering his incantations, and urging
them to stand to the fight. Four men only, and three hundred women and children, were taken prisoners. The
small number of men who surrendered, give an impressive
view of the desperation with which they fought. The assault by the troops from East Tennessee upon the Hillabee
clans, after they had sued for peace on our own terms, had
caused them to relinquish all confidence in our humanity,
and to trust to nothing but bravery and despair. Our loss,

including the friendly Indians, was fifty-five killed, and one hundred and forty-six wounded. Among the former was Major Montgomery, a brave and promising young officer of the 39th regiment, and Lieutenants Moulton and Somerville, who fell early in the action.

The General sunk his dead in the river; for he had found by experience, that when they were buried, the savages raised the bodies, stripped, and scalped them, presenting the scalps among their own people, as trophies of victory, and thus tending to inspirit them with these horrid badges of triumph, to prolong the war. Having made the necessary arrangements for carrying off his wounded, he returned safely to fort Williams.

On the 2d day of April, the General issued a very spirited address, in the form of congratulation to his soldiers. Understanding that the enemy were embodied in considerable numbers at Hoithlewalee, a town not far from the Hickory Ground, he was desirous to recommence operations as soon as possible. Too much weakened by sickness, and the loss of the late battle, and some soldiers discharged, to open the campaign as efficiently as he could choose, with his own forces, he wished to form a junction with the army from Georgia. The North Carolina troops, under the command of General Graham, an experienced revolutionary officer, and those of Georgia, under Colonel Milton, were announced to be some where not far south of Tallapoosa, and could not be very distant.

On the 7th, with all his disposable force, he commenced his march, with the double view of effecting this union and of attacking on his route the enemy's force collected at Hoithlewalee. Could the enemy, at the point they now occupied, be brought to fight, and a decisive advantage obtained over them, they might be induced to submit to terms, and the war be ended. But if suffered to escape, they might again collect, and give battle at some fortunate moment, and protract the war. This could in no way be so effectually prevented, as for the Tennessee troops to advance upon them from the north, and the Carolinians and Georgians from the south, making such a dis-

18

position as would prevent their escape by crossing the river, and passing off by the Escambia to Pensacola.

It was some time before he could procure confidential messengers to convey the information of his intended movements to the southern army. He wrote by expresses, sent on two different routes, that on the 7th he should march with eight days' provisions for Hoithlewalee, which he expected to attack on the 11th; and he urged the necessity of proper concert on their part to meet this movement. High waters prevented his reaching his destination until the 13th, before which the enemy had been sufficiently apprised of his approach to flee. The rear only of the retreating savages was overtaken, and twenty-five of them made prisoners. The next day part of the town of Hoithlewalee was destroyed by a detachment of the army; but the inhabitants and warriors had fled.

The next day the long desired junction with the southern army was effected. The Tennessee army was in a state of famine. Colonel Milton, who commanded the southern troops, proposed to lend General Jackson a temporary supply, but felt himself under no obligation to furnish any. To this courteous proffer, the General answered, by ordering him immediately to send him five thousand rations, and to join him by ten the next day at Hoithlewalee. The junction was accordingly effected. The necessary steps were taken to bring down provisions from fort Decatur, and no further inconvenience was felt for want of supplies.

The principal chiefs of the Hickory Ground tribes, and the Creek chiefs generally, came in with protestations of friendship, and applied for peace. The answer was, 'that those of the war party, who wished to put an end to the contest and become friendly, must manifest it by retiring in the rear of the army, and settling themselves to the north of fort Williams. Fourteen chiefs were willing to furnish still further evidence of their desire for peace. They assured the General that their aged king, Tous-hatchee, would have come with them in person, but was on his way with his followers, to settle north of fort Williams, according to the information which he had received from the General by a flag.

It was expected that the Indians would make a final stand at the Hickory Grounds, in the forks near where the Coosa and Tallapoosa unite. The army continued its march for this place, without hearing of any embodied enemy. At the old Toulossee fort on the Coosa, not far from the confluence, and where the two rivers approach within one hundred poles of each other, a fort was directed to be raised, to be named after the commanding General. Here the hostile chiefs arrived daily, with assurances of friendship, and proffers of submission. They concurred to state, that those of the hostile chiefs who were still opposed to peace, had fled to the gulf coast and Pensacola. To these applications an answer was returned similar to the former.

To test the sincerity of their professions, they were directed to bring the notorious chief, Weatherford, bound to the camp. He was one of the most influential chiefs of the nation, and had been the principal actor in the butchery at fort Mimms. Soon after, the General was surprised by a personal visit from that chief, who had come voluntarily, and without being known, and had been admitted to the General's quarters. He entered with a calm front, and said 'that he had come to ask peace for himself and his people.' The General expressed his astonishment that he, whose conduct at fort Mimms had been so well known, and who must be conscious that he deserved to die, should venture to appear in his presence. 'I had directed,' he continued, 'that you should be brought to me confined. Had you appeared in this way, I should have known how to have treated you.' Weatherford replied, 'I am in your power. Do with me as you please. I am a soldier. I have done the white people all the harm I could. I have fought them, and fought them bravely. If I had an army, I would yet fight, and contend to the last. But I have none. My people are all gone. I can now do no more than weep over the misfortunes of my nation.'

This man had probably penetrated the character of General Jackson so far as to be aware that this was the

only mode of address in which to please that intrepid soldier. Somewhat softened, the General informed him how
his nation could be saved, and peace restored to it, and
that there was but that alternative; informing him, however, that if the alternative was not acceptable, no advantage should be taken of his voluntary surrender, and
that he was at liberty to depart, and unite himself to the
war party when he pleased; but that, if taken, his life
would pay the forfeit of his crimes. Otherwise, he
was assured, if he chose to remain, that he should be
protected.

Weatherford answered, 'that he desired peace, that his
nation might be relieved from their sufferings; that, independent of other sufferings, consequences of the war, their
cattle were destroyed, and their women and children destitute of provisions. But,' he continued, 'I may well be
addressed in such language now. There was a time
when I had a choice, and could have answered you. I
have none now. Even hope has ended. Once I could
animate my warriors to battle. But I cannot animate the
dead. My warriors can no longer hear my voice. Their
bones are at Talladega, Tallashatchee, Emuckfaw, and
Tohopeka. I have surrendered myself deliberately. While
there were chances of success, I never left my post, or
supplicated peace. My people are now gone, and I ask
peace for my nation and myself. On the miseries and
misfortunes brought upon my country, I look back with the
deepest sorrow, and wish to avert still greater calamities.
If I had been left to contend with the Georgia army, I
would have raised my corn on one bank of the river, and
fought them on the other. Your people have destroyed
my nation. You are a brave man. I rely upon your
generosity. You will exact no terms of a conquered people, but those to which they are willing to accede. Whatever they may be, it would now be madness and folly to
oppose them. If they are opposed, you shall find me
among the sternest enforcers of obedience. Those who
would hold out, can only be influenced by a mean spirit
of revenge; and to this they must not, and shall not sacrifice the last remnant of their country. You have told

us where we may go and be safe. This is a good talk,
and my nation ought to listen to it, and they shall listen
to it.'

Such was the oration of Weatherford. The earnestness
and bold independence of his after conduct, left no doubt of
the sincerity of his intentions.

The necessary blow had been struck, and the war in
effect was closed. The spirits of the Creeks were broken
down. All who were disposed still to fight, had taken
protection with the Spanish on the coast. Little remained
for General Jackson to accomplish, but to give stability
and perpetuity to the results already obtained. The
Creek country was scoured by his troops, to find any
gatherings of hostile Indians, or lurking adherents to them.
Knowing the natural perfidy of these people, and that no
guarantee for their future fidelity, but their fears, could be
expected, he was stern in adhering to the original purpose, to consider all the Indians who did not remove to the
north of fort Williams, as enemies. By the establishment of fort Jackson, a line of posts was formed from
Tennessee and Georgia to the Alabama. The required
remove of the Indians interposed this line between them
and their communications with the Spanish at Pensacola,
and placed them properly within the control of the United
States.

On the 20th, General Pinckney arrived in camp, and
assumed the command of the army in person. The measures that had been adopted by General Jackson, in regard
to the future fidelity of the Indians, met his entire approbation. The Indians were retiring with their families,
where they were directed. Much of the property plundered at fort Mimms and along the frontier, was restored,
and every thing indicated on their part sincere desires of
peace. A sufficient force was retained for garrisoning
the posts already occupied, and orders were issued on the
21st for the troops from Tennessee to be marched home
and discharged. It was a cheering reflection to them, that
having seen, inflicted, and suffered so much misery, they
were now retiring to their homes, carrying with them the
sweetest consolation to the mind of a citizen soldier, that

18*

in the trying situations in which they had been placed, they had acted with honor, had done their duty, and were returning to their retired and peaceful dwellings, covered with glory.

It is matter of regret, that even while these arrangements were making, the friendly Creeks were engaged in pursuing and destroying their fugitive countrymen, with the most unrelenting rigor. To have been at fort Mimms, was a ground of accusation against a warrior, that at once placed him out of the pale of mercy. They viewed, or affected to view, this unprovoked outrage with more vindictive feelings than even did our own troops. A Creek party was on its way to our camp, for the purpose of making their submission. The friendly Creeks, understanding that they had accompanied Weatherford in his attack upon fort Mimms, met them on their way, and put them all to death.

All necessary arrangements having been made for garrisoning the posts, and for the future security of the country, and the proper reports made to General Pinckney, the commanding officer, after an impressive parting address to the troops, General Jackson despatched them to their homes. The freshness of the laurels which he had gathered in this war, will never fade. He had every thing to encounter, and he overcame every difficulty. He was the only one of the army that never despaired of the cause. Such was the promptitude and celerity of his movements, that he was often upon the savages before they had any intelligence of his approach. He was one of the few men who inspire universal confidence, and have the secret to command victory.

Humanity will naturally recoil from the contemplation of the misery and ruin inflicted upon these deluded savages. We may surely take to ourselves the consolation, that our country had exhausted forbearance before she inflicted vengeance. For more than twenty years, the Creeks had been perpetrating cruelties and murders along our frontiers. Many a parent still lives, whose sad remembrance treasures a child that had bled beneath their murderous hands. Cold Water, on Tennessee river, had long been a den, whence they issued to prowl and murder. As early as 1787, General Robertson collected a force of volunteers, and destroyed this settlement. Those who escaped from this place, retired upon the Black Warrior, harboring revenge, and seeking every favorable opportunity for murder, until the winter of 1813, when their towns on that river were assailed, and destroyed.

In the war that ensued between our country and Great Britain, the prowess of that nation was prodigiously magnified in their eyes. Their prophets contributed to the illusion. They were led to think that the 'Great Spirit' had taken cause with them, that they were allied with an invincible power, in the British, and that they should ultimately drive away the Americans from the country. The tomahawk and scalping knife were used with unrelenting and unsparing vengeance. A more horrid massacre than that of fort Mimms, never occurred in the annals of savage barbarity. The Indians were acquainted with the difficulties which General Jackson had to encounter, and drew encouragement from them. They soon found what kind of character they had to deal with in him. Instead of confining his plans to the guarding our own frontiers, as under all his trials would have been as much as another man would have contemplated, General Jackson with his troops burst into the centre of their country, and swept over it, as with a storm. One fatal battle after another convinced them that their prophets were imposters, and that neither the British nor the 'Great Spirit' protected them from our just vengeance. Their courage was broken down along with their power, and such results obtained, that we may confidently hope they will never again, as a nation, raise the tomahawk against us, within the limits of our country.

CHAPTER XII.

MONUMENTAL REMAINS OF THE PAST, IN THE MISSISSIPPI
VALLEY.

INNUMERABLE observers, in penetrating the bosom of the earth, in all the recorded periods of time, have come upon the remains of organized animal and vegetable bodies, the ruins of a gone-by world, the monuments of generations of rationals, whose history, whose annals, whose recorded traces, are as completely extinct as though they had not been. These monuments present materials for meditation of the profoundest interest, and the most inextricable perplexity. The monuments of present tropical existences, are found deep under the soil of the temperate and polar regions,—impressions, petrifactions of the date, fern, bread-fruit tree, bamboo, lion, tiger, hippopotomus,—under the snows and frosts of the bitterest winters. It is but recently, that some French writers, as St. Pierre and Buffon, began to class these remains. Baron Cuvier, the historian of the animals of a past world, entered, in the industry of great talent and profound research, into this walk, and from noting the conformation of organic remains, has been enabled to classify the generations of the past, and to write the history of the changes which our world has probably undergone. Dr. Buckland has found, that the caves of England, France, and Germany, are abundantly stored with the remains of animals, that at present only inhabit the tropics. The ferns of Mexico, India, and the South Sea isles, are found imbedded in English meadows. What a world must that have been, what species of men must have been the spectators, when the mammoth and megalonyx trod the plains; and the monstrous lizards, whose bones are now rescued from the soil, reared their heads from the rivers and lakes! What must have been the terrors of rivers and swamps inhabited by lizards of tremendous teeth and powers, eighty feet in length, and possessing the wings attributed to the fabulous dragon!

It has been the custom with European writers to speak of America as the *new world,* and of our own geologists to describe the great Mississippi valley as the most recent formation of this new world; and, in fact, as so lately reared from its submersion, as almost to bear on its surface the slimy traces of its emersion. More recent and better collated examinations, assign to this region an antiquity far beyond any recorded annals of human history or tradition. It is but a few years since some hardy antiquarians began to speak of finding the impress of the leaves and flowers of the bread-fruit tree, and the bamboo, and the fern, in our peat beds, and fossil coal formations. They were met by the public with incredulity and unsparing ridicule. But as these experiments multiplied; as they became too numerous to be attributed to imagination or deception; as they were so multiplied as to cease to be curiosities; as the testimony of so respectable and unquestioned a writer as Dr. Buckland, was added to prove the same facts in the old world, doubt began to change to perplexed admiration and astonishment. Our bowlders of granite in disruption, our vast masses of lead ore out of place, our stratified rocks, earths, and sands, our innumerable specimens of tropical organic animal and vegetable remains, our regular walls, stoned wells, brick hearths, medals, characters, apparently alphabetic, written on the cliffs, the brick hearths found deep below a soil which could not have been disturbed for ages, our implements of iron and copper found in a hundred places, and under circumstances to preclude a recent and European origin, our mounds and their contents, clear monuments of a second and deteriorated race, our present red men, still lower in the scale of humanity, all announce that this valley, fondly deemed of such recent origin, has undergone the baptism of fire, and water, and death, and prodigious changes almost beyond the stretch of fancy; and that this country of silent forests and prairies, has already seen, at immense and unrecorded intervals of time, three successive generations of men; the primitive race acquainted with the use of iron, of alphabetical or hieroglyphical writing, of structures of brick and stone; the second and deteriorated race of the mounds but little acquainted with the softer metals, and deriving that acquaintance from the Mexican Indians, and whose most enduring monuments are these mounds of earth, partly fortifications and partly cemeteries, full of the bones and the puerile ornaments of the founders, and the present hapless race fading fast from existence and memory, who will leave no other remembrances than their bones.

Alas! our fresh world, beneath its deep forests and flowering prairies, conceals the memorials of eras of the complete extirpation of successive races. The tide of life and empire rolled where the traveller, from the rising to the setting sun, sees neither man nor human habitation. The races are entombed beneath the ruins of a world, that is past. Every thing speaks of life and death in the new world, as in the old. Our virgin and vegetable soil, which the immigrant turns up with his share for the first time, may be the mouldering remains of a human body. The dew drops, which glitter on the flower cups of the wide ocean prairies, may once have been tear drops rolling down the cheek of youth and beauty.

The monuments of the primitive race, consist of regular stone walls, of wells stoned up, of medals of copper and silver, of swords and other implements of iron, of the brick hearths found in digging the Louisville canal, with the coal of the last fires laying upon them; of characters found on the limestone bluffs, which cannot but be deemed as either alphabetic or hieroglyphical, are discovered in too many places in the west, and under circumstances too various to be attributed to any other origin than a primitive race, whose whole history of civilization our brief limits will not allow us to give, only in the fact, that they knew the manufacture and the use of iron. But though this history may be brief, it comprises volumes in regard to their civilization, compared with any races between them and us. Among the same class of inexplicable antiquities, we place the groves of ancient live oaks set in regular park-forms in Florida, together with remains of cities, fortifications, and dwellings, near them. We have seen these strange and ancient swords. We have seen the iron shoe of some tiny animal of the horse class, encrusted with

the rust of ages, and found far beneath the soil. Fragments of wood dug from beneath the peat beds, bear the
evident marks of having been cut by an implement of iron
not unlike our axe. We recently saw a copper axe, which
weighed, we should judge, over two pounds. Its edge was
singularly tempered and polished, and worked not unlike
an edge of steel. Its place for the insertion of a handle,
was made by the rolling over of the two outer rims, leaving place for a helve at the point of insertion of the width
of a man's hand. These monuments, together with the
western medals, we refer to a class anterior to the founders of the mounds, and much farther advanced in civilization. To this era belong the remains of the ancient city,
of towers and temples, recently discovered in the Hercu-
laneum of the new world, in Peru.

The second era of American habitancy, is in the immense stone Teocalli of Mexico, and the earthen mounds
discovered in every point of the valley, from lake Erie
and West Pennsylvania and Virginia, to the savannas of
Florida, and arising on the solitude of the western prairies
quite to the Rocky mountains. Whether the mass of them
was constructed for fortifications, observatories, temples,
or tombs, is a matter of conjecture alone. That some of
them served the latter purpose, we have conclusive proof,
in their abounding in skeletons and human bones. They
show little art, though immense labor. Many of them are
of regular mathematical figures, parallelograms, ellipses,
sections of circles, showing the remains of gateways and
subterranean passages. Some of them, after the lapse of
ages, and with trees growing on them of a date of 500 years,
are still 70 or 80 feet high. A circumstance the most inexplicable of all is, that these huge and rude erections are
generally of a soil not furnished by the ground in the immediate vicinity, which at least is the general opinion, and
such is their aspect to us. Some are found on hills,
some on the fertile prairies; and they are generally most
frequent on rich alluvial grounds, near portages, between
long rivers, contiguous to fishing grounds and productive
hunting regions. They are most abundant at points where
has been since most convenient to build the towns and

form the settlements of civilized man. We have seen them rising in their striking loneliness amidst the mountains of western Virginia, along the shores of the beautiful Ohio, on the prairies of the Missouri, and on the lower courses of the Mississippi. Some are cone shaped. Some rectangles. One at Grave creek is between 70 and 80 feet in height. One among the hundreds near Cahokia, in the prairie of the American bottom, was large enough to furnish a garden and a residence to some monks of La Trappe, under a vow of perpetual silence. Where could these dreamers have meditated more profoundly in their silence, than in these flowering prairies, amidst nature's luxuriance of useless vegetation, in the wide solitude, and above the bones of a world, whose inhabitants were all passed away!

There are very interesting mounds near St. Louis, and a little north of the town. Some of them have the appearance of enormous stacks. The mound, called the Falling Garden, is pointed out to strangers at St. Louis as a great curiosity. One of these mounds was levelled in the centre of Chillicothe. In digging it down, cart loads of human bones are said to have been removed. The town of Circleville is laid out between a couple of mounds, the one circular, the other square. Skeletons have been found in digging under one in Cincinnati. A thin circular piece of gold, alloyed with copper, was discovered in this mound last year.

In passing over our vast prairies, in viewing our noble and ancient forests, planted by nature, and nurtured only by ages, when we have seen the sun rising over a boundless plain, where the blue of the heavens in all directions touched and mingled with the verdure and the flowers; when our thoughts have traversed rivers of a thousand leagues in length; when we have seen the ascending steam boat breasting the surge, and gleaming through the verdure of the trees; when we have imagined the happy multitudes that from these shores will contemplate the scenery in days to come, we have thought that our great country might at least compare with others in the beauty of its natural scenery. When on an uninhabited prairie we have fallen at night-fall upon a group of these mounb and have thought of the masses of human bones that moulder beneath; when our heart and imagination evoked the busy multitudes that here 'strutted through life's poor play,' and asked the phantoms who and what they were, and why they have left no memorials but these mounds, we have found ample scope for reflections and associations of the past with the future. We should not highly estimate the mind or the heart of the man who could behold these tombs of the desert prairies without deep thought.

Among the second class of Indian antiquities may be classed the idols, vases, and culinary utensils, of which such numbers are found in the western country, as that they are no longer regarded as curiosities. The beautiful three-headed idol, the most remarkable specimen of Indian pottery and moulding that has yet been found, was taken from a mound in Tennessee. It consists of three heads of proportions of considerable accuracy, representing countenances of different expressions and ages. The whole workmanship is surprising, when viewed in reference to the common notion of Indian art. We possessed a beautiful and perfect specimen of Indian pottery in the shape of a drinking gourd. The aperture represented the mouth of a squaw, which the thirsty drinker would naturally kiss with a degree of eager appetite. In digging a ditch round a garden below St. Charles, in the forks between the Mississippi and Missouri, we came upon great quantities of fragments of this ware. Much of it in fine preservation has been dug from the chalk banks below the mouth of the Ohio. It is found in fact every where between Pittsburgh, lake Superior, and New Mexico. The material is clay, with a considerable intermixture of sand, sometimes flinty, sometimes calcareous, but generally of a snowy whiteness. They were all moulded by the hand, without any aid from the potter's wheel. The shapes of natural objects were happily imitated, and they were hardened by the heat of the sun. Sculptured and inscribed rocks are among the most common of Indian antiquities. On the side of a mountain in Tennessee, are the marks of the footsteps of men and horses in the limestone, in great numbers, and as though they were the tracks of an army. Some of

19

the tracks show, as if the party had slipped in miry clay.
All have the appearance of being an actual impress in soft
clay, which afterwards hardened to stone, retaining a perfect impression.   Characters of great freshness of coloring, are marked upon many of the high bluffs, that impend
the western rivers.   Inscriptions of this sort are found in
Missouri, on the Illinois, and in various other places.   A
remarkable track of a human foot was found in a solid
block of limestone, on the bank of the Mississippi, at St.
Louis.   The most ancient traditions of the west, do not
touch the origin of these mounds or characters.

Human skeletons have been found in great preservation in nitre caves in Tennessee and Kentucky, some of
them enveloped in robes made of cloth of nettles curiously
overlaid with beautiful turkey feathers.   Every one has
read of the cemetery of pigmy skeletons on the Maramec,
not far from St. Louis.   Similar ones are found in Tennessee, not far from the Cumberland.   Organic remains of
various animals, and among others the megalonyx and
mastodon, and other huge and unknown animals, are found
in various places, particularly at Big Bone Lick, in Kentucky.   Whole skeletons have been completed from them
in the museums of the curious.   Indeed this country offers
a far more curious field for the discovery and classification
of organic remains, than any other known.   The museums at Cincinnati and St. Louis abound in collections of
western organic remains and Indian antiquities.   We have
found space only to admit a few of the most interesting.   In
journeying through dark forests or wide prairies, we cannot but be aware, that extinguished races, with their monuments and arts, are beneath our feet.

The recent excavation of the Louisville and Portland
canal, afforded an impressive display of ancient remains.
In the alluvial stratum immmediately above the compact
bed of slate limestone, and from nineteen to upwards of
twenty feet below the surface, brick hearths were brought
to view, with the coals of the last social domestic fires still
visible.   The bricks, as we have heard them described,
were hard and regular, differing from those of present
make, in being longer in proportion to their width and

thickness. Along with organic remains of animals, similar to those found at Big Bone Lick, were skeletons of men in great numbers. Among others, was that of a man standing erect in the earth, one arm raised to an angle of forty-five degrees with the shoulder, and holding in the hand a semi-globular, or rather elliptical stone, striated with gay colors, beautifully polished, and of the size of half an orange. When those perforations and examinations into the interior strata of the soil, which every where take place, consequent upon habitancy and improvement, shall have been made, we doubt not that innumerable testimonials to the past habitancy of this country, like those recited above, will come to light. Such remains cannot fail to elicit profound reflection and solemn thought. But it is out of the question to think of deriving from them any theories or conclusions more specific than that the country was formerly inhabited by races of animals, most of which are now extinct; and by races of men, in form and structure like ourselves.

CHAPTER XIII.

BRIEF NOTICES OF SOME OF THE WESTERN PIONEERS.

AFTER all, our most interesting remains are the transmitted examples and characters of our hardy pioneers, of whom but a very few now remain.

From a near relative of Daniel Boone, we are enabled to add a few facts, in relation to his life, in addition to those that have already been recorded in this work; and which dates subsequent to the period of his leaving Kentucky.

Boone was a man of the keenest sensitiveness; and, it is said, used to show great satisfaction at hearing any one read the flattering and rather exaggerated and sophomorical account of him, which, as original and authentic matter ap--

proved by himself, has already been incorporated in these pages. 'All true,' he used to exclaim. 'No mistake there.' But, though ardently sensitive, he was not disposed to be querulous and repining, although he used to speak sometimes with strong indignation of those legal intricacies and quibbles, by which he lost all the rewards of his exposures, labors, sufferings, and dangers, in the first settlement of Kentucky.

But having expended his indignation in a transient paroxysm, he settled soon back to his customary mental complacency and self-possession; and as he had no pledge of consequence remaining to him in the soil of Kentucky; as it was, moreover, becoming on all sides subject to the empire of the cultivator's axe and plough; and as Missouri, still an unpeopled wilderness, lying along an almost unexplored river, exceeding a thousand leagues in length, offered to his imagination a new Kentucky, almost promising indemnity for that he had lost, he determined to remove there; and, in the year 1804, he moved with his family from Kentucky to Missouri. His character for honesty, courage, and fidelity, followed him. The country had just passed by cession from the then French republic to the United States. But the Spanish and French system still being in force, he was appointed commandant of the district of St. Charles by the Spanish commandant. This was the second district, in point of importance, in the territory; and he retained his command until the government of the United States went into effect. His first position was at Boone's Lick, not far from Franklin, and about 180 miles north-west of St. Louis, near Missouri river. Here he made salt, hunted bears and buffaloes, and trapped beavers, undisturbed by white cultivators, as in the halcyon days of salt making on the Blue Licks.

But these times were too happy to last; and French *hunters, and voyageurs, and coureurs du bois,* began to scour the forests, kill the bears, drive off the buffaloes, and cut down the bee trees; and with their fleets of periogues ascend the Missouri to points, beyond where the stiffened sinews, and the time-worn frame of the Kentucky hunter permitted him to follow. The volatile and babbling

French, with their little, and to him despicable shot-guns, could bring down a turkey or a squirrel, where the rifle bullet, formerly so unerring, now directed by his dim eye, could not reach. It was in vain, that the hind sights were rendered more conspicuous by shreds of white paper. No vigor of will, no internal ardor of desire can repair the immedicable and irresistible influence of time. And, however the heart and juvenile remembrances of Boone might follow these brisk and talkative hunters to the Rocky mountains and the Western Sea, the sad consciousness that years were stronger than the subduer of bears and Indians, came over his mind like a cloud.

Other sorrows came also with age. The British war, with its influence upon the savage auxiliaries of Britain, extended even to the remote forests of the Missouri. The Boone's Lick establishment was broken up by the incursions of numerous bands of murderous savages. Boone was no longer able to make one of the rangers, who pursued them, and in some instances retaliated ample measures of revenge. But he sent numerous substitutes in his children, relatives, and neighbors. Where he passed his time during the war, whether at the block-house at *Cote Sans Dessein*, or at St. Charles, St. Louis, or in Kentucky, does not appear. Though it is believed he made salt at Boone's Lick no inconsiderable part of the time, solacing his aged ear with the music of his young days,—the howl of the nocturnal wolf, and the war song of the prowling savages, heard far away from the companionship of the whites.

When the writer lived in St. Charles in 1816, Colonel Boone, with the return of peace, had resumed his Kentucky habits, and resided on the Missouri, surrounded by the plantations of his children and connexions, farming, and still falling the trees for his winter fire, into his courtyard; and every autumn retiring to the remote and moon-illumined cities of the beavers, for the trapping of which, age had taken from him none of his capabilities. He could still, by the aid of paper on his rifle-sights, bring down an occasional turkey; at the Salt Licks he still waylaid the deer; and he found and cut down bee trees, as readily as in his morning days. Never was old age more green, or gray hairs more graceful. His high, calm, bold forehead, seemed converted by years to iron. Decay came for him without sorrow, infirmity, fever, or pain; and, surrounded and cherished by kind friends, he died as he had lived, composed and tranquil. This event took place in the eighty-fourth year of his age, at the house of his son-in-law, Colonel Calloway, not far below Boone's Lick, in the year 1818.

He was five feet ten inches in height, of a very erect, clean limbed, and athletic form, admirably fitted in structure, muscle, temperament, and habit, for the endurance of the labors, changes, and sufferings, he underwent. He had what phrenologists would consider a model head, with a forehead peculiarly high, noble, and bold, thin and compressed lips, a mild, clear blue eye, a large and prominent chin, and a general expression of countenance, in which fearlessness and courage sat enthroned, and which told the beholder at a glance what he had been, and was formed to be. Though ungratefully requited by his country, he has left a name identified with the history of Kentucky, and with the founders and benefactors of our great republic. In all future time, and in every portion of the globe; in history, in sculpture, in song, in eloquence, the name of Daniel Boone will be recorded as the patriarch of Backwoods Pioneers. It is no humble fame to be thus commemorated by Lord Byron:

> Of all men, saving Sylla the man-slayer,
> Who passes for in life and death most lucky,
> Of the great names, which in our faces stare,
> The General Boone, backwoodsman of Kentucky,
> Was happiest among mortals any where,
> For killing nothing, but a bear or buck; he
> Enjoy'd the lonely, vigorous, harmless days,
> Of his old age, in wilds of deepest maze.
>
> Crime came not near him; she is not the child
> Of solitude; health shrank not from him, for
> Her home is in the rarely trodden wild,
> Which, if men seek her not, and death be more
> Their choice than life, forgive them, as beguil'd
> By habit to what their own hearts abhor—
> In cities cag'd. The present case in point I
> Cite is, Boone liv'd hunting up to ninety:

And, what is stranger, left behind a name,
For which men vainly decimate the throng;
Not only famous, but of that good fame,
 Without which glory's but a tavern song;
Simple, serene, the antipodes of shame,
Which hate or envy e'er could tinge with wrong;
An active hermit; even in age the child
Of nature, or the Man of Ross run wild.

'Tis true, he shrank from men even of his nation,
 When they built up unto his darling trees;
He mov'd some hundred miles off, for a station,
Where there were fewer houses and more ease.
The inconvenience of civilization
Is, that you neither can be pleased, nor please.
But where he met the individual man,
He show'd himself as kind as mortal can.

He was not all alone; around him grew
A sylvan tribe of children of the chase,
Whose young, unwaken'd world was always new;
Nor sword, nor sorrow, yet had left a trace
On her unwrinkled brow; nor could you view
A frown on nature's, or on human face.
The free-born forest found, and kept them free,
And fresh as is a torrent or a tree.

And tall and strong, and swift of foot were they,
Beyond the dwarfing city's pale abortions;
Because their thoughts had never been the prey
Of care or gain; the green woods were their portions.
No sinking spirits told them they grew gray,
No fashion made them apes of her distortions.
Simple they were; not savage; and their rifles,
Though very true, were not yet us'd for trifles.

Motion was in their days; rest in their slumbers;
And cheerfulness the handmaid of their toil;
Nor yet too many, nor too few their numbers;
Corruption could not make their hearts her soil;
The lust, which stings; the splendor, which encumbers,
With the free foresters divide no spoil.
Serene, not sullen, were the solitudes
Of this unsighing people of the woods.

Such is the splendid tribute of the prince of modern po-
ets to the patriarch of backwoodsmen. Among the great
numbers of this country and foreign countries, who have
made the Kentucky hunter the theme of their narrative
romance, or song, we ought not to forget the poem to his

memory, entitled, 'The Mountain Muse,' by our amiable and excellent countryman Bryan—a poem, which critics having found unequal, and not always striking or beautiful, have consigned very unjustly to oblivion. We wish, before we dismiss this most interesting character, to set one point at rest, which no biography of him, with which we have met, has settled. He married Rebecca, daughter of Joseph Bryan, Esq. of Virginia, oldest son of Morgan Bryan, head of a very respectable family. She was born near Winchester, in that state. But, while she was still young, her father emigrated to North Carolina, where, on the banks of the Yadkin, Boone saw, loved, and married her.

Frequent enquiries and opposite statements have been made, in regard to the religious tenets of the Kentucky hunter. It is due to simplicity and truth to state, that Boone, little addicted to books, knew but little of the bible, the best of all. He worshipped, as he often said, the Great Spirit—for the woods were his books and his temple; and the creed of the red men naturally became his. But, such was the truth, simplicity, and kindness of his life and character, there can be no doubt, had the gospel of the Son of God been proposed to him, in its sublime truth and reasonableness, that he would have added to all his other virtues the higher name of a christian.

We have only to add, that the bust of Boone in Washington, the painting of him ordered by the General Assembly of Missouri, and the engravings of him in general, have, his family being the judges, very little resemblance. They want the high port, and noble daring of his countenance. In the judgment of the writer, there is no better resemblance of him extant, than the coarse wax figure of him, in the attitude of his fight with the bear, in Letton's Museum, in Cincinnati.

Next to the name of Daniel Boone, we know of no other more conspicuous in the early annals of the Pioneers, than that of Simon Kenton. He was born May, 1755, in Fauquier county, Virginia. Stout in heart, robust in limb, he was taught neither to read nor write; and his only heritage was the physical powers and capabilities of a back-

woodsman. At sixteen the precocious infant was violent-
ly smitten with a backwoods coquette. Another youth, by
the name of Leitchman, seems to have been equally favored. Leitchman, aided by his friends, watched his opportunity, and beat Kenton severely. The following
spring, their mutual claims were decided by a drawn battle. It was a desperate encounter, in which biting,
scratching, kicking, thumping, and all sorts of backwoods
annoyance, were practised to the utmost. Leitchman had
very long hair, which the rustic fair of that day admired.
Kenton found means, during the fight, to fasten him, Ab-
salom-like, by this long club of hair, to a sapling; and then
Simon feasted love and revenge to the full; and leaving
his rival for dead, fled for Kentucky.

From that time until the Indian wars ceased, by the decisive victory of General Wayne, no romance can furnish
more striking incidents of desperate and mortal encounter
with the Indians, hand to hand, and often when the only
alternative was the death of one party or the other. The
Indians finally killed his only companion, Montgomery,
and took him prisoner. Beating, torture, and menace,
were now his daily portion; when at length a white renegado among the Indians, told him with a curse, that he was
to be burnt. From this dreadful fate he was saved at that
time by the intervention of Simon Girty, who had been
his companion in the days of his boyhood; and to whom,
in this extremity, he made himself known. He was destined a second time to the flames, and was rescued this
time by the mediation of Logan, the same chief whom Mr.
Jefferson has immortalized. Still a third time the Indian
council adjudged him to the flames; and he was saved this
time by Dewyer, British trading agent among the Indians.
He ran the gauntlet, and was thrice bound to the stake,
where the faggots for burning him were collected. For
weeks his case vibrated between life and death; and more
singular and apparently fortuitous escapes have never
been recorded. Reckless in bravery, and perfectly acquainted with Indian stratagem, he was present in most of
the western encounters with the Indians, every where inspiring confidence, and always in the fore-front of the bat-

tle. He still survives on the upper waters of the Miami, in Ohio; and, like Boone, has retained for his old age neither lands nor tenements; the only fruit of his toils and dangers being remembrances, and the consciousness of having deserved well of his country.

General Benjamin Logan occupies a prominent place among the western pioneers. He was of Irish extract; and his father first settled in Pennsylvania, and afterwards moved to Virginia, where the subject of this notice was left an orphan. Inheriting all his father's landed estate, by the then law of primogeniture, he generously ordered it sold, and the proceeds equally divided among his brothers and sisters. Thence he became a back-woodsman and Indian fighter on the Holston. In 1775, he removed to Kentucky, and established a small settlement, not far from Harrodsburgh, called Logan's Fort. From this time, his name becomes identified with all the Indian contests. Many of his exploits have already been recorded in these pages. In fact, we have incidentally introduced the prominent exploits of the greater number of the western pioneers; and, as they are now in various ways made known to the public, we shall touch upon the biography of some of those commanders, commissioned by the United States, who led more considerable forces against the Indians; and who, though they conducted armies, and fought battles, decisive in regard to the final conquest of the Indians, are, perhaps, less known to western readers than these Indian fighters, who aspired to no more than partizan warfare.

At the head of these we place General George Rogers Clarke. This distinguished western hero performed exploits which would fill a volume. He was born in Virginia in 1750. We have no notices of him, previous to finding him a Colonel, in the service of Virginia. In 1778, he conducted a number of families to the Falls of the Ohio, whom, to secure them from Indian assault, he settled on an island in the Ohio, near that place. His exploits at Kaskaskia and Vincennes, have already been recorded. In 1781, he received from Congress the rank of General, and the chief command of Kentucky. To prevent the Indians crossing from the north shore of the Ohio, to assail the settlements of Kentucky, he hit on the ingenious expedient of a row galley, carrying some swivels and artillery, and rowing up and down the Ohio. The result justified the wisdom of the expedient. A formidable Indian expedition was arrested by it; and, in fact, no considerable body of Indians dared cross the Ohio, while this floating battery was in operation. With a small body of troops at fort Washington, now Cincinnati, surrounded by hordes of still hostile Indians, among whom were 300 fierce Shawnese, who exhibited much insolence and menace, he dictated the terms of a treaty; and astonished his officers and companions by the calmness of his demeanor, amidst dangers calculated to appal the stoutest heart. He died at Locust Grove, near Louisville, the scene of his early achievements, in February, 1817, in the sixty-sixth year of his age. Bravery, which nothing could daunt, and a perseverance which nothing could relax, decision, promptness, and great force of character, together with peculiar kindness of nature, were the characteristics of this most fortunate and distinguished veteran.

Of General Harmar we only know, that in September, 1790, he was appointed by Congress to the command of the United States' troops at fort Washington; that he conducted an expedition against the northern Indians, in which he was defeated with the loss of a number of gallant officers, among whom were Major Wyllys, Major Fontaine, and Lieutenant Frothingham, and 183 men.

General Arthur St. Clair commanded the revolutionary forces at Ticonderoga, in the year 1777, and conducted a retreat, marked by disaster, to the main American army at Stillwater. He seems to have been uniformly unfortunate, though sustaining important commands through the revolutionary war, and never forfeiting the confidence of Washington. In 1791, he was appointed to the command of the north-western army. His forces consisted of three United States' regiments of infantry, two companies of artillery, and one of cavalry, and over 600 militia. He was defeated near the St. Mary, with great slaughter, losing four-fifths of his officers, and having half his men either killed or wounded. Of private soldiers, 550 were left dead on the field. General St. Clair was acknowledged to have commanded on this occasion with great judgment and presence of mind, and to have exposed himself without any sense of personal danger. Eight balls passed through his hat and clothes, and several horses were killed under him during the action, in proof of his personal exposure. General Washington was blamed for appointing to this command an aged, and more than all, an unfortunate officer. In fact, his misfortune seems to have been, to have inherited that malign destiny, which was formerly supposed to result from an evil star. He was tried by a court martial, at his own request, and was honorably acquitted—and he was afterwards Governor of the northwestern territory.

General Anthony Wayne was born in Chester county, Pennsylvania, in 1745. His father was distinguished by various offices in that province. The subject of this notice was appointed to the command of a regiment by Congress; and he was sent under General Thompson into Canada. In the defeat which signalized that invasion, he was wounded; but displayed both gallantry and ability, in bringing off the shattered American forces. He served under General Gates, in the distinguished campaign in which Burgoyne was made prisoner. In addition to uncommon bravery, he showed talents as an engineer; and for his eminent services, at the close of the campaign was made a brigadier general. At the battle of Brandywine, he displayed his accustomed heroism; but his detachment being defeated with severe loss, he demanded a trial by a court martial, and was honorably acquitted. In the battle of Germantown, he signalized himself, received two wounds, and had two horses shot under him. In the battle of Monmouth, his conduct received the particular approbation of General Washington. From his glorious achievement in the capture of Stony Point, one of the most brilliant affairs of the revolution, he has been denominated 'the hero of Stony Point.' He was here wounded in the head—it was at first supposed mortally. He called to his aids to carry him into the fort, that he might die in the scene of his glory. A number of the garrison were killed, and 543 made prisoners. For this achievement, Congress presented him with a gold medal. From his letter, announcing the capture of the fort, it would appear that Commodore Perry's famous bulletin was not altogether original.

"Dear General—The fort and garrison, with Colonel Johnson, are ours. Our officers and men behaved like those determined to be free.   ANTHONY WAYNE.

His Excellency, &c. George Washington."

He bore a conspicuous part in procuring the surrender of Lord Cornwallis. He was eminently successful afterwards, in reducing the British and loyalists in Georgia, where he had a number of severe partisan engagements. For his great services there, the legislature of that state rewarded him with a valuable farm. On the peace, he retired to private life. But we find him afterwards a member of the convention of his native state; and his vote was in favor of adopting the present constitution.

In the year 1792, he was appointed to succeed the unfortunate General St. Clair. We have seen in what manner he terminated the glorious Indian campaign, that restored peace to the western country. The Indians never experienced a defeat so severe, as from the hero of Stony Point, who, from his reckless bravery, was known among the soldiers by the name of 'Mad Anthony.' He died in a log hovel at Erie, on the shore of the lake, formerly Presqu' Isle, in his native state. Not long since, the bones of the hero were removed to his native county, where a monument, with a brilliant inscription, was raised to his memory by the Society of the Cincinnati.

20

CHAPTER XIV.

SKETCH OF THE INDIAN WAR ON THE NORTH-WEST FRONTIER IN 1832.

It had been confidently hoped and predicted, that the savages, within the limits of the American territories, would never again raise the tomahawk against us. In this hope, the event disappointed us. The Sacs and Foxes, who inhabit the waters of Rock and Fox rivers, claimed a great portion of the country embracing the lead mine district, of which Galena is the centre. The greater portion of these tribes were fiercely hostile to us, and took part with the British in the late war; and these Indians seem never to have entirely abandoned the hate generated in that contest. They had, however, made a treaty with us, by which our claims to the lead mines were well defined. The hostile Sacs and Foxes had become parties to the treaty of cession, and had affected to be reconciled to us. But it is now evident, that they still fostered deep and settled purposes of revenge. These purposes were secretly fanned, by the circumstance that these tribes had become an asylum for refugees of quarrelsome, reckless, and murderous characters, who were outlaws from the other tribes about them. Their hostile feelings had been still further exasperated, by their being obliged to give up to punishment the murderers of some Indians under the protection of the United States. In addition to these causes of hostile feeling, the great source of Indian dread and hate had opened every where in the vicinity of their country. They saw the white settlements on all sides approximating and surrounding them. Galena, in their immediate vicinity, had become a considerable town, with at least thirty stores, and two or three thousand inhabitants. The country about the mines was rapidly filling with inhabitants, who had planted themselves in that healthy wilderness, either as miners, connected with mining operations, or as farmers to furnish produce to the numerous laborers collected at the mines. A number of considerable villages in that vicinity, had grown up as rapidly as Galena.

In another direction, above the Sacs and Foxes, settlements were extending from Green Bay on lake Michigan, south-west towards the settlements at Galena. In a word, the north-west frontier of Michigan, Illinois, and Missouri, which all bound on the lead mine country, had become to the Indians what Kentucky and Ohio had been forty years ago.

The war with these tribes, was ushered in with precisely the same harbingers that used to accompany the Indian wars of those days. The savages were first seen prowling about among the remote habitations of the whites, moody and menacing in their deportment. This conduct slowly settled into aggressions, such as stealing horses, killing cattle and swine, and entering dwellings to demand whiskey; and, in the absence of the male members, menacing and affrightening the women. This order of things continued nearly a year, before they proceeded to actual murders. These slow processes of obtaining revenge, suited not the thoughts of the reckless and murderous fugitives, and the abandoned young warriors among them. With them, the first object was to goad on the tribe to that gratuitous outrage, and those burnings and murders, which should place them out of the pale of longer endurance, and involve the absolute necessity of a war.

The leading war chief of the Sacs and Foxes at this time, was a warrior known among the whites by the name of Black Hawk, which is only the translation of his name in the Sac dialect. His influence over his fierce people was confirmed by the aid and counsels of his brother, the Prophet, a chief still more insidious, cruel, and revengeful, than Black Hawk himself. Both these chiefs are supposed always to have been in heart decidedly hostile to the Americans. United to the Sacs and Foxes under these chiefs, were fragments of tribes of the Sioux and Winnebagoes. They had long practised horse-steal-

ing, burned some houses, and committed some solitary
murders, when their hostility was brought to a head by
the following events. A party of the Illinois militia was
collected near a body of these Indians. The parties came
in collision; some skirmishing ensued, and two or three Indians were killed. In the exercise of their accustomed
policy, the party fled, to draw the militia into an ambuscade. As soon as they began to retreat, the militia followed them tumultuously, two or three only together, and
at wide intervals; and one collection rushing by the other,
as they happened to excel in the fleetness of their horses.
In this way they pursued their foe over a wide prairie,
until about midnight, they found themselves decoyed into
the centre of an Indian camp, whence a deadly fire was
opened upon them, by which from 12 to 20 of their number were killed. The remainder fled with still more haste
and disorder than they had advanced.

Aware that they were now in a position of open war
with the whites, they commenced their accustomed assaults, burnings, and massacres, along a frontier of 300
miles, from the borders of Illinois to Green Bay. As in
former times, their vengeance was indiscriminate and unsparing. Old and young, mothers and infants, the sick
and decrepid, were alike the victims of the merciless tomahawk. Burning and devastation completed their work of
murder. On Indian creek, a tributary of Fox River, they
destroyed a little settlement, murdering 15 persons. M. de
St. Orain, Indian agent to these Indians, and of course, by
their usages, a person considered inviolable, journeying in
company with seven or eight men, was fired upon; and,
along with two others of the party, slain. A series of
murders, the details of which have not yet been presented
to the public, were perpetrated in Vermillion county, on
the Wabash, and along the northern frontier of the mine
settlements; and such was their audacity, as to fire upon a
steam boat descending from Galena to St. Louis.

A harmless Dunkard minister, well known to them, on
a mission in that country, was assaulted and slain, when
on his solitary route.

Among a series of assaults too numerous to particular

ize, none excited more sympathy and regret, than that
upon the family of Mr. Hall, living on Indian Creek. It
was an educated family, advanced in condition and manners beyond the rougher backwoods settlers about them.
Of this numerous family, two sons, that were at work in
a distant field at the moment of the assault, were spared,
and two daughters were made captives. The rest were
all murdered, including the husband, wife, and children.
The young ladies taken prisoners, are said to have possessed, at least one of them, uncommon personal beauty.
In carrying them off, the Indians placed each upon a horse,
led by an Indian. Others walked beside them to keep
them, in the difficult places on their route, from falling off.
At night, a lodge was set apart for them, detached from
the sleeping places of the warriors; and elderly squaws
were assigned to sleep on each side of them. They were
offered their full share of the usual Indian food, which continual weeping, and the natural grief incident to their condition, prevented them from taking. In no instance did
the warriors offer them the slightest indelicacy of deportment.

They terminated their journey in the interior of Black
Hawk's camp, a position on a sort of island in a vast swamp,
inaccessible on every side, save one; and that could be
approached only through a miry and dangerous ford. No
post could have been selected more secure and impregnable. They were ransomed through the mediation of the
Winnebagoes, who seem to have been a sort of equivocal
allies both to the Americans and the Sacs and Foxes, according as success or interest preponderated. But the
ransom was found an affair both of difficulty and expense.
A young warrior of rank claimed the handsomer captive
as his prize, and showed the utmost reluctance to giving
her up. A ransom to the value of 2000 dollars was offered, and ten horses in addition for the young lady claimed
by the warrior. To all this, the Winnebagoes, whom the
Sacs dared not affront, were obliged to add menaces of
joining the Americans, and rescuing the young ladies by
violence. They were finally ransomed. But the young
warrior, fierce, avaricious, and forlorn, insisted, as a sou-

20*

venir from his fair captive flame, instead of her scalp, up
on cutting off a lock of her hair, which he said he intended
to keep, as a trophy at once of his valor and his love.

The sparseness of the settlements in that quarter, and
the great distance from our military resources, rendered
the chastisement of these murderers slower than could have
been wished; though, taking the circumstances into view,
it was more prompt than could have been expected. The
Illinois militia was promptly called out, and volunteers
flocked to our standard. The corn crop in that quarter
had failed the preceding year, and it was found difficult to
obtain sufficient resources to keep the militia embodied.
Nevertheless, they were soon driven by General Dodge
from the frontiers to their fastnesses in their own country.
A steam boat, trading on the waters of the Mississippi to
Prairie du Chien, on the first of August 1832, and while
40 miles above that place, discovered a large body of Sacs
and Foxes on the eastern shore of the Mississippi, supposed to be their main force. The company considering it
their duty to be first in the attack, fired upon them, killed
a number, and put the rest to flight. We quote the account of this affair, as related by the party, and as an amusing bulletin in its kind.

"Prairie du Chien, Aug. 3, 1832.

DEAR SAMUEL:—I arrived at this place on Monday last;
and was despatched with the Warrior alone, to Wa-pa-
shaw's village, one hundred and twenty miles above, to
inform them of the approach of the Sacs, and to order
down all the friendly Indians to this place. On our way
up, we met one of the Sioux band, who informed us, that
the enemy was on Bad-axe river, to the number of four
hundred. We stopped, took in wood, and prepared for
action. Yesterday, at four in the afternoon, we found
them, where he stated he had left them. As we neared
them, they raised a white flag, with which they endeavored to decoy us. But we were too old for that trick, and,
instead of landing, ordered them to send a boat on board,
which they declined. After fifteen minute's delay, to give
them time to remove their women and children, we let
slip a six pounder, loaded with cannister, followed by a

severe fire of musketry; and if you ever saw straight blankets, you would have seen them there. I fought them at anchor most of the time; and we were all much exposed. I have a ball, which came in close by where I was standing, and passed through the bulkhead of the wheel room. We fought them more than an hour, until our wood began to fail; and night coming on, we left them, and went to the prairie. This affair cost them twenty-three killed, and a proportional number of wounded. We had a single man wounded. The next morning, before we could get back again, on account of a heavy fog, our whole army was upon them. We found them at it, and walked in, and took a hand ourselves. The first shot from the Warrior laid out three for them. The army had eight or nine killed, and seventeen wounded, whom we took down with us. One died on deck last night. I assure you, my friend, there is no sport in fighting Indians, particularly at this season of the year, when the grass is so bright. We brought down thirty-six women and children, who were prisoners. We had sixteen regulars, five riflemen, and twenty of ourselves. There was no small whizzing of bullets. Every man, and even my cabin boy, fought well."

The officers of the militia in the vicinity, among whom General Dodge stood conspicuous, rendered continual and the most active services in this campaign. Generals Atkinson and Scott, of the United State's army, with their commands, hurried to the scene of action. General Scott, with a respectable force from the quarters of New York and the lakes, was unfortunately delayed, and his forces diminished, by the breaking out of the cholera, in a very mortal form among them. He at length arrived at the scene of action; and his troops being united with those of General Atkinson and the partisan militia, formed a force sufficient to look down all opposition. The brave militia had kept them at bay; but were not in sufficient force to penetrate into their fastnesses. As soon as they discovered what was their inevitable fate, if forced to a contest, they attempted to retreat to the vast wildernesses west of the Mississippi; and with a well imagined policy, and a perfect knowledge of that difficult country of alternate mountains and swamps, took to these wild, and as they fondly deemed, inaccessible routes to a regular army. But they mistook. Their enemy hung close upon their rear, over mountain and moor, and through the ravines and defiles. Seeing the probable issue of the war, the Sioux and Winnebagoes fell upon them in the hour of their extremity—the latter most thanklessly; for, it is affirmed, that their counsels to the Sacs and Foxes, from the beginning, had been to fight it out. A party of Sioux fell upon one of their retreating bands, gained a most decisive victory, killed two hundred, and took forty prisoners, among whom was Na-o-pope, the prophet, and brother of Black Hawk. About the same time, a detachment from Cassville encountered a war party of Sacs, and defeated them, killing twelve and taking some prisoners.

The battle, to which allusion was had in the steam-boat bulletin, is given in the accounts of the day to this amount. On July 28 and 29, Generals Atkinson, Posey, Alexander, and Dodge, crossed at Helena, to the north shore of the Ouisconsin, whence they marched in a northerly direction, and in a short time discovered a large Indian trail, leading north of west. A forced pursuit was immediately commenced; and on the morning of the second of August, they were overtaken five miles from the banks of the Mississippi. General Dodge's squadron led the attack, and the Indians were driven from hill to hill, until they came to the river, where they made a desperate stand. Finding themselves, however, defeated at every point, they plunged at length into the water,—men, women, and children,—in the hope of escaping the fire of their assailants by diving. The conflict lasted three hours. The troops of the United States lost twenty-seven in killed and wounded. The Indian loss could not be exactly ascertained; but it must have exceeded one hundred and fifty slain; and fifty of their women and children were taken prisoners. Black Hawk is said to have fled up the river in the midst of the fight, leaving many of his valuables behind him, which were found on the battle ground.

This battle was decisive of their fate. They never

made an effort to rally in force again. Their renegado allies had already shrunk from them. The Sioux, many of whom had shown equivocal deportment and double dealing between them and us, begged to be allowed to go in pursuit of the fugitives. The Winnebagoes had taken most decisive steps against them; and, after their barbarous usages, were daily bringing in their scalps. They killed Stack-ar-ka-pee, a leading Fox warrior. The Menomonees, too, came in to hunt them down. Some prisoners brought in, informed, that before the encounter in which General Dodge had defeated them, on the twenty-first of July, they had lost two hundred warriors, beside the women and children, drowned by the sinking of their canoes in the Mississippi. Not long afterwards, the head chief, Black Hawk, Ne-o-pope, the prophet, and eleven other head chiefs, together with fifty warriors of less note, were taken prisoners by the Winnebagoes, and delivered up to the Indian agent at Prairie du Chien. The fifty captive warriors were dismissed, on their giving pledge, that they would remain hereafter peaceable. The Black Hawk, Ne-o-pope, and the other eleven chiefs were sent down the Mississippi in a steam boat to St. Louis; whence they were sent to Jefferson Barracks, there to remain prisoners, and hostages for the peaceable conduct of their tribes, until a permanent peace should be established with them. Among the effects of Black Hawk, left behind on his retreat after the battle of the second of August, and which fell into the hands of the Americans, were certificates of his good character, and of his having fought bravely against the United States, in the late war with Great Britain, signed by British officers.

The war of the Sacs and Foxes was, unquestionably, one of pure aggression, and entirely unprovoked, the lands which they claimed, having been sold by themselves, and the consideration amply and promptly paid. Never were savage aggressions more cruel and wanton, than theirs, upon the inoffensive settlers of the frontiers of Illinois and the north-western territory. Many families were massacred, and settlements broken up, before retribution reached them. But when it did come, it was decisive and final. These tribes, which, for thirty years past, have hovered round our frontiers, like wolves, sometimes restrained from murder through fear or interest, or transient policy, but always hostile at heart, at length provoked their fate, and are now so broken down, as never to be able again to raise the tomahawk, except as solitary and vagabond murderers. The pioneers of civilization in those remote forests and prairies of the north-west, need never fear that their tranquility will be again disturbed by the Sacs and Foxes. The uncertain and equivocating Winnebagoes, and Sioux, and Menomonees, have had a stern lesson before their eyes, of the promptness and power of American chastisement; and the impossibility of escaping it by being cheered by the smiles of the British traders, or by their contiguity to the range of the British north-west trading company—a lesson, which, we trust, will awe them to quietness, until our settlements in that quarter shall be so dense as to leave no apprehensions from savages in their vicinage, however diposed towards us.

Black Hawk and Ne-o-pope are shown at Jefferson Barracks, as fair samples of the unsophisticated red men of the north-west. Black Hawk is considerably advanced in years, we believe, turned of sixty. He is well built, of the middle stature, with an aquiline nose, a plausible and rather cunning expression of countenance, in which he seems to wish to manifest moderation and benignity. The head is large, as large as a phrenologist would desire; but, unhappily, with a forehead singularly retreating, and the back part of his head greatly superior in length and volume to the fore part. Indeed, destructiveness is developed in his cranium to an inordinate degree. Yet the warrior, the commander, the chief among the fiercest of the red men, the man who could issue the most terrible war-hoop from the prairie, in view of a peaceful American settlement, or who could utter the most plausible and moderate speech before American agents—all these capabilities sit enthroned on his countenance; and are legible by an ordinary observer. Nature has strongly marked him a chief. Ne-o-pope, the prophet, is a malignant, fierce looking savage, in whose countenance knavery, and pretension to sanctity, and the instinct blood-thirstiness of a wolf are curiously combined.

We need hardly add, that within two or three past years, a new experiment is making upon the red people included within the territorial limits of the United States. Territories, marked by specific geographical limits, are assigned them in the immense regions west of the Mississippi, and of the settlement of the whites. These locations place them between our exterior settlements and the Rocky mountains, where a boundless region of prairie opens before them, furnishing the only hunting grounds, that are, to any considerable degree, productive within our territorial limits. Part of the Cherokees, Chactaws, Chickasaws and Creeks, and nearly all the Shawnese and Delawares, are already removed there. It is expected, in the event of a pacification, that the Sacs and Foxes will also remove west of the Mississippi.

It is now a vexed question, debated with intense interest, and no little asperity, whether the remaining Indians in the limits of Georgia, Alabama, Mississippi, and Tennessee, ought or ought not to be compelled to join their brethren, who have already removed to the country assigned them west of the Mississippi. On the one hand, it is contended, that the country, which the Indians above specified, inhabit, is secured to them by treaties with the United States, in which they are recognized as an independent people; and that being unwilling to remove, we have no right to compel them to that course. These advocates speak of their improvements, their cultivated farms, manufactories, roads, bridges, police, and their established press. All these astonishing germs of Indian civilization, will be, they affirm, extinguished by their removal. They are at once becoming christianized and civilized. In the western prairies they will again retrograde to savages and pagans. Worse, if possible, than that; in that country of sterility, they will perish miserably either by war with the other tribes, into whose territories we have intruded them, or by famine. They add numerous affecting moral arguments against the measure, closed with the touching one drawn from the consideration of removing them from their venerated cemeteries, and the bones of their forefathers.

On the other part, the advocates of removal contend, that the states, within whose limits they reside, have perfect sovereignty in their lands, and an undoubted right either to compel their submission to their laws, or to remove them. They state, that it is impossible, that the Indians should exist, as an independent people, within the populous limits of the whites; that collisions, murders, escapes of fugitive slaves, and the operations of laws and usages so essentially different, as those of the white and red people, will forever keep alive between the contiguous parties, feuds, quarrels, and retaliations, which can never cease until one of the parties becomes extinct. They state, that commissioners, who have been sent to explore the country assigned to the Indians, who have already emigrated, find them generally in healthy and fertile countries, satisfied with their condition, and advancing still more rapidly in agriculture, wealth, and civilization, than their brethren east of the Mississippi; and, that their removal will advance, instead of retarding these improvements. They expatiate on the liberal price paid for their relinquished lands, and the ample appropriation made by the government for their removal. One party sees nothing in their removal, but oppression, violation of treaties, and of the faith of the United States, cruelty and perfidy on our part, and on theirs banishment from their homes and the graves of their fathers, poverty, famine, degradation and utter extinction, chargeable to the ingratitude and tyranny of the whites.

On the other hand, the advocates of removal see the race perpetuated in opulence and peace in the fair prairies of the west. Here they are to grow up distinct red nations, with schools and churches, the anvil, the loom, and the plough—a sort of Arcadian race between our borders and the Rocky mountains, standing memorials of the kindness and good faith of our government.

Non nobis tantas componere lites.

FINIS.

The First American Frontier

AN ARNO PRESS/NEW YORK TIMES COLLECTION

Agnew, Daniel.
A History of the Region of Pennsylvania North of the Allegheny River. 1887.

Alden, George H.
New Government West of the Alleghenies Before 1780. 1897.

Barrett, Jay Amos.
Evolution of the Ordinance of 1787. 1891.

Billon, Frederick.
Annals of St. Louis in its Early Days Under the French and Spanish Dominations. 1886.

Billon, Frederick.
Annals of St. Louis in its Territorial Days, 1804-1821. 1888.

Littel, William.
Political Transactions in and Concerning Kentucky. 1926.

Bowles, William Augustus.
Authentic Memoirs of William Augustus Bowles. 1916.

Bradley, A. G.
The Fight with France for North America. 1900.

Brannan, John, ed.
Official Letters of the Military and Naval Officers of the War, 1812-1815. 1823.

Brown, John P.
Old Frontiers. 1938.

Brown, Samuel R.
The Western Gazetteer. 1817.

Cist, Charles.
Cincinnati Miscellany of Antiquities of the West and Pioneer History. (2 volumes in one). 1845-6.

Claiborne, Nathaniel Herbert.
Notes on the War in the South with Biographical Sketches of the Lives of Montgomery, Jackson, Sevier, and Others. 1819.

Clark, Daniel.
Proofs of the Corruption of Gen. James Wilkinson. 1809.

Clark, George Rogers.
Colonel George Rogers Clark's Sketch of His Campaign in the Illinois in 1778-9. 1869.

Collins, Lewis.
Historical Sketches of Kentucky. 1847.

Cruikshank, Ernest, ed,
Documents Relating to Invasion of Canada and the Surrender of Detroit. 1912.

Cruikshank, Ernest, ed,
The Documentary History of the Campaign on the Niagara Frontier, 1812-1814. (4 volumes). 1896-1909.

Cutler, Jervis.
A Topographical Description of the State of Ohio, Indian Territory, and Louisiana. 1812.

Cutler, Julia P.
The Life and Times of Ephraim Cutler. 1890.

Darlington, Mary C.
History of Col. Henry Bouquet and the Western Frontiers of Pennsylvania. 1920.

Darlington, Mary C.
Fort Pitt and Letters From the Frontier. 1892.

De Schweinitz, Edmund.
The Life and Times of David Zeisberger. 1870.

Dillon, John B.
History of Indiana. 1859.

Eaton, John Henry.
Life of Andrew Jackson. 1824.

English, William Hayden.
Conquest of the Country Northwest of the Ohio. (2 volumes in one). 1896.

Flint, Timothy.
Indian Wars of the West. 1833.

Forbes, John.
Writings of General John Forbes Relating to His Service in North America. 1938.

Forman, Samuel S.
Narrative of a Journey Down the Ohio and Mississippi in 1789-90. 1888.

Haywood, John.
Civil and Political History of the State of Tennessee to 1796. 1823.

Heckewelder, John.
History, Manners and Customs of the Indian Nations. 1876.

Heckewelder, John.
Narrative of the Mission of the United Brethren. 1820.

Hildreth, Samuel P.
Pioneer History. 1848.

Houck, Louis.
The Boundaries of the Louisiana Purchase: A Historical Study. 1901.

Houck, Louis.
History of Missouri. (3 volumes in one). 1908.

Houck, Louis.
The Spanish Regime in Missouri. (2 volumes in one). 1909.

Jacob, John J.
A Biographical Sketch of the Life of the Late Capt. Michael Cresap. 1826.

Jones, David.
A Journal of Two Visits Made to Some Nations of Indians on the West Side of the River Ohio, in the Years 1772 and 1773. 1774.

Kenton, Edna.
Simon Kenton. 1930.

Loudon, Archibald.
Selection of Some of the Most Interesting Narratives of Outrages. (2 volumes in one). 1808-1811.

Monette, J. W.
History, Discovery and Settlement of the Mississippi Valley. (2 volumes in one). 1846.

Morse, Jedediah.
American Gazetteer. 1797.

Pickett, Albert James.
History of Alabama. (2 volumes in one). 1851.

Pope, John.
A Tour Through the Southern and Western Territories. 1792.

Putnam, Albigence Waldo.
History of Middle Tennessee. 1859.

Ramsey, James G. M.
Annals of Tennessee. 1853.

Ranck, George W.
Boonesborough. 1901.

Robertson, James Rood, ed.
Petitions of the Early Inhabitants of Kentucky to the Gen. Assembly of Virginia. 1914.

Royce, Charles.
Indian Land Cessions. 1899.

Rupp, I. Daniel.
History of Northampton, Lehigh, Monroe, Carbon and Schuykill Counties. 1845.

Safford, William H.
The Blennerhasset Papers. 1864.

St. Clair, Arthur.
A Narrative of the Manner in which the Campaign Against the Indians, in the Year 1791 was Conducted. 1812.

Sargent, Winthrop, ed.
A History of an Expedition Against Fort DuQuesne in 1755. 1855.

Severance, Frank H.
An Old Frontier of France. (2 volumes in one). 1917.

Sipe, C. Hale.
Fort Ligonier and Its Times. 1932.

Stevens, Henry N.
Lewis Evans: His Map of the Middle British Colonies in America. 1920.

Timberlake, Henry.
The Memoirs of Lieut. Henry Timberlake. 1927.

Tome, Philip.
Pioneer Life: Or Thirty Years a Hunter. 1854.

Trent, William.
Journal of Captain William Trent From Logstown to Pickawillany. 1871.

Walton, Joseph S.
Conrad Weiser and the Indian Policy of Colonial Pennsylvania. 1900.

Withers, Alexander Scott.
Chronicles of Border Warfare. 1895.